STUDIES IN INTERDISCIPLINARY HISTORY

# Population and Economy

# Population and Economy

## Population and History from the Traditional to the Modern World

Edited by ROBERT I. ROTBERG and THEODORE K. RABB
Guest Editors: Roger S. Schofield and E. Anthony Wrigley

*Contributors:*
Michael Anderson
Ann Kussmaul
Ronald Lee
Peter H. Lindert
Roger S. Schofield
Brinley Thomas
Jan de Vries
E. Anthony Wrigley

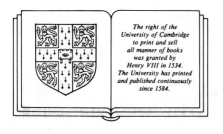

The right of the
University of Cambridge
to print and sell
all manner of books
was granted by
Henry VIII in 1534.
The University has printed
and published continuously
since 1584.

CAMBRIDGE UNIVERSITY PRESS

CAMBRIDGE

LONDON   NEW YORK   NEW ROCHELLE

MELBOURNE   SYDNEY

Published by the Press Syndicate of the University of Cambridge
The Pitt Building, Trumpington Street, Cambridge CB2 1RP
32 East 57th Street, New York, NY 10022, USA

First published 1986

Printed in the United States of America

*Library of Congress Cataloging-in-Publication Data*
Main entry under title:
Population and economy.
(Studies in interdisciplinary history series)
Contents: Introduction / Roger S. Schofield and
E. Anthony Wrigley — Through a glass darkly : The
population history of England as an experiment in
history / Roger S. Schofield — Historical demography
after The population history of England / Michael
Anderson — [etc.]
1. England—Population—History—Addresses,
essays, lectures.   2. Great Britain—Economic
conditions—Addresses, essays, lectures.
I. Rotberg, Robert I.   II. Rabb, Theodore K.
III. Schofield, Roger.   IV. Wrigley, E. A. (Edward
Anthony), 1931–        V. Anderson, Michael.
VI. Series.
HB3585.P658   1986       304.6'0941       85-26945
ISBN 0 521 32540 4 hard covers
ISBN 0 521-31055 5 paperback

# Contents

## Population and Economy

### Population and History from the Traditional to the Modern World

# Population and Economy

*Roger S. Schofield and E. Anthony Wrigley*

# Population and Economy: From the Traditional to the Modern World    This issue of *The Journal of Inter-disciplinary History* focuses upon some of the central problems in social and economic history. Until only a century or so ago land was the source not only of all food, but also of most of the raw materials needed by industry. In traditional agricultural economies, productivity per person, or per acre, was either stationary or rose very slowly. In such circumstances rapid population growth spelled disaster unless there were still large areas of virgin land to be exploited, a possibility that was no longer open to most societies in early modern Europe. For them the faster population grew, the grimmer became the struggle to exist. England was one such society, yet in the late eighteenth and early nineteenth century it experienced a series of economic changes which overcame the earlier tension between population growth and living standards. Industrialization involved changes in productivity so profound that an increase in poverty was no longer the price of an increase in numbers.

An understanding of the nature of the dynamic relationships between population and the economy, and of their transformation through industrialization, is, therefore, one of the grand themes of history, illuminating the emergence of the modern world and providing a historical perspective in which the problems of contemporary agricultural societies can better be appreciated. Such an enterprise has hitherto been hampered by the lack of adequate information about European population movements over the long run.

With the publication of *The Population History of England* it became possible for the first time to trace in some detail the demographic changes that occurred in a major European country

Roger S. Schofield is Director of the Economic and Social Research Council (ESRC) Cambridge Group for the History of Population and Social Structure and Fellow of Clare College, Cambridge. E. Anthony Wrigley is Professor of Population Studies at the London School of Economics and Associate Director of the ESRC—Cambridge Group.

throughout the early modern period and during the industrial revolution. It is thus now possible to test our understanding of the functioning of early modern economies in relation to their demographic patterns against the newly revealed empirical data. The discussion of this central historical question, first initiated by Thomas Robert Malthus in the late eighteenth century, can now be taken a substantial step further. All of the essays published here take advantage of this new possibility, either by using the English data themselves, or by reflecting on the implications of a comparison between English patterns and those found elsewhere.[1]

The most significant and pervasive issue has been, and remains, the degree of autonomy of population characteristics. On the one hand there has been a long tradition, stemming from one reading of Malthus' work, of treating population behavior as secondary to economic circumstance. The commanding heights of the historical scene were economic. Once these had been scaled, the rest of the landscape could be surveyed and was subordinate. In particular, the demand for labor has often been seen as the variable which, over the long-run, has directly or indirectly determined population trends.[2]

Over the short run, too, demographic behavior in the past has often been considered to have been highly sensitive to economic conditions. For example, the size of the harvest exercised a powerful influence each year on the number of marriages. Goubert, in a flamboyant analogy, once went so far as to describe the price of wheat as a demographic barometer, the fluctuations of which above or below normal established the demographic consequences of the harvest year in question.[3]

1 E. Anthony Wrigley and Roger S. Schofield, *The Population History of England, 1541–1871. A Reconstruction* (Cambridge, Mass., 1981).
2 "Every species of animals naturally multiplies in proportion to the means of their subsistence, and no species can ever multiply beyond it. But in civilised society it is only amongst the inferior ranks of people that the scantiness of subsistence can set limits to the further multiplication of the human species; and it can do so in no other way than by destroying a great part of the children which their fruitful marriages produce. The liberal reward of labour, by enabling them to provide better for their children, and consequently to bring up a greater number, naturally tends to widen and extend those limits. It deserves to be remarked, too, *that it necessarily does this as nearly as possible in the proportion which the demand for labour requires*" [our emphasis]. Adam Smith (ed. John Ramsay M'Culloch), *An Inquiry into the Nature and Causes of the Wealth of Nations* (Edinburgh, 1843), 36.
3 Pierre Goubert, *Beauvais et le Beauvaisis de 1600 à 1750* (Paris, 1960), I, 75–76.

On the other hand, causal priority could equally plausibly be reversed, since certain demographic characteristics of past populations could scarcely fail to have influenced economic behavior. For example, the age structure of a population, and therefore its dependency ratio, is largely determined by the prevailing level of its fertility. This factor in turn may have strongly influenced patterns and types of expenditure and saving.

The degree of autonomy involved in the functioning of population and economy in the past was an issue that was addressed directly in *Population History*. Peter Lindert and Ronald Lee both explore this question in their contributions to this issue. Lee, for example, makes a telling distinction between the short, the medium, and the long term. He shows the importance of the distinction to any discussion of the degree to which population characteristics are determined by the demand for labor, which he defines as itself arising from some combination of "technology, resources, climate, and the social organization guiding production and distribution" (636). He argues that, in the long run, demand for labor must have been the decisive factor; that, in the short run, other factors were often of greater importance; but that there are major uncertainties about medium term behavior, measured in decades or half-centuries. His analysis leads him to conclude that, in this time frame, it was *independent* variations in fertility and mortality which led to the marked long-term swings in population growth rates round the equilibrium rate suggested by the growth of the economy; and that such swings were strongly and negatively correlated with real income.

Lindert addresses much the same set of questions. Like Lee, he begins with Malthus and reflects upon the ways in which both subsequent empirical work and the changes in economic theory since the days of the classical economists have led to successive reassessments of the links between population movements and economic circumstances. Much of his discussion consists of an extended commentary on the battle between Malthusians and monetarists, in which he keeps a tally of the points scored as the fight develops, descending from time to time to intervene actively himself. He concludes that Malthus' original justification of the view that population growth and falling real wages were causally linked is difficult to sustain. However, he also suggests that the apparent domination of real wage trends by price behavior does not necessarily imply that population movements were unimportant in influencing real wages. He is led to this view by the consideration of a number of ways in which population trends may reenter the picture through their effect on prices and thus, indirectly, on real wages.

The esays by Lee and Lindert are preceded in this collection by another pair, by Schofield and Michael Anderson, which tackle questions of research design. In the former, Schofield sets out what might be described as the research philosophy of *Population History*. It is placed first in this collection since the book it describes was a catalyst for most of the other essays. He traces the intellectual ancestry of the enterprise back to Malthus' *First Essay on Population* (London, 1798) and also sets out its relationship to the more recent authors whose writings helped to shape its coverage and preoccupations: notably John Hajnal, Peter Laslett, Lee, H. John Habakkuk, and Vero Copner Wynne-Edwards. He is at pains to show that, in spite of the large proportion of the work devoted to "facts," it is a mistake to suppose that it is positivistic in nature. Indeed, he takes care to explain that the very status of a "fact" is contingent upon a prior set of assumptions about what is relevant; or rather, that a fruitful dialectic between fact and theory must inform and suffuse any successful piece of research.

Schofield also attempts to show that, when dealing with English population history, it is possible to borow with profit from the more traditional historical skills and from recent developments in demographic and statistical technique, or from economic theory, without at the same time introducing methodological contradictions or tensions. Equally, he describes how, for certain purposes, it proved more appropriate to use simple, intuitive models of reality rather than resort to elaborate and sophisticated constructs. His essay is a plea for the importance of avoiding both the Scylla of naively descriptive history, and the Charybdis of the more formal type of historical analysis in which the conclusions are effectively built into the assumptions used in devising the method of analysis or in constructing the model of reality employed. The challenge which he offers at the end of his article, that the tentative interpretations given in *Population History* should be tested, refined, and refuted, has been taken up vigorously by several contributors to this issue of the *J.I.H.*

Anderson briefly discusses the implications of the empirical findings, if substantiated, of *Population History* for the research agenda of demographic, economic, and social history. He concentrates chiefly, however, on the epistemological status of the research design employed and on the weaknesses and limitations of some of the assumptions underlying the work. He begins by making a distinction between the reliability and validity of the data used, noting that, although open to objection on the first head, the book is largely immune from the kinds of doubt on the second which beset much econometric and sociological analysis based on the application of models of behavior to quantitative data. Although able to offer reassurance on this point, he raises a series of questions about the propriety of other aspects of the work, notably in connection with the disentangling of causation from coincidence; over the dangers of passing from patterns observable in the mass to assumptions about individual motivation; and over the likelihood that results obtained at the national level conflate opposing tendencies in different regions, sectors of the economy, or social groups. He enters a strong plea for the value of sociological sensitivity to context to offset and enrich the rigors of demometric and econometric analysis.

The essays of Jan de Vries and Wrigley systematically exploit differences of context by drawing international comparisons in order to throw light upon the nature of the preindustrial economy of Western Europe. The Dutch Republic was the *Wirtschaftswunder* of the later sixteenth and seventeenth centuries, clearly the most successful economy of the age, in which the level of real wages was probably higher than anywhere else and much more resistant to the secular sag in standards of living that afflicted so much of Europe after 1550. As de Vries notes, there are major deficiencies in the Dutch registers as sources of information about population trends, but the outlines of Dutch population history are sufficiently clearly established to allow a comparison of the Dutch and English cases. He shows how the openness of the Dutch economy to external influences, because of its dependence upon trade generally and upon foreign food supplies in particular, ensures that models of the pattern of economic-demographic relationships which "save the phenomena" well enough when applied to England, need modification for use with Dutch data. In the course of constructing an alternative model which is more successful for the case of the Dutch Republic, he succeeds in clarifying the distinctiveness of the Dutch golden age and the nature of the weaknesses of the Dutch situation, which resulted in economic leadership passing across the North Sea for a time.

De Vries also played a major role in determining the scope of Wrigley's essay, for his work in establishing the chief characteristics of urban growth across the face of Europe between 1500 and 1850 made it possible for Wrigley to attempt international comparisons. Wrigley shows what further light can be shed on differential economic development in Europe by separating population growth into urban and agricultural components. There were not only striking contrasts between the overall rates of population growth in England and other European countries, but even more remarkable differences in rates of growth of certain population categories. Rural agricultural population in England grew less quickly than in France or Holland after about 1600, but rural non-agricultural population grew much faster. Patterns of urban growth in England and elsewhere afford still greater contrasts. By the second half of the eighteenth century, about 70 percent of urban growth in Europe was taking place in England alone, although only about 7 percent of the population lived there (709, Table 7). There were also important differences between England and the continent in the rate of growth in output per head of those engaged in agriculture.

Brinley Thomas sets these developments within the wider, and critical, context of the overcoming of constraints on the expansion of output, in the absence of which the industrial revolution could not have occurred. His essay continues the long-running debate about the key developments which enabled England to become the first industrial nation and, for a time, to achieve a dominant position in the world economy. He concentrates on points which have received too little attention, emphasizing, for example, the significance of technical developments in iron manufacture in the 1780s and 1790s, the prelude to a tremendous surge in the volume of its output and major reductions in its price. He lays stress especially on the importance of access to the products of agriculture in other lands, in his view a sine qua non of stable or falling food prices in a period of very rapid population growth. The links between the food basket of the

English masses and the American prairies, the black earth regions of southern Russia, and the Argentinian pampas in the later nineteenth century are well known. Thomas pays due heed to these developments but also underlines the extent of English dependence upon Ireland at an earlier period, notably in the era of revolutionary and Napoleonic wars.

Finally, Ann Kussmaul's essay exemplifies the splendid opportunities afforded to those interested in econometric history by the large mass of representative demographic data which was culled from parish registers in the course of work on *Population History*. She uses the well-marked regional patterning of marriage seasonality and its changes over time as a guide to the changing pattern of regional agricultural specialization. Changes in the timing of a local seasonal peak in marriages, or in its acuteness, were related to changes in the balance of agricultural activities, and afford a valuable clue to developments in agriculture, especially as direct evidence on the subject is at best fragmentary. In order to exploit this fact with confidence, however, it is first necessary to show that the observed changes could not have been due to other factors, such as altered ecclesiastical rules or practices. Having cleared the ground in this way by discussing other influences on seasonality, Kussmaul is able to show both that there were substantial and significant changes and that they can be accommodated neatly into a model of increasing regional specialization of agriculture. She relates these developments in turn to the vast growth of London and the scale of transport improvements during the period.

Several of the contributors to this special issue contest some of the interpretations that were offered in *Population History*. Nor are they always in accord with one another. Lindert and Lee, for example, are at odds over the assumptions which should be made in erecting an econometric model of the preindustrial English economy. Wrigley takes issue with de Vries about the protoindustrial explanation for the pattern of urban growth from 1600 to 1750, at least for England. Such differences of view are to be welcomed, but it would be out of place to comment upon the merits of the varying views in this brief introduction.

There are, however, certain common features implicit or explicit in this group of essays to which attention should be drawn. All eight contributors to this issue are economic historians. In their original training some were economists, some historians, and one a sociologist; yet all have also developed a strong interest in population history. All share a fascination with the circumstances which limited economic growth in preindustrial economies and with the train of events which led to the escape from these constraints with the occurrence of the industrial revolution.

In view of their intellectual background it is striking, first, that all the authors who consider the question are agreed in assigning a major independent importance to the demographic character of past communities in helping to determine economic conditions. Lee and Lindert address this issue explicitly but, in different ways, the same point is made by every author, except perhaps Kussmaul and Thomas, whose discussions do not involve this topic. Second, although in diverse ways, several of the essays pay tribute to the value of comparative history. Early modern Western Europe may have shared certain economic and demographic traits which set it apart from other traditional cultures, but it was nonetheless full of diversity.[4] In studying the economic, social, and demographic interrelationships in any one area or country, it is of great value to have similar data available for other places. Although only de Vries and Wrigley adopted an explicitly comparative theme, it is echoed in several other essays.

Third, the essays in this collection help to establish more fully the distinctiveness of the English experience. Although not all of the authors confront the question directly, collectively they represent a valuable contribution to a debate which has been lively in recent years. To know how far and in what ways English economic and demographic patterns diverged from those of continental Europe in the centuries before the industrial revolution; to establish how far industrialization simply continued past trends

4 For example, although patterns of nuptiality in Western Europe were distinctive, there were important differences in marriage characteristics among different parts of Western Europe, not simply in the timing and incidence of marriage, but in other aspects of marriage as a social and demographic phenomenon. On the general pattern, see John Hajnal, "European Marriage Patterns in Perspective," in David V. Glass and David E. C. Eversley (eds.), *Population in History* (London, 1965), 101–143. On the complexity of nuptiality differences between countries, in this instance England and France, see Wrigley, "Marriage and Population Growth in Eighteenth-Century England," in R. Brian Outhwaite (ed.), *Marriage and Society. Studies in the Social History of Marriage* (London, 1981), 174–185.

a fortiori or how far it involved abrupt, new departures—resolving such questions is of prime importance to understanding how the modern world came into being, one of the most important of all historical enterprises. Although varied in character and design, the essays in this issue all throw light on these fundamental questions. Their nature explains the title given to this issue: *Population and Economy: From the Traditional to the Modern World*.[5]

5   The debate on the distinctiveness of the English experience has flourished especially since the publication of Alan Macfarlane, *The Origins of English Individualism. The Family, Property, and Social Transition* (Oxford, 1978).

*Roger S. Schofield*

# Through a Glass Darkly: *The Population History of England* as an Experiment in History

The power of a theory lies in its capacity to explain its refutations in the course of its growth.[1]

As its subtitle reveals, *The Population History of England* is a work of historical reconstruction. It was written as an attempt to discover the main outlines of English demographic history and to relate them to economic developments and to the social context in which population developments occurred. The book is also a manifesto for a particular approach to historical investigation and historical inference. Although some of the principles that informed the work were made explicit, many were not and may be difficult to discern in so long and involved a text. In this article I provide an account of the philosophy that lay behind the attempt.[2]

At first glance the book appears to be the outcome of a mammoth exercise in historical positivism: the reconstruction of English population history "wie es eigentlich gewesen" (as it actually happened). This impression is, to a certain extent, justified, for matters of demographic fact had been much discussed and disputed in the literature, and there was a need to recover the empirical record in more detail and with much greater precision than had been achieved so far. For example, it was generally agreed that the population had grown in the sixteenth century, and in the later eighteenth century, but there was no exact knowl-

Roger S. Schofield is Director of the Economic and Social Research Council Cambridge Group for the History of Population and Social Structure and Fellow of Clare College, Cambridge.

1 Imre Lakatos, *Proofs and Refutations: The Logic of Mathematical Discovery* (Cambridge, 1972), 94.
2 E. Anthony Wrigley and Schofield, *The Population History of England, 1541–1871: A Reconstruction* (Cambridge, Mass., 1981).

edge of the rate of growth in either period, and considerable argument about whether growth was to be attributed to changes in fertility or mortality.[3]

Our interest in the demographic record went beyond the construction of a full and clear narrative of "what actually happened." First, as a matter of principle, we did not believe that a mere recital of the historical record would suffice to make its meaning unambiguously clear, as some of our more positivist colleagues have assumed. In order to understand and interpret the empirical record, concepts and theories are needed, and, far from being derived from the empirical data, explanatory concepts and theories precede them. Indeed the very acts of selecting sources and making historical observations presuppose some prior knowledge or theory about what is worth investigating. Second, there was already in existence a formidable and contentious body of theory about the relationship between population growth and economic change—a theory which embraced topics of major historical importance, such as the role of population in industrialization in the eighteenth and nineteenth centuries.[4]

The research that lay behind *Population History* was therefore undertaken in order to tackle a specific set of problems and theoretical concerns in history and demography. The reconstruction that the book contains was never intended to be a narrative covering all aspects of English population history. Rather it was focused on a particular set of issues in order to test the validity

3 Leopold von Ranke, *Geschichten der romanischen und germanischen völker von 1494 bis 1514* (Leipzig, 1874), vii. David Gaunt, "*The Population History of England, 1541–1871*: A Review Symposium," *Social History*, VIII (1983), 140–141.

4 For a discussion of the epistemological shortcomings of positivism, see Paul Janssens, "Histoire économique ou économie rétrospective?" *History and Theory*, XIII (1974), 21–38. ". . . at no stage of scientific development do we begin without something in the nature of a theory, such as a hypothesis, or a prejudice, or a problem . . . which in some way *guides* our observations, and helps us select from the innumerable objects of observation those which may be of interest," Karl R. Popper, *The Poverty of Historicism* (London, 1975), 134. See also *ibid.*, 135–136. On the cautious discussions of the relationship between population growth and economic change in two widely-read textbooks, see Charles Wilson, *England's Apprenticeship* (London, 1965), 117–118, 362–370; Leslie A. Clarkson, *The Preindustrial Economy in England, 1500–1750* (London, 1971), 25–32, 210–215. The eighteenth-century debate was critically reviewed by David E. C. Eversley, "Population, Economy, and Society," and by David V. Glass, "Population and Population Movements in England and Wales, 1700 to 1850," in Glass and Eversley (eds.), *Population in History* (London, 1965); and by Michael W. Flinn, *British Population Growth, 1700–1850* (London, 1970).

of some influential theories about the nature of demographic and economic change.

The first, and most influential theory of the relationship between population and the economy was formulated by Malthus at the end of the eighteenth century. He focused attention on the implications of a potential tension between population and food supply caused by their relative growth rates which, in his view, characterized all long-settled areas. Since population growth was a compound process, but food supplies were likely to be subject to diminishing proportional increments, he concluded that eventually the amount of food per head must fall until malnourishment raised mortality sufficiently to prevent population from rising faster than the supply of food. For Malthus, however, the operation of the positive check was a limiting case. He also recognized that a population might respond to a shrinking amount of food available per head by reducing fertility well before numbers rose to the level at which starvation became widespread. He thought that this would occur, not through family limitation, which offended contemporary morality, but by "a foresight of the difficulties attending the rearing of a family." That is, in some societies those contemplating marriage would be aware of its economic consequences and would modify their behavior accordingly. Thus the intensity of marriage would decline in response to deteriorating economic fortunes and so supply a preventive check that would lower the rate of population growth, thereby postponing, or even short-circuiting entirely, the operation of a positive check.[5]

On the one hand, where a preventive check prevailed, nuptiality and fertility would vary, keeping the tension between population and resources within reasonable bounds while living standards oscillated at a relatively high level. On the other hand, societies in which marriage was unresponsive to economic circumstances and fertility was constant would experience low standards of living and, at the limit, be wracked by spasms of high mortality. Even in this stylized and summary form Malthus' theoretical formulation of a problem common to most preindustrial societies provides a systematic conceptual framework for the examination of population history in England and in other countries.

5 Thomas Robert Malthus, *An Essay on the Principle of Population* (London, 1798), 62.

Although at first sight Malthus' theory may seem to be abstract and general, in fact it specifies the initial conditions that must obtain before one or more of its consequences will ensue. These conditions are historically specific matters, such as density of settlement, or attitudes to marriage and family formation. The theory, therefore, alerts us to what constitutes the critical conditions affecting demographic and economic change when we compare periods or societies. Far from ignoring the specific nature of historical instances or positing unconditionally valid laws, the theory furnishes a framework within which a wide range of particular circumstances can be evaluated and interpreted.

Malthus' theories provided the intellectual framework for our research to a greater degree than is apparent in the text of *Population History*. Several other scholars, both past and present, also profoundly influenced our research strategy. One early influence was Wynne–Edwards, whose theory of population control among certain species of birds and animals incorporated a territorial version of the preventive check. He interpreted their behavior in terms of a recognition of a limited number of economic positions (territories or niches), and of a restriction of the right to reproduce upon those who occupied them. We were struck by the analogy with preindustrial European societies, which possessed, on the one hand, a subsistence economy with a limited number of farmsteads and artisanal craft practices and, on the other hand, a set of social rules which both required economic independence at marriage and restricted reproduction to married couples. Wrigley explored the application of this model to preindustrial European societies in *Population and History*. We later discovered that Mackenroth had written much earlier in a similar vein. He described reproduction as confined to the occupants of a limited number of full economic positions (*Vollstellen*), the rest of the population being condemned to occupy subsidiary positions (*Hilfsarbeiterstellen*) in which they were prevented from marrying and were therefore largely excluded from reproduction. This social arrangement forced population and the economy to develop in step, and made marriage the most important of the demographic variables.[6]

6  Vero Copner Wynne-Edwards, *Animal Dispersion in Relation to Social Behavior* (Edinburgh, 1962). Malthus' other control theory, the positive check, was influential in the formulation of another biological theory: Darwinian natural selection. William Petersen,

The critical premise in such a view of the relationship between population and economy in the past is the assumption that the number of economic niches, and hence the number of reproducing couples, can be regarded as fixed. In these circumstances nuptiality is determined by the level of adult mortality, for it is the latter that determines the rate at which niches become available. The potential efficacy of such a self-regulating system of population control was demonstrated by Ohlin who calculated that, in the demographic conditions typical of preindustrial populations, the adjusting link between mortality and nuptiality could offset wide fluctuations in the prevailing level of mortality.[7]

The premise of a fixed total of niches, however, seemed too restrictive for preindustrial England, where the economy was expanding fairly quickly, and where many people lived by selling their labor. We, therefore, preferred to follow Malthus in taking a wider view of economic opportunity in relation to the preventive check and to consider marriage to have been responsive to the level of real incomes rather than determined solely by access to a niche. Since, according to another postulate in Malthus' theory, real income was influenced by the pressure of population on resources, the preventive check was conceived as responding not to fluctuations in mortality, but rather to the economic consequences of earlier rates of population growth.

Malthus was acutely aware of the imperfections of markets and the tenacity of custom, and so believed that the preventive check operating through real incomes would be slow to work and might well overshoot the mark. Thus long oscillations would occur in which periods of population growth and declining real incomes would gradually induce less marriage and lower fertility. Population growth would slow down until it reached a point beyond which real incomes stopped falling and began to rise again. This situation in turn would provoke earlier and more frequent marriages, increasing fertility and the rate of population

Malthus (Cambridge, Mass., 1979), 219–224. Wrigley, *Population and History* (London, 1969). A little later Jacques Dupâquier applied the model to French demographic history in "De l'animal à l'homme: le mécanisme autorégulateur des populations traditionelles," *Revue de l'Institut de Sociologie*, II (1972), 177–211. Gerhard Mackenroth, *Bevölkerungslehre* (Berlin, 1953), 431,

7 Göran Ohlin, "Mortality, Marriage, and Growth in Preindustrial Populations," *Population Studies*, XIV (1961), 190–197.

growth. But once more the adjustment would be slow, so that the earlier, economically deleterious phase of the cycle, with rising population and declining real incomes, would be replaced by an advantageous one in which population fell and real incomes rose. Malthus therefore proposed an oscillatory, or negative feed-back, model that linked demographic and economic change through a preventive check which could prove applicable to a society of wage-earners. Moreover, the model was specified in a manner that enabled it to be falsified by checking its predictions against the empirical record even though, as Malthus warned, "the operation of many interrupting causes" would introduce irregularities and make the oscillations difficult to identify and measure.[8]

There were three further considerations that impelled us to take the preventive check seriously when seeking to understand population change in England in the past. First, Hajnal had shown that marriage patterns in Western Europe, at least since the seventeenth century, had differed radically from those of all other societies: women generally married at a later age, and a much higher proportion of women did not marry at all. Hajnal noted that this lower level of nuptiality entailed lower fertility, and that his work corroborated the distinction that Malthus had drawn between Europe, which was characterized by the preventive check, and "the less civilised world," where the positive check prevailed.[9]

Second, the research of Laslett and Wall into household structure had revealed that marriage in preindustrial England involved the setting up of a new household, thereby adding a residential dimension to the normative requirement of economic independence at marriage and implying that the economic hurdle to be surmounted was set at a testing height. Finally, a simulation

---

8  Malthus, *Essay*, 30–36. "This sort of oscillation will not be remarked by superficial observers; and it may be difficult even for the most penetrating mind to calculate its periods." *Ibid.*, 31. One of the "interrupting causes" was "the facility of combination among the rich and its difficulty among the poor, [which] operates to prevent the price of labour from rising at the natural period." Malthus called it "an unjust conspiracy." *Ibid.*, 35–36. Malthus stands out among economic thinkers of his day for his awareness of the degree to which economic relationships were affected by the power structure of a society. Nor was he the upper-class apologist of vulgar Marxist folklore. See Petersen, *Malthus*, 73–77.
9  John Hajnal, "European Marriage Patterns in Perspective," in Glass and Eversley, *Population in History*, 101–143.

exercise by Lesthaeghe left no doubt that changes in nuptiality could powerfully affect the rate of population growth. The nuptiality valve was potentially a force with which to be reckoned.[10]

There was, however, an influential body of theory that argued in the opposite direction, discounting the importance of nuptiality and fertility and emphasizing the role of mortality and the positive check. Transition theory stylizes historical development by contrasting the low, controlled mortality and fertility of industrial societies with the high, uncontrolled levels in traditional societies, which are supposed to lack the means, and perhaps the will, to intervene and limit the natural processes affecting birth and death. Moreover, the theory holds that in pretransitional societies the levels of both nuptiality and fertility are determined by inflexible social custom, and are thus constant. In such a society, therefore, there can be no preventive check, an exclusion which makes mortality the only dynamic variable, and leaves the positive check as the only mechanism by which accommodation might be reached between a population and its limited resources.[11]

England, along with most of Western Europe, experienced a demographic transition toward the end of the nineteenth century. For most of its history, therefore, England—according to transition theory—should have experienced high and unchanging levels of nuptiality and fertility, while mortality varied as the country labored under successive visitations of the positive check. Indeed, until recently most historians subscribed to this view of the demographic character of pretransitional England, apart from a few scholars, such as Marshall, Habakkuk, and Ohlin, who argued for the importance of changes in nuptiality. Many did so because

10   Peter Laslett and Richard Wall, *Household and Family in Past Time* (Cambridge, 1972). Hajnal also pointed out the implications of the European marriage pattern for household structure in "European Marriage Patterns," 132, and has recently emphasized the complementary point that rules governing the formation of households were an important determinant of the European marriage pattern. *Idem,* "Two Kinds of Pre-industrial Household Formation System," in Wall (ed.), *Family Forms in Historic Europe* (Cambridge, 1983), 65–104. Ron Lesthaeghe, "Nuptiality and Population Growth," *Population Studies,* XXV (1971), 415–432.

11   The classic formulation of transition theory is Frank W. Notestein, "Economic Problems of Population Change," in *Proceedings of the Eighth International Conference of Agricultural Economists* (London, 1953), 13–31. For invariant nuptiality and fertility see, for example, Ronald Freedman (ed.), *Population: The Vital Revolution* (New York, 1964), 3. See also the discussion in United Nations, *The Determinants and Consequences of Population Trends* (New York, 1975), 58–60.

surges in mortality were easily visible in the historical record, whereas long-run changes in nuptiality and fertility were much more difficult to demonstrate convincingly.[12]

Yet, despite its influence, transition theory has little relevance to English population history before the radical changes of the late nineteenth century. In place of an understanding of historical change, it offers assertions about population dynamics based on schematic, and wholly unhistorical, assumptions about demographic behavior. Careless of context, it lumps together all pre-transitional societies, past and present, disregarding the mediating influence of specific characteristics of economic and family strucures, institutions, and value systems.

In contrast, Malthus' theoretical framework appealed to us precisely because it treats population change in its social and economic context. Moreover, it is a theory that is particularly well suited to the explanation of historical change because it not only combines conceptual elements into structures, but also explicitly considers the nature of the dynamics of those structures. The theory does not merely describe how demographic and economic elements, such as rates of population growth, food prices, fertility, and mortality, are related: it goes on to tackle the question of how changes in each of these elements affected, and were affected by, changes in the other elements. Thus the theory provides a framework for understanding historical change as a coherent set of interactions between elements that have been abstracted from historical reality.

Our understanding of the nature of the links in each of the various Malthusian chains owes an immense debt to the work of

12   Thomas H. Marshall, "The Population Problem during the Industrial Revolution: A Note on the Present State of the Controversy," in Glass and Eversley, *Population in History,* 247–268; H. John Habakkuk, "English Population in the Eighteenth Century," *ibid.,* 269–284; Ohlin, *The Positive and Preventive Check: A Study in the Rate of Growth of Preindustrial Populations* (New York, 1981). For the consensus view on the primacy of mortality, see Carlo Cipolla, *Economic History of World Population* (London, 1962), 76–77; Flinn, *British Population Growth.* One scholar, McKeown, went to the extraordinary length of asserting that increases in fertility could not in principle have caused population growth rates to rise because they would have been offset by increases in parity-specific infant mortality. Thomas McKeown and R. G. Brown, "Medical Evidence Related to English Population Changes in the Eighteenth Century," *Population Studies,* IX (1955), 119–141. For a refutation of this erroneous, but for many years widely accepted, claim, see Schofield, "The Impact of Scarcity and Plenty on Population Change in England, 1541-1871," *Journal of Interdisciplinary History,* XIV (1983), 267–268.

Lee. In several articles he greatly clarified the logical structure of the various theoretical sets of relationships linking population and the economy by expressing them in symbolic form so that they could be tested empirically. His work brought out the essentially dynamic and mutually interactive character of the relations and focused attention on three important points.[13]

First, since several relations may co-exist and mutually interact, the task of the researcher is to evaluate the relative strength of the links—that is the relative responsiveness of each element to movements in other elements in the causal network. Such a perspective is both less restrictive, and potentially more powerful, than the more usual conceptualization of causation in which only two elements are considered at a time (A causes B), and in which statements tend to be formulated in exclusive terms (*either* A1, *or* A2, causes B). Moreover, when elements are conceived as being related in a complex, mutually interacting network, it is no longer tautologous to say that changes in A provoke changes in B, and changes in B provoke changes in A. The circularity is itself important information about the nature of the processes in question, as is the knowledge that a process may have a number of causes.

Second, an important feature of an interacting causal network of this kind is the interval between changes in one element and the changes that they provoke in another element. A knowledge of the length of such lags not only adds to our understanding of the actual historical processes, but may also help to disentangle multiple causal paths and allocate relative responsibility among the elements concerned.

Third, the time scale of the interactions is important, for the nature of the relationship between two elements may not be the same in both the short and the long run. For example, it is conceivable that either the preventive or the positive check may have operated in the short run, as nuptiality or mortality responded to annual fluctuations in real incomes caused by variations in harvest yields, while more gradual changes in real incomes occurring over the longer term had no demographic effects.

13  See, for example, Ronald Lee, "Population in Preindustrial England: An Econometric Analysis," *Quarterly Journal of Economics,* LXXXVII (1973), 581–607; *idem,* "Models of Preindustrial Population Dynamics with Applications to England," in Charles Tilly (ed.), *Historical Studies of Changing Fertility* (Princeton, 1978), 155–207.

Our reconstruction of the population history of England was far from being an exercise in pure positivism: the telling of a story for its own sake. It was carried out as an experiment in order to provide empirical observations that could falsify or, by failing to falsify, corroborate the theories under debate. This objective determined the nature, time period, and level of aggregation of the historical data to be assembled. First, we needed information on population growth and vital rates (nuptiality, fertility, and mortality), and on real incomes. Second, since the theories predicted the existence of long-continued, lagged, and mutually interacting relationships between the demographic and economic elements, the information had to be available for several centuries. This accessibility of data was also necessary for the investigation of relationships between short-run fluctuations in these elements, because large numbers of observations are needed to distinguish systematic signals from random noise. Third, we decided to study England as a whole, partly because both theory and earlier discussion had been formulated at a national level, but also because local studies are inevitably suspected of being unrepresentative and their findings discounted.

Although England is fortunate in possessing documentary series that extend far back into the past, they are often interrupted, or unavailable for certain localities, for shorter or longer periods of time. Nor do the concrete events listed in the records always correspond with what is ideally required. In our case both difficulties were present: the record was neither uniform, universal, nor continuous; and there was a wide chasm between what was recorded in the sources and what data were needed to examine the theoretical demographic and economic relationships under discussion.

The first part of *Population History,* therefore, was taken up with overcoming these two problems. Our prime aim was to reconstruct the demographic record in such a way that major questions could be adequately addressed. The basic requirements were for information on population growth rates and the vital processes of nuptiality, fertility, and mortality extending as far back as possible in time. In order to calculate the appropriate demographic measures, we needed to obtain information on the size of the population at frequent intervals and continuous data on births, marriages, and deaths.

Regrettably, in the period before the nineteenth century, these basic items of information either were lacking or were available only in a highly unsatisfactory form. The first national census was held in 1801; before that date there were few sources that purported to enumerate a significant fraction of the population. Although it is possible to base national estimates of population totals on these sources, they are too far apart in time, and are surrounded by too great a margin of imprecision to provide acceptable population totals for use in calculating growth rates or to act as the denominator for measuring vital rates.[14]

Estimating the flow of vital events presented almost as many problems as calculating population totals. The state system of vital registration began in 1837. Before that date, the Anglican parish registers recorded totals of events back to the mid-sixteenth century, but the latter were ecclesiastical ceremonies associated with vital events, not the vital events themselves. Unfortunately, it is unsafe to assume that every birth, death, and marriage was followed by an entry in an Anglican register, or that such registration deficiencies were constant over time.[15]

These two problems had so constrained earlier research that the key issues in long-term population development seemed beyond resolution. Most previous work was based on parish register data collected by Rickman from parish incumbents early in the nineteenth century, but the assumptions used in correcting this material varied so widely that some calculations suggested strong population growth in the early eighteenth century whereas others showed no growth at all; some pointed to a rise in fertility, others to a fall in mortality. As Flinn has remarked, all demographic measures derived from Rickman's returns were "built on such shifting sand as to make them virtually unacceptable for the purposes of modern scholarship."[16]

14  Pre-census enumerations and the population estimates that have been based on them are evaluated in Wrigley and Schofield, *Population History*, appendix 5.
15  See, in this connection, John T. Krause, "Changes in English Fertility and Mortality, 1780–1850," *Economic History Review*, XI (1958), 52–70; idem, "The Changing Adequacy of English Registration," in Glass and Eversley, *Population in History*, 379–393.
16  John Rickman collected data on two occasions, in connection with the censuses of 1801 (with later revisions) and 1841. They are published, with accompanying text, in *1801 Census (of England and Wales)*, Observations on the Results and Parish Registers (P[arliamentary] P[apers], 1802, VI); *1811 Census*, Preliminary observations and Parish Registers (PP, 1812, XI); *1841 Census*, Enumeration Abstract (PP, 1833, XXXII). The data are exhaustively evaluated in Wrigley and Schofield, *Population History*, appendix 7. Flinn, *British Population Growth*, 20. For a critical discussion of the methods applied by individual scholars see Glass, "Population and Population Movements," 221–246. The

Some of the difficulties with these data arose from the fact that they were only available for every tenth year in the eighteenth century and even less frequently before that. But even a full enumeration of Anglican events every year would still have left the two basic problems unresolved: how to estimate the numbers of vital events missing from the Anglican registers, and how to estimate changes in the size of a population which, despite heroic assumptions to the contrary, was manifestly not closed. Fifteen years ago these hurdles seemed insurmountable, and the attempt to recover long-term population change had been largely abandoned in favor of studying the short-run fluctuations that were unambiguously evident in the parish registers.[17]

Yet the need for reliable information about nuptiality, fertility, and mortality remained pressing. Hence the interest in family reconstitution, a technique devised by Henry and applied initially with conspicuous success to the registers of a Normandy parish. Family reconstitution not only minimizes the problem of under-registration through a careful selection of the registers to be studied, but also avoids the need for population censuses by applying a set of observational rules to the family records assembled from the register entries that defines for each demographic measure the number of people to be considered at risk to experience the event in question.[18]

Family reconstitution, on the one hand, can provide detailed and dependable evidence about some key demographic variables, such as age at marriage, and age-specific fertility and mortality rates. On the other hand, not only is it an extremely laborious method of analysis, which severely limits the number of communities that can be investigated, but it also yields such small numbers of well-observed families, that most demographic measures have to be estimated over long time periods, typically a quarter or half century, so as not to be affected by random variation. Family reconstitution, therefore, is not well equipped to

various estimates that were based on the parish register abstracts are further evaluated in Wrigley and Schofield, *Population History*, 576–587.

17  Glass was well aware of the need to break away from the parish register abstracts and to tackle the problems of underregistration and net migration from the country. Glass and Eversley, *Population in History*, "Introduction," 8–9.

18  Etienne Gautier and Louis Henry, *La population de Crulai, paroisse normande* (Paris, 1958). The rules for linking entries and deriving demographic measures were adapted to English registers in Wrigley, "Family Reconstitution," in Wrigley (ed.), *An Introduction to English Historical Demography* (London, 1966), 96–159.

provide continuous information about population change at the national level.

We, therefore, resolved to mount a double-pronged attack in which family reconstitution would provide instances of the detailed mechanics of demographic behavior while aggregative methods supplied a wide-angle view of the course of demographic development in the past.[19] But this combination brought us back to the problems that had already defeated so many scholars. A new procedure had to be found.

The first step was to acquire fresh data in order to circumvent some of the restrictions and problems inherent in the parish register data collected by Rickman. Accordingly, with the help of local historians, we established a new and better data base, founded on a continuous series of monthly tabulations of events in the Anglican registers of 404 parishes that met certain minimum criteria of acceptability.[20]

The early stages of our research entailed essential tasks such as checking the quality of the tabulations, finding ways of repairing temporary collapses of registration, and compensating for the fact that not all tabulations began and ended at the same date. It was also necessary to check that our 404 parishes were reasonably typical of the country as a whole and to devise a correction for a bias that emerged. The corrected parish totals were then summed and the aggregate figures were found to agree closely in their proportional changes over time with the totals of events collected for sample years by Rickman from parishes all over the country. This result allowed an inflation ratio to be calculated which, when combined with separate estimates of the numbers of events recorded in London, enabled estimates to be made of the national totals of ecclesiastical ceremonies registered each month from 1539 to 1836.[21]

At this stage we were already in a position to investigate several questions of interest, notably the nature and significance of fluctuations in the series. For totals of ecclesiastical registrations, although falling short of the true numbers of vital events,

19 Results from reconstitution studies were introduced into the text of *Population History* where appropriate. Further preliminary results have been reported in Wrigley and Schofield, "English Population History from Family Reconstitution: Summary Results, 1600–1799," *Population Studies*, XXXVII (1983), 157–184.
20 Wrigley and Schofield, *Population History*, 15–32.
21 *Ibid.*, 15–88.

provided a good guide to *fluctuations* in the underlying demographic processes, with the exception of the period immediately after major mortality crises when the population was suddenly reduced. However, two previously insoluble problems had to be overcome. First, the numbers of events missing from the Anglican registers had to be estimated in a manner which narrowed the range of any remaining uncertainty to within reasonable bounds. Second, once totals of ecclesiastical ceremonies had been converted into totals of vital events, a way had to be found of estimating the size of the population before 1801 which did not assume that net migration was zero.

After much experimentation we at last found a way round the two problems. In both cases demography provided the necessary apparatus: an interdisciplinary approach was vital to the success of the enterprise. We applied demographic modelling to the early censuses to estimate the numbers of events missing from the Anglican registers in the nineteenth century, incidentally confirming Krause's worst fears about the scale of deterioration in parish register coverage during this period. Demographic models were also used to develop a new method of calculating the size of a population that was subject to change through migration from the totals of births and deaths alone. This calculation was made by stepping backwards from a reliable census, five years at a time, backdating the population age pyramid by making each age-group five years younger, and adding the numbers estimated to have died or emigrated in that age-group in the intervening period. The critical breakthrough lay in finding a way to estimate the numbers of net migrants in each period by age, and it was achieved by capitalizing on some basic regularities and consistencies in demographic processes. This method, back projection, yielded quinquennial estimates, not only of the size of the population, but also of its age structure and of net migration, reaching back to 1541. Population growth rates were easily calculable from the population totals, and the latter, combined with birth and death totals, could be made to yield measures of fertility, mortality and nuptiality.[22]

---

22  *Ibid.*, 140–152, 195–199, appendix 15. It was also necessary to find an alternative and stable way of estimating the numbers in the highest age group five years earlier since, by definition, there were no survivors to be backprojected by adding in deaths and migrants. The demographic estimates resulting from backprojection are tabulated in *ibid.*, appendix 3 and discussed on 192–284.

We now possessed the observations needed to test historical theories of population change in England over three centuries. Their acquisition through the collection, critical assessment, and manipulation of the historical evidence constituted the experimental core of the research enterprise. In evaluating the reliability of the sources, and in moving from them to the abstract demographic measures, we had used the rules of evidence and inference of several disciplines. To the traditional methods of historical source criticism were added others taken from demography and statistics. The well-defined structure of relationships that obtained between demographic variables afforded an especially welcome aid, for it provided a discriminating tool which could be deployed to great advantage.

It seemed essential that each step in reconstructing totals of events be fully documented, and that the data be presented in considerable detail at each stage of their progressive refinement. Sufficient information had to be provided to ensure that others could either replicate the experiment or make their own alternative estimates. If our conclusions were to carry conviction, both the methods and the data had to be fully discussed, without eliding or obfuscating any stage in the sequence of operations.[23]

Although at each stage of repairing and refining the data we presented a "best estimate," it was sometimes only one of several plausible alternatives. In such circumstances it seemed important to discover how far uncertainty at any stage might affect the results later in the analysis. In some cases the later results were highly sensitive to earlier variation; in others, they proved insensitive to wide margins of uncertainty at an earlier stage, an outcome that increased confidence in the stability, or robustness, of the results. The level of uncertainty in historical discussion is often high, and the scope for disagreement is correspondingly large. Accordingly, an investigation of the sensitivity of results to alternative assumptions about the evidence can often play a valuable role by indicating the bounds of the area of dispute and so keep the argument focused within manageable limits.[24]

In order to test the various theories of population change, we needed to supplement the new demographic data with data

23  For example, *ibid.*, appendix 4 contains annual totals of events after each major stage of correction and refinement.
24  *Ibid.*, 269–284.

on changing economic circumstances. In particular we required long runs of food prices to test Malthus' central assertion that they were affected by the rate of population growth, and some measure of the standard of living against which to test the responsiveness of nuptiality and mortality. Fortunately, other scholars had already constructed series of food prices and money wages extending over a period of several centuries, although their data left much to be desired in social and geographical representativeness. Although the wage and food price series could be combined to derive a series of real wage rates, the latter was evidently an imperfect indicator of the standard of living as a factor influencing nuptiality or mortality. Ideally we would have liked to have had a measure of real income on a household basis, but the research effort that would have been involved in constructing such a measure was so great that we accepted the limitations of a real wage series as a proxy for household real incomes.[25]

The shortcomings of real wages, on the one hand, are most evident when one measures change over the long run, for they may fail adequately to reflect secular changes in consumption patterns or in the amount of work available at the prevailing wage. This failure was especially true for women and children, whose employment was affected by structural changes in the economy and varied more extensively in the long run than that of males. However, although nominal household incomes may have diverged to some extent from the course suggested by a wage series, they are unlikely to have followed a significantly different trend from the price offered for adult male labor in the market. It therefore seemed reasonable to draw some limited inferences about movements in the trend in real incomes from the real wage series.[26]

Short-run fluctuations, on the other hand, presented fewer problems. Nominal wage rates were sticky, and short-run fluc-

25 We based our real wage series on the series of prices and wages published by E. Henry Phelps Brown and Sheila V. Hopkins, in "Seven Centuries of the Price of Consumables Compared with Builders' Wage Rates," *Economica*, XXIII (1956), 296–314. They are discussed in Wrigley and Schofield, *Population History*, 407–408, 411–412, 430–435, 638–641.

26 Keith D. M. Snell, "Agricultural Seasonal Unemployment, the Standard of Living and Women's Work in the South and East, 1690–1860," *Economic History Review*, XXXIII (1981), 407–37.

tuations in the standard of living were produced overwhelmingly by annual variations in grain prices reflecting the variation in harvest yields. Short-run comparisons of real wages, therefore, avoid the difficulties concerning wages and consumption patterns that complicate an evaluation of long-run change.[27]

Having reconstructed the demographic record over a period of three and a half centuries, and having assembled some crude economic data, we could finally turn to a different level of discussion. Our observations disproved a number of earlier hypotheses and corroborated others. For example, the discovery that fertility varied considerably over the long run falsified an important part of conventional transition theory and its variants, removing at a stroke one of the arguments adduced to explain why population control in the past must have been through variations in mortality. In fact both fertility and mortality varied over time. Moreover, with the exception of three short periods when death rates were far above normal, the range of variation of fertility was about twice as important as that of mortality in determining rates of population growth. Furthermore, a comparison with demographic developments in Sweden and France in the period from 1750 to 1850 revealed differences in the movements of fertility and mortality, and in their relative importance in determining population growth rates, a finding which falsified theories that ascribed uniform demographic characteristics to preindustrial societies.[28]

The reconstituted demographic record also gave short shrift to claims that the positive check was an important element in the control system linking population and the economy in preindustrial England. Although mortality did respond to monthly and annual fluctuations in food prices in the period before 1640, that relationship became attenuated in the following 100 years, and disappeared entirely after 1740. Furthermore, there was effectively no evidence of the positive check at work over the long term.

27  The effect of fluctuations in price on the standard of living would have been reinforced by fluctuations in the earnings of some occupations. For example, the demand for labor of agricultural laborers was directly related to the size of the harvest and, therefore, was low when prices were high. Craftsmen, who produced goods with price elasticities of demand greater than that of foodstuffs, would also suffer fluctuations in their earnings that intensified the effect of price changes on their standard of living.
28  Wrigley and Schofield, *Population History*, 228–248.

Nor was the fixed-niche view of preindustrial societies consistent with the empirical record, for, although nuptiality responded to short-run fluctuations in mortality as widows and widowers remarried, in general long-run movements in nuptiality did not respond positively to mortality trends. Early modern England was evidently far from being a society of peasants and craftsmen in which economic opportunities remained constant over time.[29]

Some theories, however, were corroborated. Malthus' critical proposition that population growth would be accompanied by a rise in food prices was confirmed by the tight positive relationship between the two which persisted throughout the entire preindustrial period. Ironically, the relationship disappeared with industrialization, almost at the very moment that Malthus so forcefully drew attention to its significance. Furthermore, since money wages varied relatively little over the long run, Malthus' proposition that real wages would be inversely related to the rate of population growth was also confirmed.

Similarly his assertion that the preventive check prevailed in England in the past also held true, for not only did nuptiality respond positively to short-run fluctuations in real wages, but its secular trends formed cycles, the turning points of which echoed those of the real wage cycle with a lag of about thirty years. The extent of Malthus' commitment to the preventive check in understanding English population dynamics is often overlooked, and we ourselves only became fully aware of it on rereading his works after we had discovered the critical role that nuptiality had played in English population history. Yet already in the first *Essay*, Malthus had written that "the preventive check to population in this country operates, though with varied force, through all the classes of the community." And in 1824, after a quarter of a century of empirical study, he broadened his claim to include much of Europe:

> Probably it may be said with truth, that in almost all the more improved countries of modern Europe, the principal check which at present keeps the population down to the level of the actual means of subsistence is the prudential restraint on marriage.[30]

29 Short-run relations: *ibid.*, 348–353, 359–384; long-run relations: *ibid.*, 412–417, 466–478.
30 *Ibid.*, 402–412, 417–443. Malthus, *Essay*, 69; *idem*, *A Summary View of the Principle of Population* (London, 1830), 50. The publication was extracted from an article on population contributed to the *Supplement of the Encyclopaedia Britannica* (London, 1824).

There was clear evidence of the relationships that together comprised Malthus' model of a population control cycle operating through the preventive check, and of the long-term oscillations in population growth and living standards that he envisaged. The high rates of population growth in the sixteenth century were accompanied by steep rates of increase in food prices. The latter entailed a sharp fall in real wages, and the accompanying reduction in nuptiality helped squeeze population growth rates until they turned negative in the mid-seventeenth century. As population growth rates declined, so the rate of increase in food prices fell until real wages began to rise. Again nuptiality responded positively to changes in the real wage. After falling for 100 years, it reversed its trend in the late seventeenth century and began to rise, causing a resumption of population growth. By the late eighteenth century the cycle was complete, with strong rates of population growth, rising food prices, falling real wages, and nuptiality beginning to decline again.[31]

In testing theories against the experimental evidence of the reconstructed record we also became aware of features which had not been expected and for which new explanations were needed. For example, the discovery that the long-term swings in mortality that occurred were not related to secular changes in the standard of living raised the question of how they were to be explained. Again, the discovery that turning points in the trend cycle of nuptiality lagged behind those in the real wage cycle by thirty or so years was a puzzle. In putting forward our own tentative hypotheses, both on these two questions and more generally on the whole dynamic network of interactions between population and the economy in England in the past, we adopted a far less rigorous and systematic approach than we applied in reconstructing the demographic observations from defective historical sources. The lack of methodological sophistication in the interpretation of the experimental results was deliberate, for we considered that a simple approach was more appropriate to our present level of understanding.[32]

Certainly some interpretative discussion was required, for to have offered a purely narrative account of the empirical data would have meant that we "returned from our journey through

31   Wrigley and Schofield, *Population History*, 446–478.
32   See, for example, the discussions on exogenous changes in mortality: *ibid.*, 318, 416–417; on the real wage-nuptiality lag: *ibid.*, 430–433; on a general model: *ibid.*, 457–484.

time with no more than a traveller's impressions." At the other extreme, to reduce the complexity of the past to a stylized explanatory model brings disadvantages as well as advantages. It may direct attention to regular and coherent features in the historical record, but it introduces an unreal simplicity and renders invisible much that was important. In the search for understanding there is a constant tension between clarity and comprehensiveness; if one is to be attained, the other must be sacrificed to some degree.[33]

Accordingly, in the final chapter of *Population History* we sought a middle ground, sketching out a conceptual structure in which the interacting dynamics of demographic and economic change could be discussed with due regard to their historical context. We resisted the temptation to carry abstraction a stage further and express the structure in a series of equations, the coefficients of which would indicate the strengths of the relationships between the demographic and economic variables. This decision was not made because of any objection in principle. Indeed, coefficients had been calculated to capture relationships between short-run fluctuations in the variables. However, in the case of relationships over the longer term, both technical and philosophical considerations made us hesitate to embark upon a formal analysis.

First, the mathematical models underlying calculations of this kind involve simplifying assumptions about the nature of the links and their regularity over the full range of values that the variables may acquire. If the assumptions are false, the results may well be spurious. Since we were studying long-term relationships extending over a period of three centuries, during which English society and economy changed greatly, the risk that assumptions of constancy and regularity would be violated seemed unacceptably high. Moreover, one can have little confidence in estimates of the *long-run* parameters of a system when the observations extend over only one and a half cycles.[34]

33   The quoted phrase is from Janssens, "Histoire économique," 30.
34   In the case of short-run relationships between the variables, we were able to reduce the risk of drawing spurious conclusions by comparing the results of several methods, some of which made very weak assumptions. Wrigley and Schofield, *Population History,* 307–309, 320–332, 342–401. There were also sufficient short-run reactions for it to be possible to calculate separate estimates for each of the three centuries being studied. *Ibid.,* 373–377, 392–398. The last point in this paragraph was first made by Kenneth Wachter at the conference on British Demographic History (1982).

Second, rather than strive for formal rigor of expression, it seemed more fruitful as a first step to propose ideas and explanations grounded in our understanding of social and economic history, however informal or tentative they might be. For, although formality and rigor are necessary in testing existing ideas against the empirical record, the generation of new ideas owes more to intuition and imagination controlled by a sense of context. The need for creative thinking is especially strong in history, so much of which occupies an uncharted space between the better defined territories of other disciplines. In the absence of any unifying scientific theory of social structure and change, historical explanation is bound to be informal and eclectic. Moreover, the incorporation of the partial and sectoral theories of other disciplines within a wider historical explanation requires an awareness of the substantive context to ensure that the initial conditions, upon which the validity of each theory depends, are in fact fulfilled. So while we began our experiment by subjecting existing theories to a severe test, we finished in a more exploratory vein.[35]

Several scholars have already embarked upon the task of examining the implications of our ideas. Some, for example, have pointed to the need to break down the national demographic and economic aggregates, the functioning of which we investigated, into their regional components. There is no doubt that such an initiative is needed, although the calculation of long-term regional demographic trends poses daunting problems.[36] Yet it does not follow that the relationships involved can *only* be properly understood at a regional or local level, even if the experience of the national aggregate proves not to have been typical of any one part of the country. For "nation," "region," and "locality" are abstrac-

35  The structural dilemma of how to combine analysis and synthesis, which all historians face, has been well expressed by Janssens: "In maintaining its global and synthetic perspective history would appear to be the most ambitious and imperialist of the human sciences. . . . Synthetic by vocation, history is forced into specialisation because its explanatory models are only sectoral. But sooner or later the historian has to meet the challenge of synthesis that he finds facing him in concrete reality." Janssens, "Histoire économique," 34–35. For the crucial role played by initial conditions in all scientific theories, and their importance in bounding the validity of historical explanations, see Popper, *Poverty of Historicism*, 122–130.
36  The most serious problem is the difficulty of calculating the numbers of events missing from the Anglican registers in the early nineteenth century. Since net migration was unlikely to have been zero in many regions and localities, the methods applied to the censuses at the national level cannot be used. Wrigley and Schofield, *Population History*, 103–136.

tions, and each level of abstraction has its own meaning. To move from a national investigation to a regional one is, therefore, to add a new level of understanding. The latter need neither negate nor supersede the earlier, rather as the conceptual relationships of chemistry are neither negated nor superseded because they are reducible to those of physics.[37]

Other scholars have noticed the critical role accorded to the preventive check, and have wondered why we did not do more to investigate the web of attitudes that affected marriage behavior. Indeed, it may seem ironic that a book which began by tackling "the wide open spaces of demography and mathematical lifelessness" should end by focusing attention on "the marshlands of sex and family life." But the progression was deliberate and reflected our commitment to the view that, since no theory or explanation can be proved to be true, scientific understanding must advance through elimination. Since the dominant explanations were cast in the form of theories of population change, only some of which contained an attitudinal component, the first task was to find some way of testing the encompassing theories; for only then would it become clear which aspects of behavior and attitudes in the past should be the focus of attention. As the theories were essentially quantitative, the initial attack on the problem had to be statistical rather than attitudinal, temporarily neglecting the individual in favor of the mass.[38]

The research upon which *Population History* was based was an application of the experimental method to a specific set of historical problems. Although this method is an essential ingredient of any scientific discipline, there are areas of historical enquiry to which it is inappropriate. Not every interpretive idea that brings order into our view of the historical record can be formulated in terms of a testable theory or hypothesis. Although such an idea cannot be refuted, so that we can never know whether it is false, it may still be of value in furthering our understanding of the past.

The problem with which we began, however, was one of making sense of a field of enquiry in which there was a plethora

37 On complexity, abstraction, and levels of explanation, see Popper, *Poverty of Historicism*, 139–140.
38 Gaunt, "Review Symposium," 141; Popper, *The Logic of Scientific Discovery* (London, 1959).

of competing explanations which were in principle testable, but which could only be tested effectively with more reliable data than any then available. Our experiment in reconstructing the English demographic record was designed to bring the historical *explicandum* into sharper focus, primarily so that those existing theories, speculations, and prejudices that did not accord with observation could be removed from the universe of historical discourse. But new observations can generate new theories and explanations that suggest where the next round of critical empirical investigations can most effectively be made. Our own contributions to this second phase of the experimental dialectic have deliberately been cast in the form of tentative interpretations rather than formal hypotheses. We hazarded them in the hope, and expectation, that other scholars would take up the challenge, refining them and, where possible, testing and refuting them by new observations or experiments.[39]

39  For a fascinating discussion of an epistemological dialectic of theory and experiment, which involves a continuing process of the "retransmission of falsity" in "concept-stretching refutations," see Lakatos, *Proofs and Refutations,* 47–76, 92–99.

*Michael Anderson*

# Historical Demography after *The Population History of England*

One of the earliest reviews of *The Population History of England* was entitled "History will never be the same again." In this article I consider three aspects of that claim: how far long-debated questions have been definitively answered; which questions should now occupy the attention of historical demography; and, more widely, whether the book represents a model which historians should seek to emulate in the future.[1]

If the figures and interpretations offered in the book are broadly correct, the potential importance of the findings of *Population History*, not only for demographic but also for economic and social history, are enormous. For the first time, we can make reasonable estimates of the population history of a Western country for all of the last 440 years. We can also do much more: we can identify the changing patterns of demographic fluctuations and crises; we can estimate population age structures, birth and death rates, expectations of life, and, with less certainty, patterns of nuptiality and migration. We can explore the mechanisms by which changes in birth, death, marriage, and migration produced changes in the size of a national population; and we can begin to posit links to economic and social changes knowing that at least some of the elements in our model are of reasonable reliability.

Moreover, if we accept the figures, many of the old topics of debate and methods of procedure now need fundamental reconsideration; old debates have been moved to a new level. No longer do we have to speculate about whether population size actually fell in the seventeenth century, or whether the 1590s saw

Michael Anderson is Professor of Economic History, University of Edinburgh. He is the author of *Approaches to the History of the Western Family, 1500–1914* (London, 1980).

The author is grateful to Rosalind Mitchison, Elspeth Moodie, and Robert J. Morris for their perceptive comments on an earlier draft of this article.

1 E. Anthony Wrigley and Roger S. Schofield, *The Population History of England, 1541–1871: A Reconstruction* (Cambridge, Mass., 1981); Leslie Clarkson, "History will never be the same again," *Times Higher Education Supplement* (Feb. 5, 1982).

massive population decline. Nor do we have to wonder about the timing and path of population growth in the eighteenth century. No longer do we have to argue about whether the eighteenth-century population growth in England was more the result of fertility or of mortality changes; instead we have to ask what it was that produced the nuptiality changes which underlay the dominant rise in fertility.

The relative unimportance of demographic crises in long-term population change raises a new question. Was England's "fertility-dominated low-pressure system" really so different from that of other parts of Europe and even from other parts of the British Isles and, if this was in fact the case, what explains the difference? No longer can we extrapolate experience from one European country to another; indeed we now must ask whether the same processes even operated in different regions of the same country.[2]

The enormous potential of back projection as a way of converting series of births, deaths, and marriages into a range of more useful demographic measures gives us an important new technique to evaluate and with which to experiment. Methodologically, back projection brings aggregative analysis back to a central place in demographic method; its strengths and weaknesses are shown to complement the strengths and weaknesses of the equally partial technique of family reconstitution.

Substantively, back projection raises two major questions at either end of the period studied. First, did 1871 really see the beginning of a new demographic system in which the previously strong bonds between demographic and economic variables were dissolved? If this were indeed the case, what does it imply for our interpretation of the fertility decline in late nineteenth-century England? And, if we accept Wrigley and Schofield's view that demographic systems before the decline were differently configured throughout much of Europe, what are the implications for

2 The quoted phrase comes from Wrigley and Schofield, *Population History,* 451. Contrast, for example, the pattern suggested for Scotland by Michael W. Flinn et al., *Scottish Population History* (Cambridge, 1977), 201–438. Of particular interest is the suggestion of continued high mortality in Scotland until the very late seventeenth century and the tentative calculations which indicate that both fertility and mortality were, in the mid-eighteenth century, at much higher levels than are estimated by Wrigley and Schofield for England (although the mid-nineteenth-century figures are almost identical).

our understanding of the parallel fertility declines elsewhere in Europe?

Second, at the other end of the period, the question arises of the longevity and origins of the mid-sixteenth-century regime of high population growth rates and high levels of fertility. Was it the last gasp of an earlier "high pressure system" with high fertility offsetting high mortality, as Wrigley and Schofield seem to imply, or simply part of an earlier phase of the "low pressure system" visible after 1541, but with fertility temporarily elevated in a lagged response to the very high "real wage" levels of the late fifteenth century? And if the low-pressure interpretation is valid, what are the implications for our understanding of English medieval demography?[3]

For the economic historian, the implications are also considerable. Those who see population only as a figure from which it is possible to estimate output per head now have figures which, whatever their faults, are more reliable than any output figures for any period before the mid-nineteenth century. Those who want to see population as an important demand-side input can now reasonably assume that there was a regularly fluctuating but steadily rising growth curve over the whole period from the mid-seventeenth to the early nineteenth centuries; the check of the 1720s is little more than a hiccup in an accelerating trend.

On the resource input front we have the additional important information that, although the scene may have differed regionally, nationally the classic industrial revolution period saw a steady worsening of the dependency ratio right up to 1826, with clear implications for the standard of living debate. Thereafter, however, there were thirty years of rapid improvement in dependency, not an insignificant factor in the economic development of the really crucial phase of growth in output.[4]

Most fascinating of all, we are offered the possibility that within a century, from about 1640 to 1740, "the economy was able to profit from the advantages that flow from a rising level of real income and to undergo structural change in consequence without provoking a population rise fast enough to threaten fur-

3 See, on this point, Elspeth M. Moodie's contribution to the review symposium in *Social History*, VIII (1983), 159–168.
4 Cf., for example, Nicholas F. R. Crafts, "British Economic Growth, 1700–1831: A Review of the Evidence," *Economic History Review*, XXXVI (1983), 177–199.

ther progress. The unusual length of this benign period was in part the gift of the economic/demographic regime which characterised early modern England." Such a view would clearly add weight to the case of those who argue that the origin of economic expansion in the eighteenth century owed much to processes of social and economic reorganization in the century before.[5]

Finally, for the social historian, there is much to ponder and much new work to do, both in exploring some of the familial and community background to the demographic changes, and also in considering the implications for individual and family life cycles of the long-run changes in the demographic variables. Some specific issues are discussed below, but one general implication can be mentioned here. In the past, the family has usually been seen both by sociologists and by historians as responding to wider economic and social changes rather than as having an independent dynamic and impact of its own. Although not so dramatic as recent speculations by Todd, Wrigley and Schofield's work has brought marriage and the family back to the center of the social science stage, with nuptiality patterns and systems exerting profound influences on population, and population in turn being seen as playing a new role in economic change.[6]

All of these implications depend on whether Wrigley and Schofield's figures are plausible, and on whether the new direction that they have given to historical demography is the right one. It is to these problems that I now turn.

In *Population History* the authors describe their work as "a reconstruction." Exercises in reconstruction are not new to historians. Indeed, whether they realize it or not, historians do just that whenever they take the scattered remnants which survive from the past and use them to construct an interpretive account of past behavior. In doing so they always evaluate the reliability, and the validity for their purposes, of the materials to hand and, where they believe that problems exist, they make adjustments to allow for bias and random error due to small numbers. *Population History* conforms to classical principles in this respect.

---

5   Wrigley and Schofield, *Population History*, 439.
6   Emmanuel Todd, *La Troisème Planète: Structures Familiales et Systèmes Ideologiques* (Paris, 1983).

The attempt to recover long-term population trends is fortunate in being largely free from one of the most important problems affecting many recent exercises in quantitative research in economic and social history. In any piece of research we have first to evaluate both the *reliability* of the data as indicators of the phenomena that we wish to analyze (to ensure that they are consistently measured across observers and over time) and their *validity* (the extent to which they are meaningful indicators of the underlying concepts which we wish to explore).[7]

Later, in the data analysis stage, we have a further problem: to find ways of modeling with our data the social or economic relationships or processes that we wish to explore. Most of the debate which has surrounded recent cliometrics stems either from questions about the validity of the indicators employed, or from the oversimplified models that are used to build equations which can be solved with the data and computational techniques available. In historical demography there are clearly problems with the reliability of the data—but these are, at least in theory, susceptible to arithmetical adjustment. In contrast, there are fewer problems of validity, since we share with contemporaries the idea that burials normally imply a dead body, and baptisms a birth, and it is births and deaths that we wish to measure.[8]

The models used in demographic analysis—for example in back projection—can often, conceptually, if not always operationally, be relatively simple. The main demographic relationships involve dichotomous variables which can be shown in the real world to have remarkable tendencies to conform to distributions with relatively simple arithmetical properties. It is thus important for even the most ardent opponent of recent tendencies in econometric history to realize that, in the early chapters of *Population History*, Wrigley and Schofield are dealing with a very different type of analysis. Their approach, in spite of any superficial dis-

7   Readers unfamiliar with this important distinction will find useful discussion in almost any standard sociological methods textbook (e.g. Renate Mayntz et al., *Introduction to Empirical Sociology* [Harmondsworth, 1976], 17–23).
8   The very real problems of under-recording are problems of bias and not of validity; contrast the debates over the legitimacy of the cost benefit analyses employed by much recent cliometrics, or the ongoing debate over the standard of living during the British industrial revolution, which to a great extent turns around the validity of different conceptualizations and measurements of the standard of living.

similarities, is much closer in methodology and technique to traditional history, but it is immensely and impressively more explicit and rigorous.

There are considerable shortcomings with the basic data set in *Population History* and there is ongoing controversy over whether the adjustments made in moving from a sample of 404 parishes to estimates of national frequencies were appropriate ones. My comments focus on the wider significance of two ways in which the data were treated.

First, as the introduction makes clear, the information on the 404 parishes which underlie the whole exercise was originally collected for the very different purpose of identifying registers suitable for family reconstitution. London, small parishes, and those with major discontinuities in registration were excluded from the beginning; in addition, the fact that local volunteers did much of the work of counting and were given considerable freedom over where they worked further skewed the "sample" toward certain areas and kinds of community. One result was that the number of parishes contributing to the data set and the number of observations in any year in the middle decades of the sixteenth century and again after 1812 were rather small. Another result was an uneven regional coverage (at the extremes and after reweighting for parish size biases in the original collection of data). For example, 12.5 percent of the parishes are from Bedfordshire and none is from Cornwall.

The authors argue that they have developed valid procedures for incorporating London and that the biases in the original data collection after adjustment do not seriously distort the trends. For the central period (from 1662 to 1811), during which all 404 parishes were included in the observations, they may well be right, although some of the biases are, at face value, unfortunate. Although the occupational profiles of the sample parishes match the population very well, one intuitively regrets the absence of any parish from Cornwall, with its high nineteenth-century adult male mortality, or of any of the great disease-ridden, manufacturing and commercial cities of the nineteenth century. Moreover, in the late eighteenth and early nineteenth centuries, there are major problems of underregistration which, together with the inevitable problems of shifting between ecclesiastical and civil registration in 1837, counsel caution in accepting uncritically the precise size and nature of trends in the early nineteenth century, as outlined in the book.

Again, at the beginning of the series, in the sixteenth century, it is possible that the overall trends are not particularly skewed by the small numbers of parishes in observations. But the fact that manipulation and inferences have to be based on such a small amount of data must increase our uncertainty about this important period. Although considerable work would have been involved in extending the data set to reduce these biases, it is nevertheless a source of regret that, at the point where it was decided to change the uses of the data so far collected and to proceed to full-scale aggregative analysis, a full reappraisal of the research design was not undertaken. Even if the results would not have looked very different, confidence would have been increased. There is, perhaps, a lesson here for the future.[9]

Second, the implications of *Population History* as a potential model for future developments in historical demography make it important to raise some fundamental questions of interpretation of quantitative historical data. For example, do the authors not accept too readily that a correlation must indicate a causal connection between two variables? In so doing they may be overlooking the possibility that posited associations may be spurious, produced by a third variable that is positively and causally related to both of the original variables so that the connection between the original variables disappears when the effect of the third variable is controlled for. In a study that spans more than three centuries and embraces at least one major economic transformation, is it reasonable to prefer a single explanatory model, or should we not take more seriously the possibility that a number of different sets of forces may have been operating at different times, even that at certain periods the basic resource to population link may not have been reversed? Finally, what is the justification

---

9  Moodie, in *Social History*, VIII, 160, has pointed out that the parishes in observation early in the series do seem to have higher mortality in the later sixteenth and seventeenth centuries relative to mortality in the early eighteenth century than was the case with the parishes which come into observation later. There are other reasons for doubt about the early period, as the authors themselves note, both because of the uncertainty over the frequency of remarriages and because, as one moves back in time, more and more of the population estimates have to be derived from what are at best guesses about the courses of fertility and mortality from 1446 to 1540, which would by no means satisfy all late medieval historians.

for assuming, as the authors implicitly do, than an explanation of individual and family behavior can legitimately be sought through variables measured at a national level?[10]

One possibility, with regard to spurious correlations, is that they may have been generated by measurement errors in the index of real wages that was used—an index of building workers' wages. Demand for the kinds of building in which these workers were previously involved is likely to have been sensitive both to increases in income levels among the very rich in periods of expansion and, to a possibly lesser extent, to population levels directly, thereby increasing the possibility that a spurious association may have arisen.[11]

But even if measurement were not a problem, is it not possible that a third variable of a different kind might have produced the observed effects? In any long cycle, for example, economic expansion, begun for exogenous reasons, might well have been mirrored initially in rises in real wages with no immediate effects on the structure of the labor force or on population. If the rise were sustained, however, as the slack in the existing system was used up, the expansion would have begun to draw a larger proportion of the population into the growing sector of the economy and possibly also into a proletarian or pseudo-proletarian sector. Because, in the first case, the expanding sector would have contained more new opportunities and, in the second, the property restraint on marriage would have been reduced for those involved, nuptiality would then probably have risen. Economic growth

10  For a useful methodological discussion of the concept of spuriousness, see Hubert M. Blalock, *An Introduction to Social Research* (Englewood Cliffs, 1970), 69–72. Although the authors claim (411) that their research casts doubt on the relevance for the English early modern period of Ester Boserup's *The Conditions of Agricultural Growth*(London, 1965), an alternative reading of Fig. 10.4 (410) could lend considerable support to Boserup's view, at least as it relates to the critical late sixteenth- and early seventeenth-century period.

11  The problems with this index, created by E. Henry Phelps Brown and Sheila V. Hopkins in "Seven Centuries of the Price of Consumables, Compared with Builders' Wage Rates," *Economica,* XXIII (1956), 296–314, have recently been summarized by Donald Woodward in "Wage Rates and Living Standards in Pre-Industrial England," *Past & Present,* 91 (1981), 28–45. Woodward demonstrates that wages formed only a part of income in this period so that living standards will have been cushioned from the full impact of wage and price changes. However, to my mind, he fails to establish the point that the index is a poor indicator of the direction of trend in living standards over the medium term, and it is for this purpose that it is used by Wrigley and Schofield.

would thus have produced changes in economic opportunities and these changes would have produced a lagged response in nuptiality. There could also have been a rise in living standards as the economy expanded but, with a stable or slow-growing population, the link between changes in living standards and population growth would be very different from that posited by Wrigley and Schofield (the direct connection being spurious, and the correlation being the result of simultaneous association with a third variable).

It would require considerable research to establish the plausibility of this proposition, but its plausibility is not the issue here. The question is a methodological one: How, given the evidence available to us, do we decide whether to prefer it or the explanation offered in the book? It would clearly be a mistake for readers to assume, because the interpretations offered in *Population History* are part of a book of which much of the methodology is very advanced, that the ideas used to link population to resources are in any fundamental way superior to those of old fashioned history. The interpretations depend largely on the intuitive plausibility of deductions, made in a basically ad hoc manner, from an observed, rather rough, cross-time relationship between two phenomena. Little direct evidence is produced for the linkage, nor is it analyzed in a statistically profound way. Thus the content of the interpretative chapters is very different from the methodological sophistication of the earlier parts of the book. This distinction is not intended to decry the effort, rather to show how far we have yet to go.

Whatever the complexities of analysis, a prior question that needs to be addressed is that of the level of generality at which the data are to be collected and explained. Whether we are testing for a Malthusian positive or preventive check, or whether we are investigating Wrigley and Schofield's own model, would we necessarily expect to be able to identify their workings with national level data?

There are two potential problems. First, within the national totals, significant changes in distribution of the variables were surely occurring: for example, in the distribution of income and wealth; in the proportion and degree to which the population was dependent on wage labor; and in the relative importance in incomes of wages and of goods in kind. Changes may have occurred in the distributions of nuptiality which, because of the asymmetry of fertility over the life course, could have had important consequences, even if the mean age of marriage remained constant. We know little about any of these shifts, except for superficial impressions that they may have occurred most rapidly in periods of major economic transition. However, in so far as these distributions changed markedly, movements in the "average" indicators may reflect very different, and possibly conflicting, compositional trends. The aggregate could well be little more than a statistical artifact.

Second, consider the underlying models which Malthus produced and those which Wrigley and Schofield imply as connections between marriage and the real wage. Both models involve individuals and their families confronting resource opportunities and constraints which do not in reality affect them homogenously at a national level, but rather affect them heterogenously at the level of the community, its migration field, and the individual family. Moreover, at a point in time, different individuals, even within the same region, do not confront the same resource constraints: a rise in prices does not produce the same impact on all individuals; nor are the resources required to establish a new household an absolute—they too can change over time and can differ between families.

Thus, statistically, on average, if prices rise faster than wages, the average level of available resources will, in the absence of technical developments, decline so that the "average" person implied by the model will have to wait longer to acquire the "average" resource level which would precede marriage. In practice, however, given the distribution of individuals across different regions and sectors of the economy, the consequences of rising prices will be very diverse. The squeeze on resources may lead some to starve and others to delay marriage; it may also push more individuals into the labor force, thereby possibly raising the likelihood of marriage; or it may make people reluctant to leave their own villages and thus keep them tied to the land, thereby probably reducing nuptiality. Or it may simply force more subsidiary labor on to the market or expand the foraging economy, so that marriage chances remain unchanged. Some individuals will benefit from the rising prices by receiving higher incomes: they may acquire more land or more cheap workers and may as a result marry younger and have more children; or their expectations of an adequate standard of living may change as a new reference group comes into view, with the paradoxical result that a rise in real incomes may lead to delayed marriage.

In any period of economic expansion or contraction some areas will be affected more than others; not all sectors of the economy will benefit or lose equally. Thus, not merely are the average values of real wages based on an aggregation of different distributions over time, but the level of prosperity necessary to establish a household through marriage may not be related linearly to changes in the real wage. Thus, an interpretation couched in national terms may fall into "the fallacy of the wrong level" because of the implicit assumption that what happens to the average is also happening to the individuals underlying it.[12]

There are two pieces of evidence which lend support to the view that the aggregate may be an average artifactual result of many conflicting tendencies, with the result that a national level correlation could be misleading. The first piece of evidence comes in the family reconstitution results, only some of which are published in detail; these results do, however, reveal some differences in tendency among parishes, especially in nuptiality and in infant and child mortality. The second piece of evidence, which is even more striking, is the remarkable variation in the timing of recovery from the mid-seventeenth-century crisis as revealed in Table 6.1 of *Population History*. Although some of the figures may reflect differences in local patterns of under-registration, they do suggest that the national average figures are an aggregate of different underlying tendencies. Yet the causal model developed by Wrigley and Schofield does not address differences of time, place, and economic structure, apparently assuming a homogeneous underlying experience.[13]

There is one final point of methodology that follows from any consideration of alternative hypotheses. In evaluating a historical investigation based upon data of this scale and complexity, readers are at a disadvantage when considering the effects of

12 A useful discussion of the "fallacy of the wrong level" can be found in Johan Galtung, *Theory and Methods of Social Research* (London, 1967), 45–48, 79–80.

13 See, for example, Wrigley and Schofield, "English Population History from Family Reconstitution: Summary Results, 1600–1799," *Population Studies*, XXXVII (1983), 157–184. *Idem, Population History*, 163.

adjustments made to raw data and when exploring possible internal variations within the data set if they do not have access to the computer programs as well as the data used by the authors. This problem raises important issues of historical practice for, if work of this kind is to become widespread, it will be impossible to verify independently alternative interpretations without access of this kind. However, computer programs of the type used on this project are historically specific tools which may not be easily transportable from one site to another. They only remain useful if maintained through time across generations of computer systems.

*Population History* raises in an acute form some basic and enduring questions about the processing, evaluation, and interpretation of historical data concerning economic and social behavior over long periods of time. It also reveals new areas urgently requiring research which fall outside the scope of demographic history as conventionally defined. Although the book may stimulate researchers to develop better real wage indicators, there are theoretical and methodological reasons for doubting whether a significant contribution to our understanding of long-run, national demographic change will result. For many purposes, indeed, a higher priority may be to learn more about the occupational and sectoral distribution of the labor force; about numbers of apprentices, journeymen, and domestic servants; about who entered service and how long they stayed there; and about how many people and of what type depended, on what occasions, on poor relief and charity. How did all of these matters differ by region and change with developments in agrarian systems and agricultural techniques and with developments in industrial production and urban life?

On the familial side, we need to know much more about the conditions under which households were established; about the minimum resources which had to be obtained before marriage at different periods, and how they were obtained (for example the relative importance of inheritance, loans, and saving from earnings); about courtship and matchmaking, and the role of sex in precipitating or retarding movement into matrimony; about the situations under which remarriages occurred; and about changes in the distribution of ages at marriage. We need, if possible, to explore how these factors varied regionally, occupationally, and by socioeconomic circumstance. And we need to establish whether there was something special about these familial matters which supported or produced the English low-pressure demographic system. This problem clearly needs comparative research on an international scale.

To understand the population history of England requires an integration of economic, social, and demographic history. This requirement in turn sets a challenging agenda for the development of new methods: multi-source record-linkage studies at the local level to explore the conditions under which marriage and household formation occurred; the linking of late medieval and early modern demography across the 1541 parish-registration divide; an investigation of how we link what will at best be ordinal level social data with demographic data susceptible to higher levels of measurement; a search for techniques by which we can statistically link findings from a number of small-scale studies in ways more sophisticated than simply taking means, or means of means. Finally, the development in Britain of something like the Scandinavian and German ethnographic approach, with its strong ecological base, might well aid our understanding of the household economics of pre-twentieth-century English society and deepen our understanding of the dynamics of demographic and economic history.

*Peter H. Lindert*

# English Population, Wages, and Prices: 1541—1913

Malthus was certain of it. Population growth brought costly food, scarce land, low wages, pauperism, and misery. Poor relief could only prolong the agony by spreading an insufficient food supply among more families and encouraging the poor to procreate. More people would continue to mean more suffering and shorter lives. Only prudential checks on marriage and fertility could hold the masses above the subsistence margin.[1]

For all his conviction, Malthus had a difficult time finding enough demographic and economic data to parry critics. The early censuses did not yield the proof that he sought: they failed to show that England, with her generous poor relief, had any more marriages or larger families than the rest of Europe, as he admitted. The 1801 census helped his cause by counting more Britons than most observers had expected, but it lacked the historic sweep that his arguments needed. Without a broader data base, even the food scarcity of the French war years left many unpersuaded by his emphasis on overpopulation. In a debate that comes back to haunt us, Malthus had to struggle again and again with those who "have attributed the dearness of provisions to the quantity of paper in circulation." Lacking good data on population, prices, and wages from a variety of historical settings, he could not show the dependence of food prices and other signs of scarcity on population pressure.[2]

Better population data are now at hand. Wrigley and Schofield have quantified 330 years of English population history without leaning heavily on the shaky census estimates available to

Peter H. Lindert is Professor of Economics at the University of California, Davis. He is the author of *Fertility and Scarcity in America* (Princeton, 1978).

The author wishes to thank the National Science Foundation for financial support and Thomas Renaghan and Ricardo Silveira for research assistance. Helpful criticisms and suggestions were also given by Ronald D. Lee, Thomas Mayer, Donald McCloskey, Anna Schwartz, Kenneth Sokoloff, Jeffrey Williamson, and E. Anthony Wrigley.

1  Thomas Robert Malthus, *An Essay on the Principle of Population* (London, 1798; reprinted 1970).
2  Patricia James, *Population Malthus* (London, 1979), 90–91, 138, 200, 201.

Malthus. Although Wrigley and Schofield may have slightly mis-estimated vital rates before 1840, their estimates of the annual level of population square with all other evidence and represent the best guesses available. We can now follow English population across decades of Tudor inflation, alternations of war and peace, the industrial revolution, and the modern demographic transition. Their figures provide excellent opportunities for testing Malthus' assertions—that remain controversial today—about the economic consequences of rising population.[3]

Following in Malthus' trail with fresh data proves to be a challenging and enjoyable intellectual journey. The trail takes some surprising twists and turns. It is more difficult to demon-strate the influence of population on real wages and relative prices than scholars have usually acknowledged. Straightforward tests using the data at hand leave doubts about the basic Malthusian belief that extra population depresses wage rates. These doubts spring from weaknesses in the available wage data and from the strong correlation between population movements and price movements before 1815, a correlation that complicates any at-tempt to isolate the effects of English population growth. One of the tasks of this article is to mark this boundary of our empirical knowledge.

To advance beyond this boundary, we must, like Malthus, pass through a monetary area that might have seemed remote from the population-food-wage nexus. To unravel the sources of the early modern price movements that influenced wages, we need to ponder what monetarism and Malthusianism may be able to teach each other. By improving our focus on these issues, the new Wrigley-Schofield population estimates give new urgency to the pursuit of three kinds of fresh data for England and the Continent before 1871: wage rates, money stocks, and better Continental population estimates.

FROM POPULATION TO REAL WAGES: INITIAL TESTS    The key to Malthusian faith continues to be the belief that population growth lowers living standards. Investigation of this belief has rightly

3   E. Anthony Wrigley and Roger S. Schofield, *The Population History of England, 1541–1871: A Reconstruction* (Cambridge, Mass., 1981), appendices 5, 6. On their possible misestimation of vital rates, see the issues and suggestions raised in Lindert, "English Living Standards, Population Growth, and Wrigley-Schofield," *Explorations in Economic History,* XX (1983), 134–149.

centered on the real low-skilled wage rate as a proxy for living standards. The net effect of population on a more global measure of living standards, such as gross national product (GNP) per capita, is ambiguous. Although adding more mouths and more hands to a fixed stock of capital and land should reduce product per person, population growth may stimulate capital formation, the advance of knowledge, and the development of market connections. These stimuli might easily erase any net effect on product per capita, as suggested by the absence of a negative correlation between population growth and product-per-capita growth in modern international comparisons or in British history. Yet wage rates could be depressed even in the absence of a negative effect on overall product per capita, so long as the stimuli to capital formation and knowledge do not raise the demand for labor as much as population growth augments labor supply. For these reasons, and because real wage data extend further back in time than data on product per capita, it is appropriate to focus on the alleged negative effect of population on wage rates.[4]

Malthus himself applied the wage test to English experience. Drawing on the historical work of Sir Frederick Morton Eden and others, he gave the history, as outlined in Table 1, of the ability of agricultural day laborers to buy wheat. Malthus' interpretation of these movements is revealing. He dwelt on the two periods of corn-wage decline, in Tudor times and in his own lifetime, asserting that population must have grown in both periods, thus explaining the growing misery of laborers. He insisted that the corn-wage declines were not due to inflation of the money supply, but he offered no test for showing the superiority of his demographic hypothesis over the monetarist views of inflation that were already three centuries old when he wrote. He showed discomfort when confronting evidence of rising corn wages, attributing the high wages of the fifteenth century to unknown "temporary causes" and avoiding any comment on the high wage rates of the eighteenth century before the French Wars.[5]

4 Simon Kuznets, *Modern Economic Growth* (New Haven, 1966), 56–68; Richard A. Easterlin, "Effects of Population Growth on the Economic Development of Developing Countries," *Annals of the American Academy of Political and Social Science,* CCCLXIX (1967), 98–108; Jean-Claude Chesnais and Alfred Sauvy, "Progrès économique et accroissement de la population: une expérience commentée," *Population,* XXVIII (1973), 843–857; Julian L. Simon, *The Ultimate Resource* (Princeton, 1981), 260–261.
5 Malthus, *Principles of Political Economy* (London, 1836; 2nd ed.; reprint, New York, 1951), 241–251.

*Table 1* Malthus' Evidence on English Wages and Prices, c. 1350–1811

| YEAR | DAILY WAGE (WITHOUT MEALS) (PENCE/DAY) | PRICE OF WHEAT (PENCE/PECK) | "CORN WAGE" (PECKS/DAY) |
|---|---|---|---|
| c. 1350 | 1.5–2.0 | 2.00 | 0.75–1.00 (fell to 1377, rose to 1398) |
| 1413–1444 | 3.0 | 3.25 | 0.92 |
| 1444–1500 | 4.0–4.5 | 2.25 | 1.78–2.00 |
| 1485–1509 | 4.0–4.5 | 2.38 | 1.68–1.89 |
| 1571–1575 | 8.0 | 8.25 | 0.97 |
| 1601 | 10.0 | 15.50 | 0.65 |
| 1650–1655 | 14.0 | 24.00 | 0.58 |
| 1656–1661 | 14.0 | 18.50 | 0.76 |
| 1665–1700 | 10.5–12.0 | 15.94 | 0.66–0.75 |
| 1700–1720 | 10.0–10.5 | 15.00 | 0.67 |
| 1720–1755 | 12.0 | 12.00 | 1.00 |
| 1767–1770 | 15.0 | 14.00 | 1.07 |
| 1807–1811 | 30.0 | 36.00 | 0.83 |

Lee has recently used better data and better techniques to confirm what Malthus suspected. Regressions on differing data sets spanning the early modern period show that higher population meant lower real wages, higher relative prices for food, and higher rents. In these regressions the part of labor demand was played by a non-linear transformation of time itself, proxying the accelerating advance of technology and capital formation. Real wages were raised by the upward march of this demand proxy and lowered by population increase, as we would expect. All is well, it might appear, for conventional wisdom.[6]

Persuasive as the evidence may seem, a critical closer look exposes two weaknesses that lead us to fresh discoveries. The first is that the true impact of labor-demand trends not induced by population itself has yet to be found. Time trends and other artificial proxies are imperfect reflections of true labor-demand shifts from capital formation and technical progress, and not all

6 Ronald D. Lee, "Population in Preindustrial England: An Econometric Analysis," *Quarterly Journal of Economics*, LXXXVII (1973), 581–607; *idem*, "Methods and Models for Analyzing Historical Series of Births, Deaths, and Marriages," in his *Population Patterns of the Past* (New York, 1977), 337–370; *idem*, "A Historical Perspective on Economic Aspects of the Population Explosion: The Case of Pre-industrial England," in Easterlin (ed.), Population and Economic Change in Developing Countries (Chicago, 1980), 517–566.

of the latter are necessarily independent of population growth itself. The second is that Malthusian lessons have been read into English experience by a consistent ignoring of the effects of price inflation on the real wage. When these inflationary effects are taken into account, Malthusian faith in diminishing returns to population and labor is surprisingly hard to sustain without fresh interpretations.

The first problem, relating to the specification of trends in labor demand, can be illustrated in Figure 1 and with some illustrative regressions. Before 1800, the real wage series follows the swings of the Wrigley-Schofield population series around a steady or slightly accelerating (ungraphed) upward trend. This pattern might be interpreted as the natural interplay of supply and demand trends. If the demand for labor drifted steadily upward from 1541 to 1800 in response to steady capital accumulation and overall productivity gains, then this demand drift can be taken as equivalent to a time trend, with the population swings around that trend neatly explaining the swings of the real wage rate.[7]

The simple demand-supply view of real wages before 1800 can be reexpressed in regressions that allow the demand to grow nonlinearly with time, conforming to our belief that capital ac-

7  In Figure 1 and all that follows, we use the Phelps Brown-Hopkins wage (and price) series for craftsmen in southern England (which is essentially a fixed multiple of their series for common building laborers' wages). E. Henry Phelps Brown and Sheila V. Hopkins, "Seven Centuries of the Prices of Consumables Compared with Builders' Wage Rates," *Economica*, XXIII (1956), 296–314. It has been noted that their price series probably contains some pessimistic biases. It slightly overstates the upward movement of prices in all centuries. See David Loschky, "Seven Centuries of Real Income per Wage Earner Reconsidered," *Economica*, LXVII (1980), 459–465. The wage series probably understates the rise of nominal earnings for the late sixteenth century. Donald Woodward, "Wage Rates and Living Standards in Preindustrial England," *Past & Present*, 91 (1981), 29, 45; D. M. Palliser, "Tawney's Century: Brave New World or Malthusian Trap?" *Economic History Review*, XXXV (1982), 349–350.

Yet the case against the Phelps Brown-Hopkins real-wage index should not be overstated. That building craftsmen had other sources of income detracts little from the usefulness of the index. If a craftsman is both a wage-earner and self-employed, the wage rate does show the (amenities-adjusted) purchasing power of an extra day of his work at *any* pursuit, building work or otherwise. And since property incomes stem in part from savings out of earnings, movements in the real wage index should affect even the property incomes of craftsmen, albeit with a lag. Furthermore, the behavior of the real-wage index after 1755 does not seem extreme when compared with many other real-wage series. Lindert and Jeffrey G. Williamson, "English Workers' Living Standards during the Industrial Revolution: A New Look," *Economic History Review*, XXXVI (1983), 1–25. There are no clear signs that its departure from the living-standard trends for laborers is so great as to distort any of the conclusions of this article. More serious is the short-run stickiness of the Phelps Brown-Hopkins nominal wage rates, discussed in the text below.

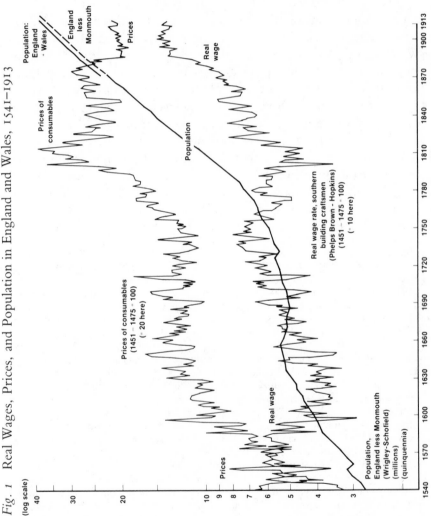

*Fig. 1* Real Wages, Prices, and Population in England and Wales, 1541–1913

cumulation and technical progress slowly accelerated, at
across the eighteenth and nineteenth centuries. Suppose, fc
ample, that we hypothesize that the natural log of the real ‹
ln(w/p), depends on the positions of aggregate labor suppl·
demand curves as follows:

$$\ln(w/p) = a_0 + a_1\ln N + a_2 t + a_3 t^2 + e$$

$$(+) \quad (+) \qquad (+) \quad (+)$$

where ln$N$ is the natural log of the labor force, $t$ is time, t
are coefficients, and $e$ is an error term that may or may not cc
serial correlation. This is similar to, although not identical
equations used by Lee. Equation (1) in Table 2 shows, fc
generally preindustrial era from 1546 to 1800, that real ·
were lowered 1.268 percent for each percentage point of g1
of the labor force, but were raised 0.56 percent a year by
sort of upward drift in labor demand.

These results are within reason. The trend drift of 0.5
cent a year is fairly close to the rate of shift in labor de
implied by the eighteenth-century trends in productivity gr·
although it is surprising to find no acceleration of this drift
1800. The −1.268 elasticity of the wage rate has the expecte
and reassuring significance. Yet it does seem high, implying
a low labor share of output or a low elasticity of substi
between labor and other inputs.[8]

Difficulties with labor-demand trends become glaring
we try to extend our view across the full nineteenth ce
Figure 1 shows that real wages rose along with the grov
population from 1800 to 1913, making it more difficult f

8 The belief that capital accumulation and technical progress slowly accelerate
founded, despite some problems with the underlying data. These recent esti
national capital-stock growth and total-factor-productivity growth for Great Br1
resent the current consensus view:

(growth rates in % per year)

| Period and scholar | Capital stock | Total factor productivity |
|---|---|---|
| 1710–1740 (Crafts) | 0.6 | 0.24 |
| 1740–1780 (Crafts) | 1.0 | 0.3 |
| 1761–1800 (Feinstein) | 1.0 | 0.2 |
| 1780–1800 (Crafts) | 2.0 | 0.8 |
| 1801–1830 (Feinstein) | 1.4 | 1.3 |
| 1831–1860 (Feinstein) | 2.1 | 0.8 |

See Roderick Floud and Donald N. McCloskey (eds.), *The Economic History of B*
*1700* (Cambridge, 1981), I, 8, 139, 140. One can blend these two series toget!

eye to separate positive demand effects from a negative influence
of labor supply on wages. Equation (2) in Table 2 offers a slight
resolution on the demand side, but Malthus would not have been
pleased. The time-squared term shows that labor demand probably accelerated across the full Wrigley-Schofield period, as hypothesized in the text equation above, yet labor supply no longer
shows a significant influence on the wage rate.

The second difficulty with past searches for Malthus' message
in the English historical experience relates to the role of the price
level in the determination of real wages. Even if real wages tend
toward an equilibrium dictated by basic labor-market forces, we
know that unexpected movements in the price level can cause
sustained disequilibria. Any attempt to account for yearly real-
wage movements must give the price level its due.

The short-run power of the price level over real wages before
1800 is shown in Figure 1 and by Equation (3) in Table 2. The
price terms completely dominate the determination of the real
wage, leaving no significance to or impact on either the labor-
supply term or the time terms proxying labor-demand trends.
This dominance reflects the multicollinearity that is made clear in
Figure 1: the price level moved in step with the population and
labor force before 1800, aside from short-run price movements
that were mirrored in the real wage.[9]

---

rough proxy for shifts in aggregate labor demand, weighting the capital stock growth by
capital's share of national product. The resulting amalgam would show the steady acceleration noted in the text.

9  The sets of price terms in Equation (3) in Table 1 imply that the natural log of the
nominal wage, $w$, depends on a weighted average of the natural logs of the price levels
of the last 10 years ($p_0$ = the log of this year's price, . . . , $p_{10}$ = the log of the price level
ten years ago). This dependence can be written as

$$w = \sum_0^{10} a_i p_i + \text{other terms.}$$

This is equivalent to the real-wage equation shown in Equation (3):

$$w - p = \sum_0^9 b_i(p_i - p_{i+1}) + b_{10}p_{10} + \text{same other terms,}$$

where each $b_i = \Sigma_0^i a_j - 1$. Equation (3)'s results thus show, in effect, that a permanent
100% price rise still had only a tiny 1% effect on the nominal wage rate ten years later,
because nominal wages were so sticky. That is, Equation (3) is equivalent to a nominal-
wage equation showing that neither price nor population succeeds in moving the nominal
wage rate much when both are forced to compete side by side, leaving to the text below
the task of deciding what interpretation of price-population covariation seems most plausible. The striking parallelism between price level and population and labor force has been
noted before. See Wrigley and Schofield, *Population History*, Fig. 10.1; Lindert, "English
Living Standards," 149–151.

*Table 2*  Determinants of the Real Wage in England:
Exploratory Regression Results, 1541–1871

| INDEPENDENT VARIABLE | EQUATION AND SAMPLE PERIOD | | |
|---|---|---|---|
| | (1) 1546–1800 | (2) 1541–1871 | (3) 1546–1800 |
| ln (labor force) | −1.268(.21)** | −0.013(.01) | −0.067(.25) |
| time | .0056(.02)** | − .0011(.001) | .0026(.0037) |
| time squared | .0000022 | .0000074 | .0000075(.000001) |
| | (.0000040) | (.0000032)* | |
| Inflation | | | |
| fr last year (t-1) to this (t) | — | — | −0.886(.036)** |
| (t-2) to this (t-1) | — | — | −1.096(.059)** |
| (t-3) to this (t-2) | — | — | −1.055(.082)** |
| (t-4) to this (t-3) | — | — | −1.091(.105)** |
| (t-5) to this (t-4) | — | — | −1.072(.125)** |
| (t-6) to this (t-5) | — | — | −1.016(.145)** |
| (t-7) to this (t-6) | — | — | −0.997(.164)** |
| (t-8) to this (t-7) | — | — | −0.984(.183)** |
| (t-9) to this (t-8) | — | — | −0.987(.200)** |
| (t-10) to this (t-9) | — | — | −0.977(.216)** |
| ln (price ten years ago) | — | — | −0.991(.218)** |
| Constant (after $\rho$): | 6.886 | −0.079 | 0.437 |
| Adjusted $R^2$/std. err. of est. | .189/.113 | .082/.110 | .731/.063 |
| DW/$\rho$ | 1.914/.60 | 1.998/.76 | 2.207/.93 |

* = significant at 5% level.
** = significant at 1% level.
(standard errors in parentheses)

The dependent variable is $\ln(w/p)$, the natural log of the Phelps Brown-Hopkins real wage rate for building craftsmen in southern England ($1850 = \ln(1) = 0$). Unreported regressions using the rate for common laborers gave the same results.

ln(labor force) = natural log of the potential labor force, determined by applying participation rates by age and sex to the Wrigley-Schofield population series. For further details, see Lindert, "English Living Standards," 154.

Time = the year minus 1541.

Inflation from each Year $t$-1 to Year $t = (\ln p_t - \ln p_{t-1})$, where $p$ is the Phelps Brown-Hopkins price of consumables.

DW = final Durbin-Watson statistic after Cochrane-Orcutt transformation on the residuals to reduce serial correlation. The residuals were of the form $u_t = \rho u_{t-1} + e_t$, where $e_t$ has no clear serial correlation. (Preliminary regression runs without such a transformation showed Durbin-Watson statistics far below the 2.00 norm.)

There are four possible responses to the bothersome results of Equation (3) in Table 2:

(1) we can suspect the data, especially the wage rate series;

(2) we can try to imagine ways in which the powerful price level could have been partly a response to population;

(3) we can insist that the model of Equation (3), like any regression model, might be misspecified in some other way that

hides the true dependence of real wages on population(Lee's article in this issue is an example of this response, concentrating as it does on other exogenous-price specifications using the same data series);

(4) we can accept the single-equation model as an anti-Malthusian truth.

The order of attractiveness of these responses is the same, in my view, as the order in which they are listed here. In particular, responses (1) and (2) seem most promising for the next stage of research, and these are the ones pursued here.

Some of the dominance by price levels stems from a shortcoming in the Phelps Brown–Hopkins wage series for southern building craftsmen. Although this series has made an enormous contribution to knowledge, it is constructed in such a way as to overstate wage stickiness. In fact, it is *designed* to be as sticky as possible. Faced with wage data of varying depth across seven centuries, Phelps Brown and Hopkins "looked for rates which we could regard as representative because they were recurrent." The result is not an average but a mode that changes only once, on average, every dozen years between 1541 and 1914 (with occasional gaps requiring interpolation). This procedure hides some of the true responsiveness of the average nominal wage to more basic forces. It is essential that scholars search for other long-term wage series to ease the strain of overreliance on the classic Phelps Brown–Hopkins series.[10]

While we await better wage data, we should concentrate on the most intriguing and underexplored possibility—that the price level itself was partly a response to population, the second possibility listed above. We can consider endogenizing the price level, making it a reflection of population movements rather than a separate force. The rest of this article does so.

EXPLAINING PRICE MOVEMENTS

*A. Malthusians and Monetarists* A demographic interpretation of the price level has already been offered by scholars writing in the 1950s and 1960s about the price revolution of the sixteenth

10   Phelps Brown and Hopkins, "Seven Centuries of Building Wages," *Economica*, XXII (1955), 196. Wage stickiness refers to the fact that wages do not change rapidly enough to keep the labor market in equilibrium.

and early seventeenth centuries. The flavor of this view is epitomized by Ramsey:

> The main argument is that English population expanded substantially during the sixteenth century, while agricultural production failed to match this growth. Inevitably food prices rose, the increase being accelerated in bad harvest years like those of the 1550s and 1590s. A corollary might be that neither agriculture nor industry expanded its labour force enough to absorb the increasing numbers of workers available. . . . [With enclosures and other labor-saving changes in agriculture and lackluster growth in industrial productivity] the result was growing unemployment and underemployment.
>
> This theory, based on expanding population and relatively inelastic food supplies and job opportunity . . . would go far to explain why prices rose before the monetary supply was affected by either American silver or debasement, why food prices rose faster than others, and why wages lagged behind prices—just those features which monetary theory left unexplained.[11]

This view does not really add up to an explanation of the overall price level, for reasons stressed anew by economic historians joining the monetarist revival in the 1970s. It is hardly even a theory of relative price movements, and does not begin to explain why these movements have to be accompanied by overall price inflation relative to a unit of money, the market for which has hardly been discussed. The reference to rising unemployment is at best a vague Keynesian gloss meant to explain that population growth could not lower industrial prices because there was institutional resistance to price cuts. Yet industrial prices actually rose during the price revolution era and fell many times thereafter. Furthermore, there are good theoretical reasons for suspecting that population growth should *lower* prices by supplying more

11   See the introduction by Peter H. Ramsey and the chapters by I. Hammerstrom, Y. S. Brenner, J. D. Gould, and C. E. Challis in Ramsey (ed.), *The Price Revolution in Sixteenth-Century England* (London, 1971), 10, for the quotation. These authors draw upon earlier works by Phelps Brown and Hopkins, yet the latter took care to offer a demographic interpretation of *relative* prices, real wages, and real rents, rather than a theory of the price level itself. See Phelps Brown and Hopkins, "Wage-Rates and Prices: Evidence for Population Pressure in the Sixteenth Century," *Economica*, XXIV (1957), 289–307; *idem*, "Builders' Wage-Rates, Prices, and Population: Some Further Evidence," *ibid.*, XXVI (1959), 18–38.

real output (Y) or real transactions (T): since $MV_y = PY$ or $MV_T = PT$, then Y up or T up should mean P down. Thus, recent scholars stressing the role of population in the price revolution have left their arguments almost as weak as those of Malthus.[12]

Yet there are plausible reasons for believing both that population growth could have raised prices generally and that it increased the relative price of food. First, rapid population growth might have caused shifts in age structure which would have increased the demand for goods relative to the demand for money, thus raising the price level. The driving force would have been the higher ratio of children to adults brought about either by higher fertility or by a differentially large decline in child mortality. More children per household mean that a given income per earner must be stretched over more people. This typically means lower savings. A lower ratio of household wealth to household income implies a greater demand for consumer goods and services relative to demand for money holdings, raising the price level. This argument is supported by the reasonably close correlation between the child/adult ratio and the price level in England between 1541 and 1913.[13]

12  McCloskey, "Review of *The Price Revolution in Sixteenth-Century England,*" *Journal of Political Economy,* LXXX (1972), 1332–1335; Dennis O. Flynn, "A New Perspective on the Spanish Price Revolution: The Monetary Approach to the Balance of Payments,"*Explorations in Economic History,* XV (1978), 388–406. There is a similar debate over "real" versus monetary explanations of price swings between 1815 and 1914, with a similar lamentable vagueness on the side of the antimonetarists. W. Arthur Lewis and Walt W. Rostow, for example, push the defensible notion that the forces behind real food scarcity and other not-so-monetary events in individual markets help explain inflation and deflation, yet they leave themselves open to monetarist counterattack on both theoretical and empirical grounds. See Lewis, *Growth and Fluctuations, 1870–1913* (London, 1978), 33–93; Michael Bordo and Anna J. Schwartz, "Money and Prices in the Nineteenth Century: Was Thomas Tooke Right?" *Explorations in Economic History,* XVIII (1981), 97–127.
13  Readers may imagine a longer list of links from population to the general price level. But some possible links require assuming the Malthusian conclusion that population depresses real wages, and should be omitted from a listing of arguments supporting that conclusion. One example is the possibility that population growth, by depressing real wages and workers' food reserves, would cause workers to shift from holding cash to hoarding food in a world where poor market mechanisms failed to assure food at an affordable money price during local famines. This shift from holding money to holding food supplies would raise the price level. Another example is the possibility that a higher population, by depressing real wages and raising rents, depresses all conventional saving, including the demand for cash. If workers cannot afford the luxury of saving, in money or in other assets, while landlords have their savings desires met by perceived capital gains

The same change in the ratio of children to adults would also raise the relative price of food by channeling an increased proportion of a fixed level of earnings into food. Moreover, *if* a higher population means lower wage rates and higher rents on non-human property, the relative demand for food could be raised by the resulting redistribution of income. This result seems likely. The elasticity of demand for food appears to decline as we move from poor to rich nations. If the same is true within a nation, then the marginal propensity to consume food (which equals the share spent on food × the income elasticity of food demand) must decline sharply with income. If population growth is inegalitarian, it must raise the relative demand for food.[14]

A second plausible population-to-price link can be called the "Goldstone variation." Goldstone, a sociologist, has recently proposed an ingenious basis for believing that population growth could actually raise monetary velocity and prices. Population in-

---

on land, then consumption demand can be elevated and the demand for money depressed, raising the price level. Again, however, this assumes that extra population directly depresses real wages.

The child/adult ratio can be calculated for 1541–1871 from the quinquennial estimates in Wrigley and Schofield, *Population History*, Table 3.1, 528–529. The revisions in their population estimates pondered in Lindert, "English Living Standards," 144–149, would dampen the pre-1840 swings in the child/adult ratio but would otherwise leave its chronology the same as in the Wrigley-Schofield original.

14  Malthus added a twist, relating food demand to poor relief. If society redistributes income toward the destitute during times of population-induced hardship for laborers, then their high marginal propensity to buy food with the parish's help will again raise the relative price of food. His point is well taken for the food crisis during which he wrote, when poor relief expenditures were perhaps 3% of national product, but it is less relevant to the Tudor era, when relief expenditure probably never reached 1% of national product. On the supply side of the economy, the relative inelasticity of the supply of agricultural land is crucial. This means that more labor will bid up the relative prices of land and agricultural products even if the extra labor somehow breeds extra capital in proportion. This point should not be confused with the questionable assumption that food production was less labor-intensive than the rest of the economy. It was probably more labor-intensive as well as rural-land-intensive, but less capital-intensive than the rest of the economy. What little we know about income and employment patterns in the seventeenth century and later suggests that agriculture took a slightly greater share of the labor force than it contributed to national income. Wrigley, "Urban Growth in Early Modern England," this issue; Lindert and Williamson, "Revising England's Social Tables, 1688–1812," *Explorations in Economic History*, XIX (1982), 385–408, Tables 1–4, with assumptions on the share of laborers employed in agriculture; Glenn R. Hueckel, "War and the British Economy: A General-Equilibrium Analysis," *Explorations in Economic History*, X (1973), 384–385; Phyllis Deane and W. A. Cole, *British Economic Growth, 1688–1959* (Cambridge, 1969).

creases bring increased population density, urbanization, and stratification within agriculture. In greater contact with one another, households specialize more and more, and monetized transactions crowd out consumption of the household's own produce. It is not yet obvious that these changes should raise monetary velocity or prices. Perhaps population growth merely raises the demand for M and for real T, without raising V or P. Goldstone adds network-theoretical reasons, however, for believing that the larger scale of monetary transactions triggered by rising population density and household specialization should bring economies in the holding of cash, thanks to more frequent and smaller individual transactions among individual households. Thus, he argues, V is likely to respond to population faster than T or the demand for money will respond. This argument is applied to the task of explaining a likely rise in velocity and prices during the English price revolution and the inflation of the later eighteenth century.[15]

Goldstone's argument has its greatest power in settings where the marketplace is underdeveloped. But after a point, households become almost completely specialized, marketing nearly all that they produce, removing any reason for velocity to respond to population growth or other early influences on monetization. Meanwhile, greater contact with markets where money can buy anything (or be borrowed) at relatively predictable prices reduces the incentive to hoard grain to cover possible food shortages (which population growth might have made more likely in premodern times). In such a market economy Goldstone's theorems about rising V/T are less compelling. Yet, for medieval and early modern England, population growth *might* have raised V/T enough to have been a major source of price inflation.[16]

*B. MV = PY in England*     The most direct way to delineate possible monetary, demographic, and other sources of English price movements is to work from the national-income versions of the equation of exchange, $MV = PY$, in which Y is real national

15 Jack A. Goldstone, "Urbanization and Inflation: Lessons from the English Price Revolution of the Sixteenth and Seventeenth Centuries," *American Journal of Sociology*, LXXXIX (1984), 1122–1160.
16 Goldstone's argument is akin to several economists' conjecture that population or any other force shortening the payment period reduces the demand for money holdings. For a recent reminder of this possibility see Milton Friedman and Schwartz, *Monetary Trends in the United States and the United Kingdom . . . 1867–1975* (Chicago, 1982), 222.

product and V is the income velocity of money. Accounting for movements in the price level (P), we first give monetary forces proximate credit for changing the price level by the percentage by which the money stock (M) changed. Any net change in the ratio P/M is also a change in V/Y, one that we should try to explain. We reflect here on the possible role of population growth in the observed changes in V and Y.

The money stock rose faster than the price level between the start of the seventeenth century and the middle of the twentieth. It rose faster even than the national income (PY) of England and Wales. This rise in M/PY implies the long-run decline in velocity shown in Table 3 and Figure 2. Economists studying velocity trends after 1870 have already offered explanations that probably also apply to earlier centuries. Over the course of more than three centuries, England dramatically improved her money-supply institutions, building an ever more efficient network of deposit banks around the Bank of England. With reliable money thus in progressively better supply at declining real interest rates, the nation shifted toward using money as a liquid store of value in place of hoarding grain and other commodities.[17]

This plausible sketch of the history of English monetary velocity trends thus far owes little or nothing to the history of population. The increase in the money supply exceeded any increase in prices (i.e. the real money stock rose). If the percentage growth of the money stock were an exogenous force capable of explaining the same percentage of price increase, and money and population were the only forces considered, there would be no room left for the argument that population growth separately raised prices.

The best chance for believing that population growth raised prices lies in setting aside the years after, say, 1815. Recall that the theoretical reasons for positing such a link seemed better suited to earlier settings, before the full integration of fluid financial and commodity markets. Before 1815 the price level received an extra

17 Bordo and Lars Jonung, "The Long-Run Behavior of the Income Velocity of Money in Five Advanced Countries, 1870–1975," *Economic Inquiry*, XIX (1981), 96–116; Friedman and Schwartz, *Monetary Trends*, 138–304. Between 1760 and 1860, for example, the money stocks in Table 2 show much faster growth than holdings of circulating capital, land, or total wealth. See Charles H. Feinstein, "Capital Formation in Great Britain," in Peter Mathias and Michael M. Postan (eds.), *Cambridge Economic History of Europe* (Cambridge, 1978), VII., pt. I, 42, 68, 88.

*Table 3*  Price Level and Some Possible Price Determinants, England and Wales, Selected Years, 1526–1913

| BENCHMARK YEAR | PRICE OF CONSUMABLES $(P_c)$(1700 = 100) | NATIONAL INCOME (PY) (£MILL. PER YEAR) | MONEY STOCK (M) "±ME" (£MILL.) | VELOCITY $v = PY/M$ "±ME" (PER YEAR) | PRICE INFLATION % PER ANNUM SINCE LAST BENCHMARK | PRICE INFLATION % PER ANNUM NEXT DECADE | POPULATION OF ENGLAND AND WALES (MILLIONS) |
|---|---|---|---|---|---|---|---|
| 1526 | 21.34 | from 4.1 to 10.4 | 1.67 | from 2.43 to 6.20, and $\leq v$ 1603 1.39 | 1.28 (since 1500) | 0.16 | 2.65 |
| 1603 | 68.27 | from 18.8 to 37.7 | 3.49 | from 5.39 to 10.80 | 1.52 | 1.45 | 4.53 |
| 1688 | 81.03 | 54.4 | 12.0 | 4.53 | 0.20 | 2.66 | 5.20 |
| 1760 | 97.63 | 68.8 | 20.2 | 3.41 | 0.26 | 1.54 | 6.53 |
| 1801 | 172.06 | 204.1 | 51.0 | 4.00 | 1.39 | 4.03 | 9.28 |
| 1831 | 173.36 | 355.7 | from 99 to 112 | from 3.18 to 3.59 | 0.02 | 0.23 | 13.99 |
| 1873 | 203.26 | 903.2 | 474.0 | 1.91 | 0.38 | −1.96 | 23.41 |
| 1899 | 144.27 | 1,340.6 | 727.6 | 1.84 | −1.31 | 0.47 | 31.88 |
| 1913 | 151.08 | 1,793.5 | 943.4 | 1.90 | 0.33 | 5.71 | 36.57 |

SOURCES: For sources and notes on Table 3 and Fig. 2, see Appendix.

*Fig. 2* Income Velocity of Money, England and Wales, 1526–1913 (UK after 1873)

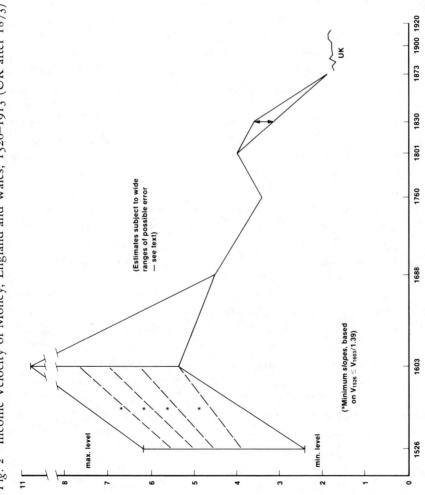

boost from increases in velocity in two periods of rapid population growth identified by Table 3 and Figure 2: the Tudor period (1526–1603) and the late eighteenth century (1760–1801). By contrast, prices and velocity rose less (or fell) in the period of less dramatic population growth between the early seventeenth century and the middle of the eighteenth. This correlation of P with V encourages the population-to-inflation view. A monetarist could try to argue that velocity and prices were raised more by the effect of money-supply expansion on inflationary expectations themselves, proxied by the inflation rates in Table 3, than by population effects. But the extent of the movement in velocity seems too large, especially in the Tudor era, for explanation in terms of the rather slight changes in the rate of inflation.

*C. An Open-Economy View*     Thus far the battle of the price level has been fought on closed-economy grounds, with the national money supply fully exogenous. Limiting the battleground in this way, however, will not do. England always traded with the Continent and achieved most of her early money-supply growth in this way. If England's money stock were an endogenous variable, subject to all the determinants of the trade balance, what then becomes of the monetary forces that are to compete against population as exogenous determinants of the national price level?

The relevant exogenous monetary variable is not the national money stock but the prices of tradable goods and services in terms of pound sterling, the national money of account. The world supply and demand for gold and silver, the international monies, exerted a strong influence over the London and Bristol prices of tradable goods and services in terms of these metals. Tradable prices in pounds sterling depended upon royal debasement of the pound, as well as upon international metallic prices. We can judge the likely impact of all monetary forces on the English price level by measuring the change in the average pound price of tradable goods and services. If this exceeds the overall rate of inflation, there is apparently no inflation (and apparently some deflation) left for population growth and other forces to explain. If not, there is some price inflation left to be explained by population and other variables.[18]

18  Scholars wishing to pursue further the comparison of tradables' prices with overall national prices should take at least two precautions relating to terms used here. First, one must be sure to recognize that goods or services, having negligible net trade balances, can

Suitable indices of the prices of tradables have yet to be constructed for England or Britain before 1795, so any conclusions about them must be tentative. We can describe a likely upper bound, however, on the price impact of international monetary forces, by unrealistically assuming (a) that they explain *all* observed movements in the prices of tradables; and (b) that non-tradables, despite their name, were perfect substitutes for tradables, so that the entire national price level was affected by monetary forces fully as much as the price index for tradables moved.

Pursuing this line of reasoning, we need next to decide which English goods and services were tradable, i.e. which could have had their price level set by international conditions. The decision must differ for different periods. For the Pax Britannica (1815–1913) most British goods and services were tradable, and rough purchasing-power-parity held between countries. Some services, to be sure, were essentially non-traded (e.g. housing). But the price movements in these sectors were generally less extreme than price movements for tradables, so that knowing the latter does not put any clear bounds on the overall price impact of monetary forces.[19]

At the other end of the historic range surveyed here, in the sixteenth and seventeenth centuries England only traded certain goods, and these had more stable prices than the economy as a whole. Her exports were dominated by woolen textiles and by the reexport of primary products from Asia and America. Her imports were more varied, but over half consisted of textiles, wine, brandy, sugar, and molasses. The most important absences from the list of heavily traded goods before 1700 are several staples which dominated such cost-of-living indices as that of Phelps

---

still be among England's tradables. A not-so-traded good is still a tradable if slight movements in international prices would cause large amounts of it to enter trade. Second, to compare the average price index of tradables with a national price index as evidence on the hypothesis of purchasing-power-parity, one must take care to use the same national expenditure-and-production weights for both sets of individual prices to avoid distortions due solely to differences in weights.

19 See, for example, McCloskey and J. Richard Zecher, "How the Gold Standard Worked, 1880–1913," in Jacob A. Frenkel and Harry G. Johnson (eds.), *The Monetary Approach to the Balance of Payments* (London, 1975), 357–385. Note that for the Pax Britannica, when paper sterling became the leading world currency, the monetary forces captured by the price of tradables were not entirely foreign. The Bank of England's policies could affect the world money supply and world price levels, and thus could affect Britain's price index for tradables. That is, Britain was not a "small country" in the sense of being a price-taker.

Brown and Hopkins: grains and bread (20 percent weight), meat (part of 25 percent for "meat and fish"), butter and cheese (20 percent), malt and hops (part of 22.5 percent) and fuel and light (7.5 percent). In general, industrial goods were much more heavily involved in overseas trade than were staple foodstuffs (other than wine, brandy, sugar, molasses, and fish). Further evidence that wheat, in particular, did not behave like a good tradable across the Channel comes from the seventeenth century: jumps in the wheat/silver price ratio on the Continent, e.g. in the 1640s, were not matched in timing or magnitude by movements in Exeter or London.[20]

That staple food prices in England were not tied to foreign prices is an important (tentative) discovery. We have already noted that during periods of inflation prices of staple foodstuffs, especially wheat, rose much faster than prices of industrial goods. If staples are rightly viewed as non-tradables before 1700, then the larger price revolution cannot be fully explained by the monetary forces driving the smaller movements in prices of tradables. If the prices of tradables moved in constant proportion with the prices of industrial goods in England, as seems possible, then monetary forces explain only a 133 percent price hike from the period 1521 to 1530 to the period 1601 to 1610, whereas the overall cost of living rose 217 percent.[21]

There is a considerable gap to be explained by such non-monetary forces as population growth. The same cannot be said of the food-led inflation of the late eighteenth century, since by that time wheat and other food staples clearly entered international trade, allowing a price index for tradables to rise at least as rapidly as the overall price index. Yet for the Tudor price revolution, the

20  Ralph Davis, "English Foreign Trade, 1660–1700," *Economic History Review*, VII (1954), 150–166; *idem, English Overseas Trade, 1500–1700* (London, 1973). Phelps Brown and Hopkins, "Seven Centuries of the Price of Consumables," 297–303. Fernand P. Braudel and Frank Spooner, "Prices in Europe from 1450 to 1750," in Edwin E. Rich and Charles H. Wilson (eds.), *Cambridge Economic History of Europe* (Cambridge, 1967), IV, 638–641.

21  Phelps Brown and Hopkins, "Wage-rates and Prices," 306; *idem,* "Seven Centuries of the Price of Consumables," 312. The same difference appears on a smaller scale between 1601–1610 and 1691–1700: industrial (and tradable?) prices rose only 29%, whereas the overall index for consumables rose 38%. Industrial prices were again more stable in the deflationary first half of the eighteenth century, but by this time wheat and other foods entered foreign trade enough to prevent any inferences about the price index for tradables.

open-economy evidence permits the same demographic view permitted by the MV = PY evidence: a significant part of the observed inflation may have been due to population growth or other non-monetary forces.

D. *A World-Economy View*     The natural next step in judging the effect of population growth on price movements is to look beyond the prices of tradable goods to the larger world money supply and demand that determine them. If prices are internationally set, let us focus on the world market in which they are set.

This next phase of early modern monetary history is difficult. Scholars have to grapple again with the vexing problem of estimating what actually happened to the money supply of Western Europe, or the world, as a whole. Existing estimates of the world stock of metallic money are wild guesses for the years before 1800, or even before 1913, as illustrated by the fact that the estimates assume that the stock was zero in 1492. Scholars who have been reluctant to posit a unified global money market before 1800 have tried to view official Spanish imports of gold and silver plus output from European mines as net increments to Western Europe's money stock. This is misleading: European privateers also imported large volumes of precious metals; not all gold and silver became money; and the outflow of silver to the east was also probably large. Furthermore, the Western European stock was itself partly endogenous, with net outflows from the region affected by European money demand to an unknown extent. The stock measure would not quantify an exogenous variable.[22]

Several of the patterns observed for England also seem to apply to all of Western Europe. Although England grew faster in most periods, the swings in population growth rates for England and the Continent are contemporaneous between 1200 and 1800, as were swings in the cost of living in England, France, Holland, and other countries, measured either in monies of account or in units of gold or silver. With minor exceptions and deviations, prices of consumables rose in England and France from the mid-

22  On estimates see, for example, Karl Helfferich (trans. Louis Infield), *Money* (New York, 1969), 86; U.S. Commission on the Role of Gold in the Domestic and International Monetary Systems, *Report* (Washington, D.C. 1982), I, 187, 195–197. A. Attman, *The Bullion Flow between Europe and the East, 1000–1750* (Göteborg, 1981).

thirteenth century to the early fourteenth, experienced a net decline to the mid-fifteenth, and then moved in all countries according to the pattern shown for England in Figure 1 above. That is, from about 1250 to 1800 the movement of prices resembles the movement of population throughout Western Europe. In most cases periods of rapid population growth and price increase were also periods in which real wages fell and the relative price of foodstuffs rose.[23]

Why were trends in population, prices, real wages, and the relative prices of food so closely correlated and so similar across countries in Western Europe? The Western European pattern underlines the suggestions already put about the behavior of velocity and the open-economy clues for England: before the industrial revolution and the refinement of modern market networks, it may well be that higher population brought lower real wages, either directly or by raising prices in the face of sluggish nominal wages.

Malthus has gained at least a standoff on the wage-price front for the period up to 1815. In fact, Malthus may be on the verge of winning by default. How can one explain real-wage declines in all countries, c.1500 to c.1610 and c.1750 to c.1815, *without* giving a strong negative role to population growth? The mere stickiness of nominal wages in the face of inflation helps, but cannot explain several decades of real-wage decline, as better wage series are likely to show. The nominal wage rates were not even rigid during inflation. Furthermore, demand–side causal forces such as enclosures or labor-saving innovations could not have reduced labor demand enough in so many countries as to outweigh the rise of labor supply.[24] The Malthusian wage argument survives for now, although the evidence has proved tricky and further research is needed.

23 Colin McEvedy and Richard Jones, *Atlas of World Population History* (London, 1978); Wrigley, "Urban Growth and Agricultural Change: England and the Continent in the Early Modern Period," in this issue. Phelps Brown and Hopkins, "Seven Centuries of the Price of Consumables"; *idem,* "Wage-rates and Prices"; *idem,* "Builders' Wage-rates"; Nicolaas W. Posthumus, *Inquiry into the History of Prices in Holland* (Leiden, 1946), cxvi–cxviii; Georges d'Avenel, *Histoire economique . . . depuis l'an 1200 jusqu'en l'an 1800* (New York, 1968–69; orig. pub. 1894–1926), 7v., for French prices beyond the period covered by Phelps Brown and Hopkins; Braudel and Spooner, "Prices in Europe," 458–484.
24 Here the text is advancing two arguments at once. First, a reading of the available literature does not suggest labor-saving changes large enough to exceed the rate of labor-

The Wrigley-Schofield population series has opened several doors for economic demography, including some that had previously been locked. This article offers four tentative conclusions.

First, new efforts must be made to test the classical belief that population increases depress wage rates. The Phelps Brown-Hopkins time series on nominal wages needs to be supplanted with new series that better reflect short-run movements in mean wage rates. We also need to rethink the role of unexpected inflation in the determination of the real wage rate. Past studies have ignored the fact that the proximate effects of price on the real wage obscure any apparent impact of population growth. England's early modern experience has been dominated by a strong temporal correlation between prices and population. We should ponder whether population could have affected the price level itself, thereby having an indirect effect on real wages via prices.

Second, population might help explain price levels before, say, 1815, according to two theories and three empirical tests. The two theories are (a) the likelihood that the higher dependency ratios accompanying faster population growth would shift demand from money-holding to staple commodities, and (b) Goldstone's argument that, before the development of modern markets, increases in population density could actually raise the velocity of circulation faster than they raise the volume of real transactions, thus putting upward pressure on prices. Three tests support these hunches: (i) the fact that velocity did rise in two

---

supply shift. Second, one cannot assert that drops in labor demand depressed the wage rate without granting the same unit impact to labor-supply shifts as to demand shifts, since both have the same elasticity-based multiplier. In a log-linear example, let labor demand (D) and supply (S) depend on shift terms ($S_o, D_o$) and the real wage (w):

$$D = D_o w^d \quad \text{(exponent } d < 0)$$
$$S = S_o w^s \quad \text{(exponent } s > 0)$$

Then, differentiating and using the growth rate operator $\overset{*}{X} = dX/X$,

$$\overset{*}{D} = \overset{*}{D_o} + d\overset{*}{w},$$
$$\overset{*}{S} = \overset{*}{S_o} + s\overset{*}{w}, \text{ and } \overset{*}{D} = \overset{*}{S},$$

so that $\overset{*}{w} = \dfrac{\overset{*}{D_o} - \overset{*}{S_o}}{s - d}$

The unit wage impact of any labor-demand shifts ($\overset{*}{D_o}$'s, e.g. due to enclosures) is simply $1/(s-d)$, the same as the unit impact of any labor-supply shift ($\overset{*}{S_o}$). Either both kinds of shift have strong impacts on wages or neither does. If demand and supply reasoning explains wage changes at all, population growth must depress wages.

periods of rapid population growth—the Tudor era and the late eighteenth century; (ii) the fact that tradable-goods price movements, which should be the main symptom of monetary change in an open economy, fell short of accounting for the overall Tudor price inflation, leaving room for population as an extra source of inflation; and (iii) the remarkable correlation of early modern price movements with population movements in all Western European countries.

Third, given all the information gathered in this look at prices, it would be difficult to explain early modern real-wage movements *without* believing that labor supply depressed the real wage. The alternative anti-Malthusian hypotheses do not add up to a satisfactory explanation of the Tudor and late-eighteenth-century wage declines.

Fourth, exploring the possible effects of population on wage rates and rents promotes a conjecture that I have voiced elsewhere: there is a good chance that population growth makes income distribution more inegalitarian. It probably widens income gaps by pushing up property rents and reducing real wage rates for common workers. This it may have done in English experience even if it had no effect at all on income per person.[25]

### APPENDIX

*Notes and sources for Table 3 and Figure 2*
The benchmark years for 1526–1873 are simply some data-yielding years. Those for 1873–1913 are cyclical peaks. The velocities after 1870 in Figure 2 are for business cycles graphed at mid-cycle.

*Price of consumables*: the Phelps Brown-Hopkins series, five-year averages centred on the benchmark year. Rates of inflation refer to this series, with the 1913 figure referring to 1901–1913.

*National income*: after 1873 the source is Friedman and Schwartz, *Monetary Trends*, 122–137. Figures for England and Wales were estimated by using the ratio of (England and Wales/UK) = 0.813 given for 1867 national product by R. Dudley Baxter, *The National Income* (London, 1868), 52, 64. For 1831, the starting point is the GNP at factor cost from Deane, "New Estimates of Gross National Product for the United Kingdom, 1830–1914," *Review of Income and Wealth*, VI (1968), 104–107, adjusted by the same ratio of 0.813 for EW/UK used for later dates. National income for 1688–1801 is from Lindert and Williamson, "Revising England's Tables," Tables 2–4.

25  Lindert, *Fertility and Scarcity in America* (Princeton, 1978), 14–36, 216–260.

The 1526 and 1603 national income figures were projected back from 1688 using lower- and upper-bound assumptions. National product in 1688 was divided into land rents of £10 million (Gregory King, *Natural and Political Observations,* in G. E. Barnett [ed.], *Two Tracts by Gregory King* [Baltimore, 1936], 52) and a remainder of £44.4 millions representing the earnings of labor and capital (1688 national income totals from Lindert and Williamson, "Revising England's Tables," Table 2). The rents were projected back to 1526 and 1603 using the rents per acre given in Eric Kerridge, "The Movement of Rent, 1540–1640," in Edith M. Carus-Wilson (ed.), *Essays in Economic History* (London, 1962), II, 216; Arthur G. Ruston and Denis Witney, *Hooton Pagnell: The Agricultural Evolution of a Yorkshire Village* (New York, 1934), 193; James E. Thorold Rogers, *A History of Agriculture and Prices in England* (Vaduz, 1963; orig. pub. 1887), VI, 716. The same rental projection was used for both the lower- and upper-bound estimates.

The lower-bound estimates projected total non-land earnings back to 1526 and 1603 assuming that

| Non-land earnings 1526 or 1603 | 1688 ave. income, laboring people and = outservants, times total families | 1562 or 1603 labor force × 1688 labor force | 1526 or 1603 wage rate, × bldg laborers 1688 wage rate, bldg. laborers |
|---|---|---|---|

where the labor-force ratios are based on Wrigley and Schofield as described for Table 1 above and the wage rates for building laborers are the Phelps Brown-Hopkins daily rates.

The upper-bound estimates for 1526 and 1603 used the same procedure, but replaced the 1688 average income of laboring people and outservants (£15) with £40, a figure above the true mean non-land income per family (£31.96). Next we can further limit the upper-bound income for 1526 by constraining the change from 1526 to 1603. Nominal non-land income per family could not have dropped in so inflationary a period. So an extra constraint is that (non-land income, 1526) ≤ (ditto, 1603) × (labor force ratio, 1526/1603). This leads to the extra constraint shown in the velocity column.

The estimates for *money stock* are subject to wide unboundable errors before 1873, and for this reason the estimates for M and V bear the warning symbol "±ME," for "plus or minus an unknown error in the money stock." This is particularly true of the money stocks for 1526 and 1603, borrowed from Challis, *The Tudor Coinage* (Manchester, 1978), 236–238, 247. Challis' use of the last 30 years of mint output as a stock estimate can certainly be wrong, as he notes, though it seems consistent with the different estimates for the coin stocks of 1688, to judge from the 1659–1688 mint output. The 1688 money stock consists of £10 million of monetary coin and bullion, from Rondo E. Cameron, "England, 1750–1844," in *idem* (ed.), *Banking in the Early Stages of Industrialization* (London, 1967), 42, 43; J. Keith Horsefield, *British Mone-*

*tary Experiments, 1650–1710* (London, 1960), Appendix 2. To this is added £2 million in banknotes and deposits, from Cameron, *Ea  y Stages,* 42.

The money stock for 1760 begins with £14.6 million in coin and bullion outside the Bank of England. This is derived by applying England-Wales shares to figures for Great Britain. The latter are derived by subtracting £2.628 million of Bank holdings (Brian Mitchell and Deane, *Abstract of British Historical Statistics* [Cambridge, 1971], 441–442) from the £20 million of estimated coin and bullion in Great Britain (Feinstein, "Capital Formation in Great Britain," 72). To the net total of £17.372 million, I applied a population-based share of 0.84 for England and Wales, yielding the £14.6 million. Next £4.936 million of Bank of England notes in circulation were added (Mitchell and Deane, *Abstract,* 441), along with £0.7 million of other banknotes (Cameron's guess for 1750, in *Early Stages,* 43).

The money stock for 1801 was derived using the same sources and procedures as for 1760. These were applied again for 1830, but here a discrepancy arose regarding total coin and bullion in circulation. Using Feinstein and Mitchell-Deane implies £42.597 million, but Cameron calculated £30 million. Neither is clearly superior to the other, and the ranges for money stock and velocity given in Table 2 and Figure 2 reflect both possibilities.

For 1873 on, the money stock figures are from Friedman and Schwartz, *Monetary Trends,* 122–137, with each figure being scaled to England and Wales using the 0.813 ratio of national income.

The population figures before 1873 start from the Wrigley and Schofield estimates for England less Monmouth from *Population History,* 531–535 and apply the ratios for (England and Wales)/(England less Monmouth) given in *ibid.,* 566.

*Ronald Lee*

# Population Homeostasis and English
# Demographic History
Classical economists viewed population size as a passive variable, which obediently traced a path defined by the demand for labor. The sometimes turbulent chronology of fertility, mortality, and nuptiality was seen as a distracting tale of epiphenomena, contributing little to our understanding of the fundamental forces shaping history. As Malthus put it:

> The actual progress of the population is, with very few exceptions, determined by the relative difficulty of procuring the means of subsistence, and not by the relative natural powers of increase . . . except in extreme cases, the actual progress of population is little affected by unhealthiness or healthiness.[1]

This point of view also offers some comfort to those viewing with concern the current rapid increase of population in the Third World: if population is growing in response to expanding economic productivity, then it will not drive nations deeper into poverty, although it may prevent them from becoming rich. However, to the extent that wages (or, more generally, living standards) exerted only a minor influence on vital rates, whereas political, social, climatic, medical, and ecological changes exerted important influences, then population size played an active role in economic and social history.

Marshall, writing in the classical tradition, concluded:

Ronald Lee is Professor of Demography and Economics at the University of California, Berkeley. He is the author of *Econometric Studies of Topics in Demographic History* (New York, 1978).

Research for this article was supported by a grant from the National Institutes of Child Health and Human Development, HD 18107. The author acknowledges helpful discussions with Kenneth Wachter, Peter Lindert, and William Hodges, and able research assistance from Patrick Galloway and Shelley Lapkoff.

1 Thomas Robert, Malthus (ed. Anthony Flew), *An Essay on the Principle of Population, and A Summary View of the Principle of Population* (Baltimore, 1970; orig. pub. 1798), 262.

We have, then, a path sketched out for the population curve by the conditions of economic progress, and oscillation about that path caused by the disturbance and readjustment of the balance between births and deaths.

However, he also wrote that

[the] balance is bound to be frequently disturbed by the action of forces which have nothing to do with social and econmic progress, measured by its capacity to sustain population.[2]

It is obvious that a great deal of the short-run variation in vital rates (the movements up and down lasting for no more than a decade) must have been due to factors other than fluctuations in real wages or incomes, as Marshall's lines suggest. And it seems clear that in the very long run—over the millennia—gross variations in population size must have been largely determined by the demand for labor—that is, by technology, resources, climate, and the social organization guiding production and distribution. It is the broad middle range, spanning changes of more than a decade or two, but less than, say, a millennium, where the issue is in doubt. Did these longer-run trends and swings in population and real wages primarily reflect variations in the demand for labor ("conditions of economic progress"), or did they instead primarily reflect disturbances in the "relative natural powers of increase," independent of economic progress? This question is, in my view, the most basic in economic-demographic history.[3]

I have investigated these issues in the past, at first using flawed English data for 1250 to 1800, and later, through the generosity of Wrigley and Schofield, using preliminary versions of their new and greatly superior demographic series for 1540 to 1840. My conclusions, broadly stated, were as follows:

1. The demand for labor was growing over the long run at between 0.1 and 0.5 percent; population growth more rapid than

2 T. H. Marshall, "The Population Problem during the Industrial Revolution: A Note on the Present State of the Controversy," reprinted in David V. Glass and David E. C. Eversley (eds.), *Population in History* (Chicago, 1965), 250. The second portion of the quotation originally preceded the first by a few lines in the text.

3 It is also possible that population size and density were themselves powerful influences on technological change, as many authors have argued, most notably Ester Boserup in *Population and Technical Change: A Study of Long-Term Trends* (Chicago, 1981).

this sharply depressed the real wage (and slower growth sharply raised it), and was the major cause of long swings in the real wage level.

2. Fertility responded weakly although positively to the real wage, and varied little over the long run; the poor quality of the fertility data rendered these conclusions uncertain.

3. Mortality exhibited no discernible response to the real wage over the long swing, and only a weak negative response in the short run; however, it underwent substantial long-run variation, evidently exogenous in origin.

4. Combining these elements suggested that population size and wages were indeed controlled by a Malthusian equilibrating mechanism. The long-run upward drift in population size was due to a secular trend in the demand for labor, as classical theory would suggest. However, over the long and deep swings characterizing these five and a half centuries, the driving force was not the demand for labor, but rather independent variation in mortality.[4]

Wrigley and Schofield, in their important book, provide unique demographic data which may be used to shed light on these issues, and they also propose an interpretation of the economic-demographic changes over their period, which addresses these questions. I have discussed the demographic estimates themselves elsewhere; here I restrict my discussion to the interpretation of these demographic series in conjunction with the wage and price series, assuming that the data are correct.[5]

The series of population size, population growth rates (and their components, fertility and mortality), and real wages, all have a distinctive characteristic: they exhibit a long and deep swing,

4 The main references here are Lee, *Econometric Studies of Topics in Demographic History* (New York, 1978); *idem*, "A Historical Perspective on Economic Aspects of the Population Explosion: The Case of Preindustrial England," in Richard Easterlin (ed.), *Population and Economic Change in Developing Countries* (Chicago, 1980), 517–557; Lee, "Models of Preindustrial Population Dynamics, with Applications to England," in Charles Tilly (ed.), *Historical Studies of Changing Fertility* (Princeton, 1978), 155–207; *idem*, "Population in Preindustrial England: An Econometric Analysis," *Quarterly Journal of Economics*, LXXXVII (1973), 581–607.

5 E. Anthony Wrigley and Roger S. Schofield, *The Population History of England, 1541–1871: A Reconstruction* (Cambridge, Mass., 1981). Lee and David Lam, "Age Distribution Adjustments for English Censuses, 1821 to 1931," *Population Studies*, XXXVII (1983), 445–464; Lee, "Inverse Projection and Back Projection: A Critical Appraisal and Comparative Results for England, 1539 to 1871," *ibid.*, forthcoming.

with two or three major turning points over the period from 1540 to 1800; this is precisely the kind of variation which we seek to understand.

Superimposed on this long swing, for all series except population size, there is also an impressive amount of short-run variation, presumably reflecting epidemics, the influence of weather on the harvest, and so on. Finally, all the series, except for population size, appear to be relatively trend free (although we must bear in mind that the swing is as much as two or more centuries long), whereas population size shows a distinct upward trend.

The approximate nature and magnitude of the swing in mortality were fairly well established prior to the appearance of these new data, through work on the British peerage and upper classes and through Wrigley's own reconstitution study of Colyton, all of which give broadly the same results. The general trend in population size was also fairly well established, but the new series adds a great deal of temporal and quantitative detail, and to some degree modifies the larger picture. For example, it now appears that population actually declined in the latter half of the seventeenth century, and experienced brief but sharp declines in the late 1550s and 1720s. Most important, whereas in the past we had a general picture and a range of uncertain estimates, we now have solid numbers.[6]

But the greatest surprise by far is the fertility series, for it exhibits even wider long swings than mortality, and apparently played the leading proximate role in shaping population trends. Whether these fertility variations were introduced by changes in the real wage, as Wrigley and Schofield suggest, or were of independent origin due, for example, to the rise of a rural proletariat, as some have suggested, is one of the major puzzles posed by the book. Another kind of explanation, more ambitious but more difficult to sustain, argues that the long cycles were themselves generated by the economic-demographic system, and are therefore an intrinsic, rather than an incidental feature of the series that we observe.

---

6 See Thomas H. Hollingsworth, "*The Demography of the British Peerage,*" supplement to *Population Studies*, XVIII (1965); Wrigley, "Mortality in Pre-Industrial England: The Example of Colyton, Devon, over Three Centuries," *Daedalus*, XVCII (1968), 546–580; William A. Guy, "On the Duration of Life as Affected by the Pursuits of Literature, Science, and Art: With a Summary View of the Duration of Life Among Upper and Middle Classes of Society," *Quarterly Journal of the Statistical Society*, XXII (1859), 337–361.

The natural starting point in estimating relationships between the variables over this period, and in interpreting the motion of the system as a whole is the interpretation offered by Wrigley and Schofield themselves.

From 1540 to 1800 or so, wages initially dropped rapidly, causing fertility to fall. The latter reached a trough fifty years after wages and then, following wages, started moving upward again. One obvious question is why fertility responded with such a long lag; more is said about this point later. Another question, however, is why wages fell in the first place, and later rose again. Presumably the answer is that population was growing more rapidly than the equilibrium rate of .3 or .4 percent per year. But why was population growing rapidly? Because fertility was high and mortality was low. But once again, why? If the answer is that high wages favorably influenced the vital rates, then the whole explanation lacks a driving force; there is nothing to make *anything* change if each part of the system is completely determined by some other part unless the system moves in self-generated cycles, a possibility which is not discussed in this article.[7]

Let us retrace our steps. Was the decline in wages non-demographic in origin? Such an explanation is possible but unlikely, since wage change appears so closely associated with population change in this instance, and in the upswing as well. But population growth is automatically (that is, non-behaviorally) linked to fertility and mortality, aside from the presumably minor role of net migration. If wages did not fall autonomously, then either fertility must have been autonomously high, or mortality must have been autonomously low. In fact, if both fertility and mortality were undergoing a long exogenous fluctuation, this would explain their peculiar relationship to the wage: it was not driving them with a long lag; rather they were driving it. And because the *rate of change* of wages should be influenced by the

---

7 The possibility of self-generating cycles should not be discarded too lightly; after all, Malthus himself expected such cyclical behavior, as did G. Udney Yule in "Changes in the Marriage and Birth Rates in England and Wales during the Past Half Century," *Journal of the Royal Statistical Society*, LXIX (1906), 18–132, and, most recently, Easterlin in *Birth and Fortune* (New York, 1980). Also see Lee, "The Formal Dynamics of Controlled Populations and the Echo, the Boom, and the Bust," *Demography*, XI (1974), 563–585; James C. Frauenthall and Kenneth E. Swick, "Limit Cycle Oscillations of the Human Population," *ibid.*, XX (1983), 285–298.

difference in the *level* of the vital rates, we would expect fluctuations in the *level* of wages in turn to *lead* fluctuations in the level of vital rates.

This argument is developed in more detail below. The main point to be emphasized, however, is that if the theory of homeostatic population advanced by Wrigley and Schofield, and elsewhere by myself and others, is correct, then theorizing must pay careful attention to exactly what exogenous variations are driving the system. (A homeostatic population is one which automatically tends toward some equilibrium.) It is difficult to estimate relationships or test hypotheses from observation of a homeostatic system since, depending on how it is perturbed, we may observe different patterns of association among the variables even though true relationships remain unchanged. This difficulty is well known for market adjustment in general: do observed covariations of prices and quantities traded trace out the demand schedule or the supply schedule? That is precisely the issue here, applied to the labor market.

In earlier research on this topic my working hypothesis was that the longer-run movements in the system were powered by exogenous variations in mortality. Indeed, even modest exogenous variations in mortality have a considerable effect on population size and wages if maintained over the long run, although the effect of short-run variations is drastically attenuated. Therefore a modest exogenous variation in mortality is a logical candidate. If this argument were correct, then estimation of wage-population relationships would be possible, as would estimation of both short- and long-run wage-fertility relationships. Our examination of wage-mortality relationships, however, would have to be restricted to the short run.

With the new Wrigley and Schofield data, showing major long swings in fertility, the question arises whether fertility might not also have been subject to substantial exogenous variation, in which case observation of long-run wage-fertility relationships would be misleading, and give rise to anomalies, such as the fifty-year lag. If so, the economic-demographic history of the period would take on a different aspect, and one different from that described by Wrigley and Schofield. If not, then we are left with roughly the theory that I have been arguing in the past: exogenous change in mortality dominates the long-run behavior of the entire system, including the behavior of fertility, indirectly, through population and wages. The only alteration in that view is that fertility responded much more sensitively to the wage than I had thought, and therefore in the *demographic* accounting, if not in the *causal* accounting, has more importance than I previously suggested.

To address these questions more systematically, I offer a model below describing the basic relationships. In the simplest terms, real wages are a function of total population size, rather than its working-age segment; fertility and mortality are represented by crude rates; and there are no leads or lags in any of the relationships. Since we look primarily at the long swing in the series, which is roughly two centuries from peak to peak, ignoring lags of a few years' length should have little effect. If there were true lags on the order of fifty years, as Wrigley and Schofield suggest, then it would be impossible to ignore them. However, the present model without lags can generate the *appearance* of a fifty-year lag of the sort hypothesized by Wrigley and Schofield.

We start with an equation describing the level of real wages (w) as completely determined by population size (P), a trend in the demand for labor (indexed by A), and swings or short-run fluctuations about that trend (indexed by $e^{\epsilon}_t$):

1.    $w_t = A_t P_t^{-\beta} e^{\epsilon}_t.$

The trend and fluctuations in the demand for labor ($A_t$ and $\epsilon_t$) change over time with capital accumulation, technological progress, land reclamation, the development of international markets, and so on. If the labor supply is independent of the wage for a given population size, then $\beta$ describes the shape of the demand for labor schedule, whereas A and the longer-run components of $\epsilon_t$ describe its expected position. Later it will be convenient to assume that the natural log of A can be represented as a polynomial in time, which permits explicit estimation.

Next consider the level of fertility as partly determined by wages (w) and mortality (d):

2.    $b_t = \sigma_0 + \sigma_1 \ln w_t + \sigma_2 d_t + v_t.$

Here the relationship to wages ($\sigma_1$) is expected to be positive, either due to voluntary control of fertility (for a variety of possible reasons), to an influence of nutrition on fecundity, or to a relationship between nuptiality and wages. Wrigley and Schofield argue strongly for the last. The logarithmic form of wages is for mathematical convenience.

We would also expect, on the one hand, the relationship to mortality ($\sigma_2$) to be positive, because high mortality promotes earlier inheritance and marriage, or it interrupts lactation, or couples attempt to replace child deaths. On the other hand, we know that the short-run association is strongly negative, presumably because the unobserved variable "poor health" both raises mortality and depresses fertility; thus this short-run behavior should not be interpreted as reflecting a true influence of mortality on fertility.

Mortality is considered as partly determined by wages (w).

3. $\quad d_t = \gamma_0 - \gamma_1 \ln w_t + \nu_t.$

Here the relationship ($\gamma_1$) represents the positive check.

The system is closed by the assumption of no net migration, which yields the identity:

4. $\quad n_t \equiv \ln P_t - \ln P_{t-1} \equiv d_t,$

where $n_t$ is the population growth rate. It will sometimes be convenient to combine equations 2, 3, and 4:

5. $\quad n_t = \alpha + \delta \ln w_t + \eta_t,$

where $\alpha = \sigma_0 - (1-\sigma_2)\gamma_0; \delta = \sigma_1 + (1-\sigma_2)\gamma_1;$

$\eta_t = \nu_t - (1-\sigma_2)\nu_t.$

If the demand for labor does not change, or if it changes at a constant rate, then the system is in equilibrium when population grows at just that rate which leaves the real wage unchanged, whereas fertility and mortality are constant at levels consistent both with that population growth rate and with the real wage level (more precisely, these conditions hold only for expected values). If we let asterisks (*) denote equilibrium values, and superscript dots (˙) indicate derivatives with respect to time, then it is easy to show that:

6. $\quad n^* = (\dot{A}/A)/\beta,$

7. $\quad \ln w^* = [(\dot{A}/A)/\beta - \mu]/\delta,$

8. $\quad P^* = (A/w^*)^{1/\beta}.$

The equilibrium values of population growth (n*) and the wage level (w*) are constant so long as the rate of change in the demand for labor ($\dot{A}/A$) is at a constant rate (or is not changing at all). But they will rise or decline if the latter accelerates or decelerates. The equilibrium population size P* will be constant only if the demand for labor is constant, which is unlikely.

Because this is an equilibrating system, there may be severe difficulties in estimating any of the relationships. If the system is not perturbed—that is, if all the disturbances ($\epsilon$, $\nu$, $\gamma$, $\eta$) are zero, and the rate of change in the demand for labor ($\dot{A}/A$) is constant—then it will settle down to a placid equilibrium in which nothing changes except population size, which grows along a smooth exponential path. No relationships can be estimated because nothing varies.

Suppose, however, that there are disturbances, and therefore that the relationships do not hold exactly. If these disturbances are random, uncorrelated errors, then we can study the behavior of the system using graphical techniques, as do Wrigley and Schofield, or we can use ordinary least squares regression without serious problems. Unfortunately, however, it is unlikely that the disturbances will be temporally uncorrelated; rather it appears that they themselves follow a swing about two centuries long, driving the system to respond accordingly.[8]

Consider, for example, the little ice age, or the rise of a rural proletariat, or the exposure to a new disease to which the population eventually adapts. Such influences may be usefully viewed as deterministic historical forces following a particular course over time. For any one of these, we could in principle derive (using the equations presented above) the behavior of the system in response to these forces. An alternative, to be pursued here, is to argue more generally in terms of stylized representations of such influences. We might portray their evolution over time as a series of connected straight line trends, or as sine waves. I illustrate here with sine waves, analytically and conceptually the simplest.

There is one key point to establish first. Suppose that the

8    There will be some simultaneity in the system if all relationships are contemporaneous, but this should not seriously bias the estimates. For procedures to avoid this problem, see Lee, "Models of Preindustrial Population Dynamics"; idem, "Economic Aspects of the Population Explosion," 517–566.

population growth rate follows a long sinusoidal cycle; the *size* of the population (actually, its logarithm) will follow the same length cycle, but it will lag behind its rate of increase by one quarter of the cycle length (since $\Delta\sin(x)/\Delta x = \sin'(x) = \cos(x) = \sin(x + \pi/2)$). This is illustrated schematically in Figure 1. Population size will continue to increase so long as its growth rate is above zero; but the growth rate does not fall to zero until a quarter cycle after it reaches its maximum. Hence the size of population peaks one quarter cycle after its rate of change, which is what we need to show.

According to Malthusian theory, the real wage should be negatively related to population size and positively related to the rate of growth of population. But in light of the quarter-cycle lag of population behind its growth rate, it is impossible for both relationships to be true at once in the observed series; if one is apparent, the other will be absent. Two polar cases illustrate this point. In one, the demand for labor (which summarizes most extraneous influences on the real wage) undergoes a long sinusoidal change, whereas the population growth rate is com-

*Fig. 1*    The Relationship of Population Size to its Growth Rate when Size and Rate follow Sine Waves[a]

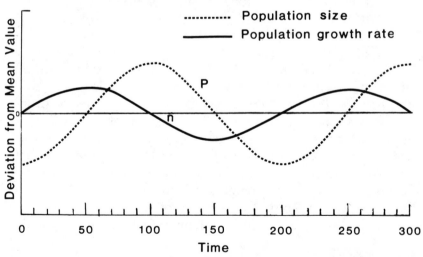

[a]In Figs. 1, 2, and 3, since the variables are plotted as deviations from their means, and each has a separate vertical scale, the relative magnitudes of the fluctuations are arbitrary as drawn.

pletely determined by the real wage. Formally we can write $\epsilon_t = c_1 \sin(c_2 t + c_3)$ and $\eta \equiv 0$, where $c_1$, $c_2$, and $c_3$ fix the amplitude, length, and position of the cycle in demand for labor.[9]

The other case is just the reverse: the real wage is determined *completely* by population size (no variation is allowed in the demand for labor, so $\epsilon_t \equiv 0$) and some extraneous influence on fertility or mortality undergoes a long cyclical swing ($\eta_t = f_1 \sin(f_2 t + f_3)$). It is easily shown mathematically that, in either case, all the observed series (log population, log real wages, and population growth rates) would also move in sinusoidal fluctuations of the same length, but perhaps with different amplitudes and relative positions. Given this result, it is possible to derive the main results of interest diagrammatically, without recourse to formal mathematics.[10]

For the case in which the demand for labor varies sinusoidally and the population growth rate is completely determined by the level of the real wage, the various series must look as they are shown in Figure 2. By assumption, the rate of population growth moves in perfect sympathy with the sinusoidal real wage. As shown earlier, population size lags behind its growth rate by one quarter cycle, and therefore behind the real wage by one quarter cycle.

Should the actual historical series that we observe look like Figure 2, in Malthusian terms we might correctly note that the population growth rate bears a close positive relationship to the real wage. A regression would yield a correct estimate (of $\alpha$ and $\delta$, the parameters of equation 5). But, with regard to the relationship of the real wage to population size, the correlation of the two series is zero, as is the regression coefficient of wages on population. Searching for the expected negative relationship, reflecting diminishing returns, we might note that, after allowing for a quarter cycle lag (here fifty years), wages are perfectly negatively related to population size (a correlation of $-1$). Thus encouraged, we might regress wages on population with a fifty-

9  Variations in the supply of labor for a given population size, arising from changing age-sex composition, institutional changes, or behavioral changes in hours of labor supplied per potential worker, will also affect the real wage, as will unexpected price changes.
10  The exact result depends on initial values of these variables, but their influence wears off quickly relative to the length of a 200-year cycle, given plausible assumptions about the values of $\alpha$ and $\beta$ in the model.

*Fig. 2*  The Demand for Labor Drives the System

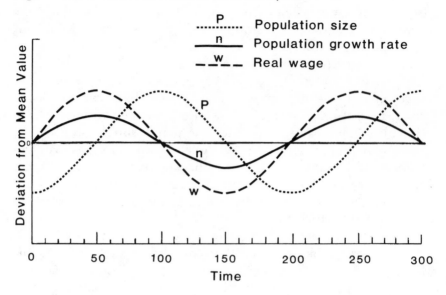

year lag. The coefficients obtained would be intended to estimate $\beta$ (in equation 1), the true effect of population on wages. But in fact, the estimate would bear no relationship to $\beta$ whatsoever; it would depend only on $\alpha$ and on the cycle length, and would be the same whether the true $\beta$ were zero or 100.[11]

The lesson to be drawn from this discussion is that, if most of the system's variation over a long swing is due to an extraneous swing in the demand for labor, then we can correctly identify the effect of real wages on population *growth rates*, but we can learn nothing about the influence of population *size* on the real wage.

The opposite case, when the demand for labor is constant and there is an extraneous swing in fertility or mortality, leading to a swing in population growth rates, is shown in Figure 3.

The population growth rate moves sinusoidally, and population size, as shown earlier, must lag behind it by one quarter

---

11 The regression coefficient would be $\alpha L/(2\pi)$, where L is the cycle length; if $\alpha$ = 0.02, a plausible value, in light of short-run estimates, then the supposed estimate of $\beta$ would be about 0.64 when the cycle length L is 200 years. There is one other point which emerges from the mathematical results: the real wage will *lead* the demand for labor somewhat (up to one quarter cycle, but generally much less) due to the offsetting effects of induced population change.

*Fig. 3* Extraneous Change in Population Growth Rates Drives the System

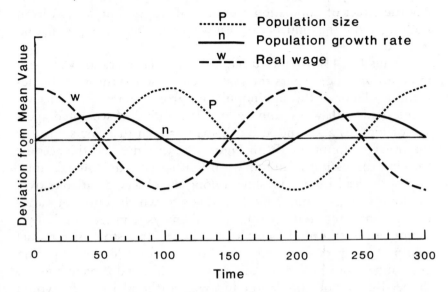

........P........ Population size

_____n_____ Population growth rate

_ _ _w_ _ _ Real wage

cycle. The real wage, by assumption, is completely determined by population size and moves inversely to it; therefore it must lead the population growth rate by one quarter cycle, as shown in Figure 3. Now we are able to identify the effect of population size on real wages, obtaining the correct value of β, either by inspecting plotted series or by regression. However, we find zero correlation between the contemporaneous population growth rate and the wage, and estimate a regression coefficient of zero. Seeking a positive relation, we might note that growth rates and wages would be perfectly correlated with a quarter-cycle lag, or about fifty years if the cycle were 200 years as in Figure 3. Thus encouraged, we might make a regression estimate of the strength of the positive and preventive check; we would find a positive coefficient, but it would in fact be entirely independent of the true relationship (described by α), and instead would reflect only the sensitivity of diminishing returns (β) and cycle length.[12]

The lesson to be drawn from this discussion is that, if most

12    The coefficient would equal $2\pi L/\beta$, where L is the cycle length; for L = 200 and β = 1 (which appears roughly correct, as is discussed below), then the supposed estimate of α would be 0.03; but this number would be the same no matter what the true α was.

of the system's variation over a long swing is due to an extraneous swing in the population growth rate, then we can correctly identify the effect of population size on real wages, but we can learn nothing about the influence of real wages on the rate of population growth.

Thus far, I have only discussed the polar cases in which extraneous variation enters the system either solely through the demand for labor or through population growth rates. Realistically, it enters in both ways, and we observe a kind of weighted average of Figures 2, 3, and 4; but it may happen that one source or the other is dominant. With Figures 2, 3, and 4 and the accompanying discussion in mind, we might suspect that an examination of the lead–lag relationships among the observed variables over the long swing would provide clues as to which source of variation is more important. More formal analysis, in terms of either the deterministic model employed above, or a stochastic model analyzed using cross-spectral methods (and no longer requiring cyclical behavior), confirms that this is so. If $\alpha$ and $\beta$ were known, the lead or lag of population and wages (the phase shift) would completely identify the relative contributions of the extraneous variation by source.

Figure 4 plots twenty-five-year moving averages of the population growth rate and of the real wage, calculated from the Wrigley-Schofield estimates, along with detrended population size, unsmoothed. The series were averaged in order to filter out the short-run variations, thus revealing the long swings more clearly. Also shown is a line corresponding to a constant population growth rate of 0.4 percent per year, which is the value about which the growth rate swings, i.e. the equilibrium rate of equation 6 $((\dot{A}/A)/\beta)$. This line corresponds to the zero line of Figures 2 and 3.[13]

Inspection of these plots suggests, on the one hand, that real wages and detrended population size are strongly negatively related with no clear leads or lags. The population growth rate, on

13 The Wrigley-Schofield real wage estimates are essentially those of Phelps-Brown and Hopkins with some interpolations. The detrended population size was calculated at $P_t e^{-rt}$, where r was estimated by a regression of $\ln P_t$ on time, using GLS to correct for second-order autoregressive disturbances; r was estimated at 0.0041. See Henry Phelps Brown and Sheila V. Hopkins, "Seven Centuries of the Price of Consumables Compared with Builders' Wage Rates," *Economica*, XIII (1956), 296–314.

*Fig. 4* Detrended Population Size, Population Growth Rate, and Real Wages in England, 1541–1813[a]

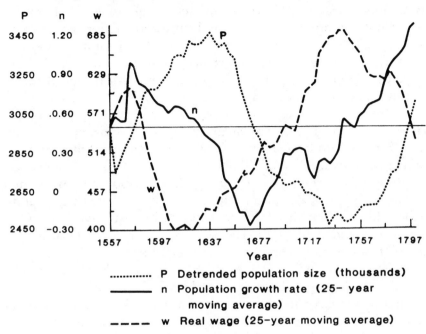

............ P  Detrended population size (thousands)

——————  n  Population growth rate (25- year
moving average)

— — — —  w  Real wage (25-year moving average)

[a]Population size was divided by $e^{rt}$, where r is a regression estimate of its long-run growth rate. The population growth rate and real wage were smoothed using a 25-year moving average. All series are plotted at 4-year intervals.
SOURCE: Population is from Wrigley and Schofield, *Population History*, 531–534. Real wage is from *ibid.*, 642–644.

the other hand, appears to lag substantially behind the real wage, at least at the only clear turning point which both series show, during the seventeenth century. Wrigley and Schofield detect three turning points in one component of the growth rate, fertility, with lags of fifty, sixty-five, and forty years behind wages. This general pattern conforms more clearly to that of Figure 3 than of Figure 2, suggesting that extraneous variation in vital rates drove the system over this long swing, and not a swing in the demand for labor. More formal statistical analysis, based on the estimated phase shift of the empirical cross-spectrum, confirms this conclusion.[14]

14  Wrigley and Schofield, *Population History*, 419.

This result is of considerable substantive interest in itself, for it amounts to a rejection of the classical demand for labor theory as an interpretation of these prominent long swings in English economic-demographic history, and substitutes a more active role for population itself. The investigation of the historical causes of the variations in fertility and mortality assumes a new importance, since these causes now appear to be fundamental, not incidental, to the history of the period.

One consequence is that we can identify the effect of population size on real wages by analyzing their relationship over the long run, as I do later. However, we cannot hope to identify the influence of wages on natural increase, or on its components, fertility and mortality, by studying their relationships over the long swing.[15] In particular, it appears possible that Wrigley and Schofield's finding that fertility responded sensitively to the real wage, but with a fifty-year lag, reflects a spurious association of the sort discussed in connection with Figure 3.

If the long swing enables us to estimate only the effect of population on wages, how can we identify the effect of wages on natural increase, or its component vital rates? This identification can be done through the study of short-run fluctuations using the same data series. The complications that afflict the interpretation of long swings arise because a small extraneous variation in natural increase is greatly amplified in its effect on population and wages, if it persists for fifty or 100 years; the longer the swing, the greater the amplification. Short-run extraneous fluctuations in natural increase, however, have little effect on population size, which is itself a kind of long cumulation of such variations. If we assume birth and death rates of thirty per 1,000, a 10 percent increase one year in the death rate would lead to a mere 0.3 percent decrease in the current rate of growth of the population in the following year, which would have a negligible effect on wages, indiscernible among the extraneous wage fluctuations due to the influence of weather. Furthermore, fluctuations in fertility have no impact on the potential labor supply for ten or fifteen years, and therefore

15 This statement is actually too pessimistic, since it is possible that, say, mortality was driving the system, whereas fertility varied passively in response to wages. Separate inspection of the series of each, however, in practice seems to rule out this possibility for this period. In Lee, "Population in Preindustrial England," 581–607, I used this assumption about exogenously varying mortality to identify the system.

no impact on wages in the short run. After suitable manipulation to remove not only the trend but also all fluctuations of more than ten or fifteen years, the associations among the series reveal the influence of wages on fertility and mortality. Unfortunately, this approach is less satisfactory than it seems at first; it is a technical solution to the problem, but only under the assumption, implicit in equations 2, 3, and 5, that short-run responses are no different than long-run ones. This assumption may not be so.

Nevertheless, I estimated the empirical cross spectrum of real wages against detrended population size for England, from 1540 to 1809. This estimate disclosed that for fluctuations of forty years in length and above, the two moved inversely with no lead or lag, as in Figure 3. Thus the regression coefficient (in this case, the gain) of wages on population should provide a good estimate of the true structural relation ($\beta$ in equation 1). Such estimates were consistently close to 1.5, for all of the longer frequencies. Ordinary regressions of the real wage on population size gave much the same result, as is discussed in more detail below.

The preceding discussions have suggested that the long-run fluctuations in the series had their origins in independent movements of the vital rates, rather than in the demand for labor. Therefore an estimation of the effect of population on wages should be possible. However, Lindert, both in his article in this issue, and in an earlier article, has argued plausibly that the rate of inflation should be included as an explanatory variable in the real wage equation, and that when it is, the role of population size (labor supply) diminishes to insignificance. Thus the Malthusian position that premodern real wage trends were largely determined by swings in population size appears to be seriously undermined. I believe, however, that on closer inspection this challenge is less serious than it first appears.[16]

"Yet impish Clio may have played another of her tricks here. The periods of rapid population growth just happened to match those with rising prices from the sixteenth century to the early nineteenth." That this close correlation exists is indisputable. But theory tells us that it is *changes* in prices which may affect real

16 Peter H. Lindert, "English Living Standards, Population Growth, and Wrigley-Schofield," *Explorations in Economic History*, XX (1983), 131–155.

wages, and theory gives no reason whatsoever to expect real wages to be influenced in the long run by price *levels*. Fortunately, the rate of change of prices is *not* closely correlated with population size over that period. In practice, however, we must also account for the fact that Lindert's regression appears to show that the rate of inflation dominates the size of the population.[17]

The simple model describing the determination of the real wage and nominal wage that I develop here will be used to explain Lindert's results, and to propose a change in the specification of his regression equation. The new estimates that follow show an important role for price changes, but an undiminished impact of population on the real wage.

Consider how the money wage was determined. In this period production in agriculture, where most labor was employed, had a large stochastic component, reflecting the importance of the weather; indeed, the standard deviation of wheat prices relative to trend was 22 percent. When labor was hired, neither its physical productivity, nor the price of its output, could be known with any accuracy; these would become clear only at the time of harvest. At a given money wage, employers of labor would presumably hire a quantity of labor such that its expected marginal revenue product equalled that wage, where the marginal revenue product is simply the price of output times the marginal physical product of labor. If every employer did so, then for the economy as a whole we would have: $W_t = E[Price_{t+1} \cdot MPL_t]$. This reasoning helps explain the stickiness of nominal wages, since discernment of genuine change in the average price level must have been difficult, and the adjustment of expectations slow.[18]

Let prices and the MPL each be expressed as the product of their individual expected values (based on observations up to time $t-1$ for the $MPL_t$, and up to t for $Prices_{t+1}$), and some contemporary disturbance. Thus $MPL_t = E(MPL_t) \cdot e^{\epsilon}_t$, where $e^{\epsilon}_t$ represents the multiplicative disturbing effect of weather on marginal productivity. The expected value of MPL depends, by hypothesis, on population size, so $E(MPL_t) = A_t P_t^{-\beta}$ in line with the earlier as-

17   *Ibid.*, 150.
18   For details, see Lee, "Short-run Fluctuations of Vital Rates, Prices, and Weather in England, 1539 to 1840," in Wrigley and Schofield, *Population History*, 377. The standard deviation was calculated for the ratio of prices to a centered 11-point moving average, from 1540 to 1840.

sumption in equation 1. In practice, $A_t$ is expressed so that $\ln A_t$ is a polynomial in time, typically of the form $\ln A_t = \mu + \rho_1 t + \rho_2 t^2$.[19]

As for prices, we distinguish between two kinds of disturbances: one, a function of $\epsilon$ due to the influence of weather on the previous harvests' outputs; the other, $e^{\theta}{}_t$, due to all other unanticipated influences and, notable among these, monetary factors. Then: $\text{Price}_t = E(\text{Price}_t) \cdot e^{-\lambda \epsilon_{t-1}} \cdot e^{\theta}{}_t$, where $\lambda$ reflects the own-price elasticity of demand for output. The expected price level may be assumed to be formulated as a weighted geometric average of past prices: $E(\text{Price}_t) = \Pi_{i=1}(\text{Price}_{t-i})^{c_i}$ where the $[c_i]$ are the weights, and must add to unity if expectations are correct when prices are constant.

Assume that weather ($\epsilon_t$) is unpredictable from year to year, and independent of non-weather related price disturbances ($\theta_t$), which are also unpredictable in the sense of being serially uncorrelated. Then we have the following:

9.  $W_t = E[\text{Price}_{t+1} \cdot \text{MPL}_t] = e^{\mu + \rho_1 t + \rho_2 t^2} P_t^{-\beta} \Pi_{i=1} (\text{Price}_{t-i})^{c_i}.$

    subject to $\Sigma c_i = 1$.

This equation describes the dependence of the money wage on past prices, population size, and the demand for labor; a multiplicative error reflecting the approximate nature of the specification may be added.

The real wage is $W_t/\text{Price}_t$, from which it follows that the log of the real wage is given by:

10.  $\ln(W_t/\text{Price}_t) = \mu + \rho_1{}^t + \rho_2 t^2 - \beta \ln P_t - \ln \text{Price}_t$

$$+ \sum_{i=0}^{\infty} c_i \ln \text{Price}_{t-i}$$

$$\text{subject to } \sum_{i=1}^{\infty} c_i = 1.$$

19   Strictly speaking the expected value of MPL depends on the quantity of labor employed, which is assumed to be a fixed proportion of the total working age population. Note also that if $E(\epsilon_t) = 0$ but the variance of $\epsilon$ is positive, then $E(e^{\epsilon t})$ will be greater than unity, and the decomposition is inexact; therefore assume that $E(\epsilon_t) \neq 0$, but rather that $E(e^{\epsilon t}) = 1$. The same point holds for the disturbance $\theta_t$ introduced in the following paragraph.

This equation is very similar to the one estimated by Lindert, except that his weighted sum of the logs of past prices goes back only ten years, rather than an infinite number, and, most important, he does not constrain the sum of $c_i$ to equal unity.[20]

Lindert's actual regression results can be summarized as follows. The coefficient on the log of current price is $-0.89$ and on price lagged one year, $-0.21$; all of the other price coefficients are essentially zero, although the sum of all coefficients is $-0.99$. The coefficient on population is insignificant and small ($-0.07$). The coefficients on time imply that the demand for labor grew at an accelerating rate, initially in 1541 at 0.26 percent per year, rising in 1800 to 0.65 percent per year. One might conclude from these results that there is no evidence that population change explains long-run real wage variation in this period, and that its apparent strong showing in my previous research results was because of an improper specification of the equations due to the omission of prices.

Given that the long-run price level was essentially proportional to population size over this period, it is easy to see why Lindert's estimates came out as they did. For the long-run price level is simply the expected value of price represented by $\Sigma_0^{10} c_i \ln \text{Price}_{t-i}$. And the "true" value of $\beta$, when prices are not in the equation, is (according to Lindert's estimate) $-1.27$, not significantly different from $-1$. Thus we have, very approximately, $-\beta \ln P_t + \Sigma_0^{10} c_i \ln \text{Price}_{t-i} = 0$. All of these variables effectively drop from the equation, and their estimated coefficients approach zero. This leaves:

11. $\quad \ln (W_t / \text{Price}_t) \doteq \mu + \rho_1 t + \rho_2 t^2 - \ln \text{Price}_t,$

which is roughly what Lindert found. This equation, however, by adding $\ln P_t$ to both sides, may be further simplified to $\ln W_t = \mu + \rho_1 t + \rho_2 t^2$. Thus, in the end, we have expressed $\ln W_t$ as a time trend, and found it insensitive to the price level or population. Now it may be debatable whether population growth depresses real wages, but it seems unlikely that the money wage level should be completely independent of the level of prices, even when this level increased by a factor of ten; and equally unlikely

20 Lindert's specification appears to be different, since it is expressed in terms of rates of inflation; however, it can be re-expressed in terms of levels of $\ln \text{Price}_{t-i}$ as in equation 10 above. Lindert, "English Population, Wages, and Prices," in this issue, 9n.

that the money wage should have risen by a factor of six or seven over this period, apparently independently of any real or monetary influences.[21]

It is possible to tighten the specification of Lindert's estimation equation by incorporating the additional constraint: that the sum of the weights used to form price expectations be unity. This incorporation of the constraint ensures that, over the long run, nominal wages will adjust completely to prices, while leaving room for inflation to erode the real wage in the short run.

One might also relax Lindert's constraint that the lagged prices go back only ten years, but I have retained that somewhat arbitrary assumption. The resulting equation for real wages is identical to equation 10, except that the upper limit "10" is substituted for "∞"; it is also identical to Lindert's, except that the $c_i$s are constrained to sum to unity, in accordance with the assumption that price expectations are correct when prices are constant.

This equation was estimated using the Wrigley-Schofield population size series, their version of the Phelps-Brown and Hopkins real wage series, and the Phelps-Brown and Hopkins general cost of living index.[22] The results are as follows:

12. $\ln (W_t/\text{Price}_t) = 15.9 + 0.000436t$
$$+ 0.0000163t^2 - 1.18 \ln \text{Pop}_t$$

$$(37.5) \quad (1.20) \quad\quad (16.37) \quad\quad (22.3)$$

$$- \ln \text{Price}_t + 0.158 \ln \text{Price}_t + 0.059 \ln \text{Price}_{t-1}$$

$$(3.38) \quad\quad (0.99)$$

$$+ 0.086 \ln \text{Price}_{t-2} + 0.079 \ln \text{Price}_{t-3} + 0.059 \ln \text{Price}_{t-4}$$

$$(1.43) \quad\quad (1.31) \quad\quad (0.97)$$

$$+ 0.073 \ln \text{Price}_{t-5} + 0.063 \ln \text{Price}_{t-6} + 0.088 \ln \text{Price}_{t-7}$$

$$(1.21) \quad\quad (1.06) \quad\quad (1.48)$$

---

21   This discussion corresponds to Lindert's second strategy of rebuttal for Malthusians to adopt, outlined in *ibid.*, 616–618.

22   It would have been preferable to use only the population of working age, rather than total population, but this was not done as it would have required interpolation within five-year periods.

$$+ \ 0.099 \ \ln \text{Price}_{t-8} + 0.071 \ \ln \text{Price}_{t-9} + 0.165 \ \ln \text{Price}_{t-10}$$

$$(1.67) \qquad (1.20) \qquad (\text{n.a.})$$

$R = .89$

$DW = .11$

First, the coefficient on population is highly significant, with a value of $-1.18$; this value is somewhat lower than my previous estimates, which clustered around $-1.5$ with the same data.[23] Second, it is clear from the coefficients $\rho_1$ and $\rho_2$ (found for t and $t^2$) that the rate of change in the demand for labor accelerates dramatically in this regression. Accordingly, the equilibrium population growth rate (calculated as $(\rho_1 + 2\rho_2 t)/\beta$) changes from 0.03 percent per year in 1541 to 0.75 in 1800, contrasting sharply with the more modest acceleration that I had found with the same data previously, from 0.28 to 0.51 percent per year.[24]

Third, a constant rate of inflation of r percent per year would depress real wages by 5.5r percent, which can be found by substituting such a trend in ln Price in the estimated equation.[25]

I have also estimated a closely related specification which is simpler, filters out most short-run variance, and allows in a more transparent way for inflation to depress real wages. The regression is run on ten-year averages of the data, reducing the number of observations from 260 to twenty-six, between 1541 and 1800.

---

23  When correction is made for autocorrelated disturbances, signalled by the low Durbin-Watson statistic, the results are altered drastically and the coefficient on population becomes insignificant. Correction was made for second-order autoregressive disturbances using Generalized Least Squares. However, the periodicity implied by the estimated autoregressive coefficients (1.91, $-0.92$) was 211 years. Evidently the long swing in real wages and population was modelled as an error process. There are signs that the correction is somehow inappropriate, e.g. the instability of coefficients and many of the t-statistics increasing by factors of 10 to 20. It is known that this kind of correction can sometimes result in less efficient estimates, particularly when trending variables are present, as is the case here. See A. C. Harvey, *The Econometric Analysis of Time Series* (New York, 1981).

24  See Lee, "Fluctuations in English Fertility, Mortality, Population, and Wages: Estimation of a Perturbed Homeostatic System," paper presented at the Conference on British Historical Demography (1982).

25  On the one hand, the truncation of the lag distribution of prices at 10 years is arbitrary, and the elevated value of the coefficient estimate for ln Price$_{t-10}$ indicates that more years should be included. On the other hand, the result that constant inflation at rate r would depress the real wage by 5.5r (half the length of the moving average times r) is not dictated by truncation at lag 10; asymmetric patterns of estimated coefficients could shift the result to any value.

The equation is:

$$13. \quad \ln \overline{W}_t - \ln \overline{Price}_t = \mu + \rho_1 t + \rho_2 t^2 - \sigma \ln P_t - \sigma (\ln \overline{Price} - \ln \overline{Price}_{t-10}),$$

where the t subscript indicates an average value for years t to t + 9. When prices are on average constant, they have no effect on the average real wage; when there is inflation, however, the real wage drops by the share $\sigma$ of the decadal rate.[26]

Table 1 shows empirical estimates of equation 13, this time using a population between the ages of fifteen and sixty; otherwise the data are the same as before.

A number of conclusions can be drawn from these results. First, the decadal rate of inflation has a highly significant negative effect on the real wage, which is reduced by 53.5 percent of the inflation in the preceding ten years (essentially the same result as obtained with single-year data). Second, the coefficient on population is highly significant, and is modified very little by the inclusion of inflation in the regression, which can be seen from a comparison of the two columns. Its value with inflation included is virtually identical to the result from single-year data. Third, when inflation is included, the estimated equilibrium population growth rate shows more rapid acceleration. Rather than remaining flat, as it does when inflation is excluded, it rises from below 0.2 percent per year at the beginning of the period to above 0.6 percent per year at its end. This pattern again confirms the marked increase found in regressions on annual data.

Figure 5 plots the decadal average values of real wages, along with the fitted values (based solely on the independent variables) from the two regressions, the results of which were reported in Table 1. The figure shows that inclusion of the inflation variable hardly alters the fitted long-run time path, but leads to successful tracking of many important fluctuations.

Taken as a whole, these results suggest that Lindert is entirely correct to argue that price variables should be included in the real wage regressions. However, when these price variables are in-

---

26 The relationship of this model to the previous one is that the price expectations for the 10-year period t to t + 9 may be viewed as a weighted sum of average prices during the period t to t + 9 and during t − 10 to t − 1, with weights $(1 - \sigma)$ and $\sigma$. If, for example, each single year expectation is formed as $E(Price_t) = \Pi_{i=1} Price_{t-i}^{1/10}$, then $(1 - \sigma) = 0.45$ and $\sigma = 0.55$. Subtracting $\ln \overline{Price}_t$ from both sides yields equation 13.

*Table 1* Regression Estimates of the Effect of Population and Inflation on the Real Wage, Decadal Averages, 1541–1550 to 1791–1800[a]

| | DECADAL AVERAGE REAL WAGE (DEPENDENT VARIABLE) | |
|---|---|---|
| | WITH INFLATION TERM | WITHOUT INFLATION TERM |
| Constant | 15.22 (13.94) | 15.63 (8.45) |
| Time | .0134 (1.34) | .0405 (2.42) |
| Time$^2$ | .00–131 | .000–404 |
| ln (Pop 20–60) | −1.17 (8.04) | −1.25 (5.04) |
| Inflation | −.535 (11.38) | — — |
| $\rho 1$ | .996 | .350 |
| $\rho 2$ | −.753 | −.146 |
| $R^2$(raw) | .87 | .79 |

[a]t-statistics are in parentheses below each estimate. Both equations were estimated by Generalized Least Squares corrected for second-order autoregressive disturbances, but results are virtually identical for Ordinary Least Squares. Time is measured in decades, starting with zero.

cluded with specifications which incorporate constraints strongly suggested by theory, the evidence for population's dominant role remains strong. Furthermore, their inclusion leads to estimation of a more rapid acceleration of the increasing demand for labor.

Classical population theory rested on two structural propositions: that population increase, other things equal, would depress living standards; and that increased living standards, other things equal, would raise the rate of population growth. Using the new data at our disposal, Lindert has questioned the first proposition, and has concluded that if population depressed the real wage at all, it was probably indirectly, through influencing the price level.

*Fig. 5* The Actual Real Wage and the Predicted Real Wage from Regressions with and without Inflation

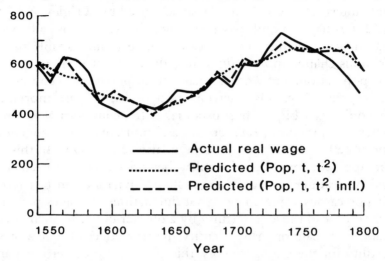

NOTE: All points represent 10-year averages starting at date shown, except Population is population aged 15 to 60 at the midpoint. Estimates are GLS with AR2 errors; predictions are independent of error structure and are based on regressions reported in Table 1.

However, in more tightly specified equations, estimates show important roles for both prices and population, with population by far the dominant influence in the long run. These new data also show clearly that the equilibrium population growth rate was rising throughout the period, which is what we would expect. Nonetheless it is not what has always been found. When price data are included in the analysis, the acceleration in this equilibrium growth rate is particularly pronounced. Thus it appears from these new data, as it did from the old, that the wage responded sensitively to deviations of population from its equilibrium growth path, and that the first classical proposition is sustained.

As for the second proposition, the situation is less clear. For short-run fluctuations in the vital rates, these new data show that fertility responded closely to price and real wage fluctuations, whereas mortality responded weakly and varied relatively independently. But for longer-run swings, the identification of relationships is treacherous. It certainly does appear from these new data that fertility was a more important proximate determinant of population change than mortality, which is a new, unexpected, and important finding. But if we attempt to go behind the *prox-imate* determinants to the causal determinants, there are two possible interpretations. In one, that advanced by Wrigley and Scho-field, fertility responds passively, sensitively, and with a fifty-year lag to wage change. In this case it appears inescapable that exogenous change in *mortality* drives the long-run changes in fertility, population, and wages, whatever the *proximate* decomposition of responsibility; this assertion must be so, because mortality is the only variable with substantial extraneous variation. In the other interpretation, *both* fertility and mortality vary exogenously and together drive changes in population and wages. In this case, the apparent long lag of fertility behind wages is a predictable, and misleading, aspect of the system's dynamics: in fact fertility change causes wage change, but fluctuations in wages perversely *appear* to lead those in fertility by a quarter cycle. In such circumstances we cannot easily identify the true effect of real wages on fertility for these long swings; this effect could be zero, negative, or positive.

Which of these two interpretations is correct? If we knew that the responsiveness of fertility to wages was structurally the same for both short- and long-run fluctuations, then we could estimate the model completely, and we would conclude that much of the fertility variation was exogenous. This conclusion would amount to a rejection of the Wrigley and Schofield interpretation in favor of the second one. But in fact the responsiveness of fertility to wages may well be structurally different for long swings and for short fluctuations.

In either case, it seems clear that it was independent variation in the vital rates, rather than the demand for labor, which drove the system over the distinctive long swing. But if it were the insubordinate behavior of fertility and mortality that kept the system out of equilibrium, this behavior was nonetheless only a sideshow. The main event was the dramatic increase in both actual and equilibrium population size, reflecting accelerating increases in the demand for labor; and there classical population theory comes into its own.

## Jan de Vries

# The Population and Economy of the Preindustrial Netherlands

In the past two decades the application of family reconstitution techniques has deepened our knowledge of past demographic behavior in several European countries. The Dutch Republic is not one of these countries because the technique has only limited application to the recalcitrant Dutch parish registers. As a result, only fragmentary and indirect evidence is available on demographic behavior in the preindustrial Netherlands.

In contrast, Dutch research emphasizes the investigation of macrodemographic questions in a regional context. This literature impresses chiefly through its resourceful use of flawed and imperfect data. And one can hope that the adaptation of newly developed techniques like back projection will enable further progress in this direction. If parish records can be assembled to reconstruct Dutch population back to the early seventeenth century (the sixteenth century will, it appears, always remain beyond our reach), Dutch historical demography will be able to build upon its strong regional studies, adding a more detailed knowledge of the nuptiality, fertility, and mortality behavior that has long been the missing element in such studies.

Even so, it is relevant to identify the issues in Dutch demographic history most in need of further investigation, and to probe the limits to the applicability to the Dutch Republic of the dynamic model of demographic-economic interaction developed by Wrigley and Schofield.[1]

THE POPULATION    The size of the Dutch population before 1795, the date of the first national census, is thought to have followed

Jan de Vries is Professor of History and Economics, University of California, Berkeley. He is the author of *European Urbanization, 1500–1800* (Cambridge, Mass., 1984).

1    E. Anthony Wrigley and Roger S. Schofield, *The Population History of England, 1541–1871: A Reconstruction* (Cambridge, Mass., 1981).

*Table 1*  Dutch Population and Urbanization, 1500–1900
(in thousands)

| YEAR | TOTAL POPULATION | POPULATION OF HOLLAND | RURAL POPULATION | PERCENTAGE URBAN >2,500 | >10,000 | >20,000 |
|------|------|------|------|------|------|------|
| 1500 | 900–1,000 | | | | | |
| 1525 | | 275[a] | 800 | 27 | 15 | 5.5 |
| 1550 | 1,200–1,300 | | | | 15 | |
| 1600 | 1,400–1,600 | 672[b] | | | 24 | |
| 1650 | 1,850–1,900 | | | | 32 | |
| 1675 | | 883 | 1,085 | 42 | | 24.5 |
| 1700 | 1,850–1,950 | | | | 34 | |
| 1750 | 1,900–1,950 | 783 | 1,150 | 39 | 30 | 21.8 |
| 1800 | 2,100 | 783 | 1,300 | 37 | 29 | 20.8 |
| 1815 | 2,292 | 764 | | 35 | 26 | 17.5 |
| 1830 | 2,613 | 894 | | 35 | 26 | |
| 1840 | 2,860 | 969 | | 39 | 28 | 21.3 |
| 1850 | 3,049 | 1,039 | 1,830 | 39 | 29 | |
| 1860 | 3,309 | 1,143 | | | | 24.7 |
| 1870 | 3,580 | 1,266 | 2,140 | | | 28.9 |
| 1880 | 4,013 | 1,484 | | | | 30.5 |
| 1900 | 5,104 | 2,113 | | | | 45.6 |

a  In 1514.
b  In 1622.
SOURCES: A. A. van der Woude, "Demografische ontwikkeling van de Noordelijke Nederlanden 1500–1800," in *Algemene Geschiedenis der Nederlanden* (Bussum, 1980), V, 102–168; W. P. Blockmans et al., "Tussen crises en welvaart," *ibid.*, IV, 42–60; de Vries, *Barges and Capitalism. Passenger Transportation in the Dutch Economy, 1632–1839* (Utrecht, 1981), 248–249; E. W. Hofstee, *De demografische ontwikkeling van Nederland in de eerste helft van de negentiende eeuw* (n.p., 1978), Table IA; M. C. Deurloo and G. A. Hoekveld, "The Population Growth of the Urban Municipalities in the Netherlands between 1849 and 1970," in H. Schmal (ed.), *Patterns of European Urbanisation since 1500* (London, 1981), 247–283.

the course shown in Table I. These estimates are based on regional studies pursued during the 1960s by Slicher van Bath and the members of the Institute of Rural History at the Agricultural University in Wageningen. The national estimates embody two distinct regional patterns: in the maritime provinces very rapid population growth in the sixteenth and early seventeenth centuries gave way, in the third quarter of the seventeenth century, to absolute decline; in the inland provinces the sixteenth-century growth was much slower and the period from 1650 to 1750 was one of continued growth. When compared to other Western European populations, the Dutch trends stand out in two respects: the high rate of sixteenth-century growth and the virtual absence of an upturn in the second half of the eighteenth century. Since the publication of these total population estimates in 1965 no one has felt sufficiently dissatisfied with them to produce alternative estimates.[2]

City populations were not a primary object of attention in the 1965 study, and historical urban demography still awaits the attention it deserves. However, enough work has been completed to establish in broad outline the course of Dutch urbanization. The estimates of urban population, just like the total population estimates, are a composite of diverse trends among the numerous cities. The seventeenth-century growth of Amsterdam and the eighteenth-century growth of Rotterdam and The Hague compensated for the sharp decline of several other cities.

Table I displays the percentage of the total population resident in cities. The high level of urbanization attained by the mid-seventeenth century is well known; that this level formed a ceiling not to be broken through for two centuries is worth emphasizing here.

Research in Dutch demographic history has yielded estimates of total, regional, and urban population that are sufficiently well founded to provide a framework for further research. It is unlikely that the contours of population change displayed in Table I will need substantial revision. When we turn to the study of fertility, mortality, marriage, and migration, however, which jointly determined the observed course of population change, no such sanguine statement is possible.

Current views about vital rates in the early modern period are based largely on fragmentary and indirect evidence. Any general statements should be thought of as hypotheses awaiting confirmation rather than as the conclusions of systematic research. In a comprehensive survey of Dutch demographic history (of which he is the leading exponent), Van der Woude offered views about the likely course of events, which can be summarized as follows:

*Mortality,* in the short run, did not exhibit the sharp fluctuations associated with *crises de subsistance* and in the long run remained roughly constant. Only the persistently high mortality of the first three decades of the eighteenth century stands as an

2 J. A. Faber, H. K. Roessingh, B. H. Slicher van Bath, A. M. van der Woude, and H. J. van Xanten, "Population Changes and Economic Developments in the Netherlands: A Historical Survey," *A. A. G. Bijdragen,* XII (1965), 47–110.

exception to this rule. The major changes in the rate of population growth were activated by *fertility,* which experienced two major turning points. The birth rate began to turn downward around 1650 and turned abruptly upwards around 1815 (see Figure 1). The *marriage age* and *celibacy rates* were the main regulators of total fertility.[3]

At present Van der Woude's views must be regarded as controlled conjectures. They are based on such data as the baptism and burial totals for several towns and villages, village baptism-marriage ratios, marriage ages and marriage rates in Amsterdam, and the comprehensive but crude data compiled in the first censuses of the early nineteenth century. For example, almost all that is known concerning the age at first marriage is summarized in Table 2.

If they could be sustained by further research, Van der Woude's views would be of special interest because they are

*Fig. 1*   Crude Birth Rates and Crude Death Rates in The Netherlands and England, 1804–1850

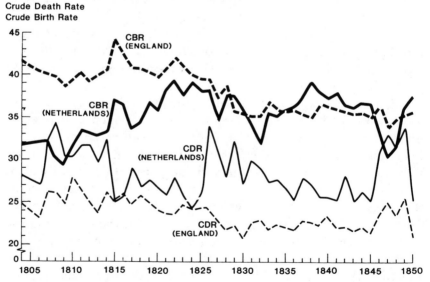

SOURCES: Hofstee, *De demografische ontwikkeling,* 196, 198; Wrigley and Schofield, *Populaiton History,* Table A3.3

3   Van der Woude, "Demografische ontwikkeling," 139–156. This section of my article relies heavily on Van der Woude's work.

*Table 2* Data on Nuptiality in the Netherlands

Percent married before the age specified, of those who ever married.

| YEARS | MEN | WOMEN | | MEAN AGE AT FIRST MARRIAGE |
|---|---|---|---|---|
| | 25 | 25 | 30 | |
| Amsterdam | | | | |
| 1578–1601 | 53% | | | |
| 1626–27 | | 60.9% | 89.1% | 24.5 |
| 1676–77 | | 44.4 | 77.7 | 26.5 |
| 1726–27 | | 36.5 | 71.0 | 27.2 |
| 1776–77 | | 35.3 | 66.5 | 27.8 |
| 1801–06 | 30.2 | 44.8 | 80.0 | |
| 1809–10 | | 42.2 | 76.4 | 26.3 |
| The Netherlands | | | | |
| 1830 | 12.4 | 22.8 | | |
| 1840 | 11.4 | 21.8 | 60.6 | |
| 1849 | 7.5 | 16.0 | 51.9 | |
| 1859 | 7.7 | 17.6 | 55.8 | |

MEAN AGE AT FIRST MARRIAGE (WOMEN)

| | |
|---|---|
| Maasland | |
| 1747 | 25.4 (Protestant) |
| 1747 | 25.9 (Catholic) |
| Duiven | |
| 1711–30 | 28.1 |
| 1731–50 | 28.9 |
| 1751–70 | 26.9 |
| 1771–90 | 27.3 |

SOURCES: Leonie van Nierop, "De bruidgoms van Amsterdam van 1578 tot 1601," *Tijdschrift voor Geschiedenis*, XLVIII (1933), 337–359; Herman Diederiks, *Een stad in verval. Amsterdam omstreeks 1800* (Meppel, 1982), 93; Van der Woude, "Demografische ontwikkeling," 156; Hofstee, *De demografische ontwikkeling*; S. Hart, "Bronnen voor de historische demografie van Amsterdam in de 17de en 18de eeuw," *Historisch Demografische Kring* (Amsterdam, 1965).

broadly consistent with the findings of Wrigley and Schofield for England. However, the turning points of Dutch fertility differ substantially from the English pattern, although an exact comparison is possible only for a limited period. Figure 1 displays Dutch crude birth and death rates from the first years that they are known. The comparable English rates are also displayed. In this late period, it is evident—as evident as crude rates can allow— that the Dutch fertility rate began to rise within a few years of the start of the decline of English fertility identified by Wrigley and Schofield.[4]

The mid-seventeenth-century turning point is more conjectural. The baptism-marriage ratios for the handful of places with records that go back far enough decline in the second half of the seventeenth century and the rather more abundant data on eighteenth-century household size and structure show clearly that families had become remarkably small. Nevertheless, any argument about fertility in this period must be regarded as highly tentative so long as we cannot control for possible changes in mortality or, in the case of marriage-baptism ratios, for changes in the frequency of remarriage.[5]

There remains one important respect in which the demographic processes governing Dutch population growth almost certainly differed substantially from the English model. That difference is in the pervasive role of migration in the Netherlands' highly urbanized society and open economy.

The population in cities of 10,000 and above nearly quadrupled between 1525 and 1650, at which date the urban population approached 40 percent of the total. The absolute size of the Republic's urban population exceeded that of England until 1700, at which date England's total population was nearly three times that of the Republic. So long as urban mortality exceeded rural mortality (and in Amsterdam alone the burial totals exceeded the recorded baptisms by an average of 1,000 per year throughout the eighteenth century), the presence of such a large Dutch urban sector was bound to influence the overall mortality rate and to make rural-urban migration an important regulator of rural population growth.[6]

---

4   Wrigley and Schofield, *Population History,* 230.
5   G. J. Mentink and Van der Woude, *De demografische ontwikkeling te Rotterdam en Cool in de 17e en 18e eeuw* (Rotterdam, 1965), 71–74; Van der Woude, "De omvang en samenstelling van de huishouding in Nederland in het verleden," *A. A. G. Bijdragen,* XV (1970), 202–440. A version of this article appeared in English in Peter Laslett (ed.), *The Comparative History of Household and Family: Studies in the Development of the Size and Structure of the Domestic Group over Time in Five Select Countries* (Cambridge, 1972), 299–318. In a study of over 4,000 households in North Holland, Van der Woude found average household size to be 3.74. A comparable study of England yielded an average size of 4.77.
6   See Wrigley, "A Simple Model of London's Importance in Changing English Society and Economy, 1650–1750," *Past & Present,* 37 (1967), 44–70; de Vries, *The Dutch Rural Economy in the Golden Age* (New Haven, 1974), 116. For another view see Allan Sharlin, "Natural Decrease in Early Modern Cities: A Reconsideration," *Past & Present,* 79 (1978), 126–138.

Even when local mortality rates remained unaltered, the growth of the urban sector could affect the national mortality rate, and when urban growth ceased, as it did in the Netherlands after 1675, the continuing inflow of rural migrants that made good the urban deficits acted to limit rural population growth. Those rural migrants can be thought to have had a demographic opportunity cost, the cost being the higher natural increase that could have been achieved had they remained in the countryside. Indeed, if current theories of protoindustrial demography are valid, the chief alternative to urban migration would have been rural proletarianization, bringing with it forms of demographic behavior that would have tended to secure high rates of natural increase. These considerations have application to many parts of Europe, but the compositional effects of urban migration will be more important in a society where urbanization rises from 20 to 40 percent than where the movement is from 6 to 12 percent.[7]

The second way in which migration plays a prominent role in the Dutch Republic's demographic history is in the international movement of people. The Republic differed from England in being a consistent net recipient of migrants. Tens of thousands of Flemings poured in between 1580 and 1620; thereafter immigrants came primarily from Scandinavia and Germany. The numbers are unknown, but immigrants were sufficiently numerous to account for one third of all persons marrying in Amsterdam in the seventeenth century and a quarter of all those marrying in the eighteenth century—183,000 immigrants in all.[8]

Many tens of thousands of immigrants entered the Netherlands during the 150 years after 1650, a period in which the

---

7 Among the many historical works illuminating the phenomenon of protoindustrial demographic behavior, see Franklin Mendels, "Protoindustrialization: The First Phase of Industrialization," *Journal of Economic History*, XXXII (1972), 241–261; Hans Medick, Jurgen Schlumbohm, and Peter Kriedte, *Industrialisierung vor der Industrialisierung* (Göttingen, 1977); David Levine, *Family Formation in an Age of Nascent Capitalism* (New York, 1977). Elsewhere I have written of an "urban safety valve" (*Dutch Rural Economy*, 117). In fact, little is known about rural-urban migration patterns, but it seems likely that the absence of populations devoted to rural industry except in the most remote districts near the borders of the Netherlands is related to the ongoing urban levees on the natural increase of the rural population. In 1795, the first national census revealed that the rural population density per cultivated hectare was much lower in the urbanized maritime provinces than in the outlying, more agrarian, provinces where soil quality was also generally poorer.

8 Hart, *Geschrift en getal* (Dordrecht, 1976), 136–143.

population of the western provinces fell absolutely and the national population was stagnant. It is not unreasonable to suppose that a population unable to growth despite persisting immigration suffers from particularly high mortality. Indeed, the combination of high urbanization and low-lying, marshy rural areas almost certainly kept the *level* of mortality above that of the surrounding countries, as was true in the first half of the nineteenth century when data are first available. What is uncertain, and appears to be denied by Van der Woude, is whether the cessation of population growth in the mid-seventeenth century was caused by a secular rise in the mortality rate.[9]

One particular kind of population loss—Wrigley and Schofield treat it as a form of migration rather than a form of mortality—undoubtedly played an important role in limiting Dutch population growth in the late seventeenth and eighteenth centuries. An analysis of the muster rolls of the Dutch East India Company (VOC) made by Bruijn uncovered the striking fact that during the life of the Company, from 1602 to 1795, one million sailors embarked from Dutch ports in 4,700 sailings, of whom at least 660,000 never returned. Almost all of them died en route or, more commonly, while stationed in Java. An average of some 3,000 men, mainly young, died in this way each year in the seventeenth century; in the eighteenth century the annual average was nearly 4,400.[10]

Until the 1720s about one quarter of VOC crews consisted of foreigners; after 1750 foreigners comprised fully half of all the Company's sailors embarking for Asia. Recruitment by the VOC must therefore have absorbed a substantial proportion of the male immigrants to the Dutch Republic. But consider the effects of this colonial enterprise on the native-born Dutch population. The absolute number of Dutch sailors employed by the VOC remained

9 For comparison with England, see Fig. 1; for comparison with Belgium, see Hofstee, *De demografische ontwikkeling*, 198–199. On infant mortality, see C. Vandenbroeke, F. Van Poppel, and Van der Woude, "De zuigelingen- en kindersterfte in België en Nederland in seculair perspectief," *Tijdschrift voor geschiedenis*, XCIV (1981), 461–491. I say "appears to be denied" because Van der Woude elsewhere emphasizes the mortality problems of the eighteenth century. See his *Het Noorderkwartier* (Wageningen, 1972), I, 255–256.
10 J. R. Bruijn, "De personeelsbehoefte van de VOC overzee en aan boord, bezien in Aziatisch en Nederlands perspectief," *Bijdragen en mededelingen betreffende de geschiedenis der Nederlanden*, XCI (1976), 218–248.

relatively constant throughout the eighteenth century and resulted in about 2,600 losses per year. The province of Holland contributed disproportionately to this ongoing drain of manpower: about 2,000 losses per year up to 1760 and 1,600 per year thereafter. Van der Woude reckons that if Holland's crude birth rate stood at about thirty-six per 1,000, and if the survivors to age twenty numbered fifty-five of each original 100, then the annual cohort of twenty-year-old men in Holland numbered about 7,000 to 8,000. In excess of 20 percent of this number were lost annually in the service of the VOC.[11]

This phenomenon affected "demographically expendable" men, but it could hardly fail to have influenced the percentage of women who married, their age at marriage, and thereby the total fertility rate.[12]

Some surviving scraps of data from Amsterdam, by far the largest recruitment center of the VOC, help illustrate the process. In the 1730s the Amsterdam parish registers record an annual average of 6,800 baptisms. This figure is certainly an underestimate of the true number; in any event Jewish births were not included. About 3,500 of the recorded births were boys whereas 3,300 were girls. The city's marrige records show that twenty-five years after these births occurred, from 1756 to 1765, an annual average of 1,100 Amsterdam-born men and 1,410 Amsterdam-born women were wed.[13]

Nearly 45 percent of women born in the city survived and stayed on to marry in the city of their birth. Given the city's high infant and child mortality, and the likelihood of some out-migration and some celibacy, one could hardly expect the percentage to have been higher. In contrast, only 30 percent of Amsterdam-born men married in the city. The higher infant and child mortality of males can explain only a small portion of the yawning gap between the number of native men and native women marrying in the city.

11   Van der Woude, "Demografische ontwikkeling," 154–156.
12   The phrase "demographically expendable" is Eric Jones', used in *The European Miracle* (Cambridge, 1981), 35, in a discussion of a comparable loss of male population in Switzerland.
13   For baptisms, "Statistiek der bevolking in Amsterdam to 1921," in *Mededelingen Bureau van Statistiek van de gemeente Amsterdam* (Amsterdam, 1923), no. 67, 136; for marriages, Hart, *Geschrift en getal*, 136.

The probable cause of this chronic demographic feature is that many men went to sea in their teens and early twenties—before marriage—never to return. The demographic "hole" created by their departure was filled by the thousands of migrants who accounted for 60 percent of all men marrying in seventeenth- and eighteenth-century Amsterdam.[14]

A sample of all Amsterdam marriages in 1801 and 1806 taken by Diederiks shows that fully 81 percent of Amsterdam-born grooms married Amsterdam-born women. But those grooms were so scarce that nearly 41 percent of all Amsterdam-born women marrying for the first time had to find grooms among migrants and widowers. What these data cannot tell us is how many found no husbands at all. But the ages at which brides married hint at the probability that spinsterhood was not unknown. Those brides who found fellow Amsterdam-born grooms married at the average age of 24.5 years; for brides marrying migrants the figure stood at 25.6 years. The few migrant women who married Amsterdam-born grooms did so at the average age of 26.6; the much larger number who married fellow migrants waited, on average, until the age of 28.4.[15]

This progression uncovered by Diederiks in the nuptiality behavior of turn-of-the nineteenth-century Amsterdam is of great interest because of its demonstration of a link between the incidence of migration and the age at first marriage, the key regulator of total fertility.

Wrigley and Schofield argue that English population change was driven by nuptiality, a demographic variable deeply embedded in economic and social life. The marriage rate was the major determinant of fertility and set the long-run course of population growth and decline. The limited data available for the study of Dutch historical demography is not incompatible with this mechanism of population change. But in the Dutch case a second variable, also highly sensitive to economic forces and social customs, complicates the analysis. Migration, in the form of rural-

14  Throughout the seventeenth and eighteenth centuries there was no 10-year period in which the number of Amsterdam-born grooms exceeded 73 per 100 Amsterdam-born brides. For the entire 200-year period the average was 69 per 100. *Ibid.*, 139.
15  Diederiks, *Stad in verval*, 77–79, 92. Hart presents evidence suggesting that both the marriage partner choice and the marriage age behavior described above for the end of the eighteenth century also applies to earlier periods. Hart, *Geschrift en getal*, 180–181, 205.

urban migration, immigration, and "emigration" to the merchant marine, apparently affected the mortality level, age structure, sex ratios, and marriage rates in ways that would have been unlikely in a larger, less urban, more closed economy.

REAL WAGES     For most preindustrial economies, the proposition that the real wages of day laborers adequately reflect the trends in personal income must be regarded as dubious. However, in the case of the Netherlands, it is less dubious than elsewhere. The high level of urbanization and the commercial orientation of agriculture in many regions endowed Dutch society with a large wage labor force. In view of this fact it is ironic that hardly anything is known of Dutch wage trends. My Dutch Labor Market Project, now in progress, aims to rectify this state of affairs.[16]

Wage and salary data from many locations, representing a variety of occupations, have been compiled and are now being analyzed. Just as in other countries, the most abundant archival data refer to craftsmen and laborers in the building trades and related outdoor employments. Since Wrigley and Schofield's study relied on real wages in the building trades—the famous Phelps Brown and Hopkins time series—to define the economic setting of English demographic history, it seems reasonable to confine myself here to analogous Dutch wage data. I have used two sources of data: one because it provides a long unbroken series; the other because it has wider coverage, but it is available only for certain groups of years.[17]

The first source, providing continuous wage records for common labor, carpenters, and masons from 1510 into the twentieth century, is drawn from the archives of the regional drainage authority of Rijnland (*Het Hoogheemraadschap van Rijnland*). This venerable institution employed, and continues to employ, scores of craftsmen and hundreds of laborers in the maintenance and

16 Support from the National Science Foundation (SOC 78-21078) for my Dutch Labor Market Project is acknowledged with gratitude. For further information, see de Vries, "The Decline and Rise of the Dutch Economy, 1675–1900," in Gavin Wright and Gary Saxonhouse (eds.), *Technique, Spirit, and Form in the Making of the Modern Economies: Essays in Honor of William N. Parker* (Greenwich, Ct., 1984), 149–189.
17 E. Henry Phelps Brown and Sheila V. Hopkins, "Seven Centuries of Building Wages," *Economica*, XXII (1955), 195–206; *idem*, "Seven Centuries of the Prices of Consumables, Compared with Builders' Wage-rates," *ibid.*, XXIII (1956), 296–314.

repair of sluices and dikes at several locations in central Holland. The series presented here refers to Spaarndam, a village near Haarlem. But laborers at nearby Halfweg, at Katwijk aan Zee, Bilderdam, and other places received essentially the same wages.[18]

The second source concerns wages in the building trades. These wages are available for many locations, but they do not all yield such long, continuous time series as do those for Spaarndam. Table 3 presents a summary of the (unweighted) mean daily summer wage paid to common labor and journeymen craftsmen in selected time periods. The numer of observations per entry varies from seven to fourteen.

To calculate real wages I have constructed a basket of consumables index. It is comparable in form to the Phelps Brown and Hopkins index, although the weights and specific commodities reflect Dutch conditions. The index was compiled from price data published by Posthumus in two invaluable works, his general monograph on the history of Dutch prices, and his study of the Leiden textile industry. Unfortunately, Posthumus' work does not provide an adequate basis for a basket of consumables index before 1575 nor after 1800. An index of foodstuffs alone must serve from 1550 to 1575 and from 1800 to 1850. A peculiar lacuna

*Table 3*  Unweighted Mean Daily Summer Wages Paid to Common Labor and Skilled Labor in the Building Trades in the Western and Eastern Netherlands, 1550–1854, in Current Stuivers (20st = 1 guilder)

|  | COMMON LABOR | | SKILLED LABOR | |
| --- | --- | --- | --- | --- |
| PERIOD | WESTERN | EASTERN | WESTERN | EASTERN |
| 1550–58 | 4.5 | 3.0 | 6.5 | 5.0 |
| 1583–92 | 9.0 | 6.9 | 11.5 | 10.5 |
| 1650–79 | 18.7 | 13.6 | 25.1 | 18.6 |
| 1745–54 | 18.1 | 13.6 | 25.2 | 18.9 |
| 1790–99 | 17.9 | 13.1 | 24.8 | 19.5 |
| 1820–29 | 17.8 |  | 25.2 |  |
| 1840–54 | 18.0 |  | 26.2 | 18.0 |

SOURCES: Dutch labor market study, in progress.

18  Hoogheemraadschap van Rijnland, Oud Archief, nos. 9510–10263; Bijlagen tot de rekeningen; nos. 10917–10932, Werklijsten.

*Fig. 2*  Real Wage Indices for Southern England and Holland in 25-
Year Moving Averages and Average Real Wage of Construction
Labor in the Western Netherlands in Selected Periods.

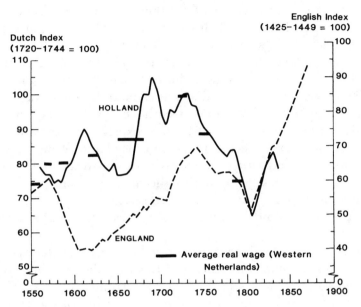

SOURCES: Dutch labor market study, in progress; Wrigley and Schofield, *Population History,*
Appendix 9.

in our knowledge of Dutch economic history is nineteenth-century prices. No comprehensive price index has ever been constructed to link Posthumus' voluminous pre-1800 data to the
twentieth-century indices.[19]

Figure 2 displays the course of real wages in the Netherlands
in the form of a twenty-five-year moving average of Spaarndam

19  My basket of consumables consists of the following items: rye (1050 kg.), yellow
peas (143.5 kg.), stockfish (25 kg.), meat (100 kg.), cheese (50 kg.), butter (50 kg.), beer
(621 liters)—for which coffee, tea, and gin are substituted in the second half of the
eighteenth century—peat (100 turf tons), and a composite of industrial product prices
weighted to equal 25% of the food sub-total in the period 1575–1599. Nicolaas W.
Posthumus, *Inquiry into the History of Prices in Holland* (Leiden, 1946–64), 2 v.; *idem, De
geschiedenis van de Leidsche lakenindustrie* (The Hague, 1908–1939), 3 v.
One attempt to construct a Dutch price index bridging the nineteenth century uses
German and English wholesale price indices to fill the gap between the Dutch series: J.
H. van Stuijvenberg and J. E. J. de Vrijer, "Prices, Population, and National Income in
the Netherlands, 1620–1978," *Journal of European Economic History,* XI (1982), 699–712.

common laborers' real wages, and averages at selected periods of the more broadly based real wages of labor in the building trades.

For comparative purposes, Figure 2 also plots the twenty-five-year moving average of southern English craftsmen's real wages as calculated by Phelps Brown and Hopkins and adjusted by Wrigley and Schofield. The English and Dutch real wage curves are indexed to separate bases periods, but I have positioned them on the graph to reflect the fact that the silver values and exchange-rate values of these Dutch and English wages were roughly equal in the mid-sixteenth century and again, more briefly, around 1800. Although this exercise is not without its dangers, it does have the redeeming academic value of calling attention to important differences in the histories of Dutch and English real wages: it highlights the differing trends and the incidence of turning points in the two series.[20]

The basic trends of Dutch real wages can be summarized as follows:

1. Real wages remained constant at best through the first three quarters of the sixteenth century. After 1575 they rose in a volatile manner to the 1680s, the rise being interrupted most notably by the many years of high prices during the wars of the 1650s and 1660s. Wage increases dominated the pattern to the 1640s; thereafter price movements generated the changes.

2. From the real wage peaks extending from the 1680s through the 1730s, a new trend of declining real wages set in that reached its nadir shortly after 1800. Price changes dominated this trend.

3. The partial recovery of real wages after the Napoleonic era was determined by price changes. Only after the 1860s did a combination of rising wages and falling prices push up the real wage to unprecedented levels. This breakthrough was concentrated in the 1870s and 1880s.

POPULATION AND REAL WAGES

*1500–1720.* Through the sixeenth and seventeenth centuries, the Netherlands experienced rapid population growth fol-

---

20 The prevailing southern English craftsmen's wage in the 1560s and the 1570s was 10 pence per day, or approximately 8 to 9 stuivers using exchange rates for Antwerp kindly furnished to me by Herman van de Wee of the Catholic University of Leuven. In the 1780s and the 1790s the southern English wage rate of 29 pence converts to about 26 stuivers at the exchange rates on Amsterdam published in Posthumus, *History of Prices,* I, 590–595.

*Fig. 3* Comparisons of Dutch and English Population and Real Wage Trends in Two Periods.

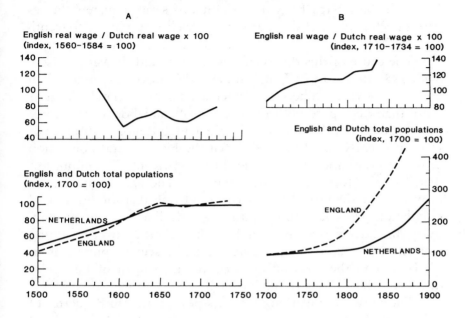

lowed by stagnation; the tempo and timing was remarkably similar to that of England. Figure 3a displays indices of the crude estimates of Dutch population and the new refined estimates for England (excepting the extension back from 1541 to 1500). The population of what would later become the Netherlands stood at 43 percent of the English level in 1500, fell throughout the sixteenth century to 37 percent in 1600, and remained at that level into the early eighteenth century. These figures suggest that Dutch growth in the sixteenth century fell short of England's, but estimates for both countries are weakest in precisely this period. In the seventeenth century, the two populations move in sweet harmony, one with the other.

Did these two societies, with their similar population histories, also share similar demographic characteristics? Anyone nurturing the belief that they did must confront the fact that the economic setting in which the English and Dutch made their decisions affecting reproduction could hardly have been more different. The Dutch escaped the nearly universal plunge of real wages that accompanied the price revolution of the sixteenth century. England felt its full force. In fact, the Dutch economy mustered a rise of real wages from 1580 to 1620, the very decades in which the Phelps Brown and Hopkins series registers the severest decline of English wage earners' well-being in the sixteenth century.[21]

The cause of this divergence is easily found. It was precisely from 1580 to 1620 that Dutch trade and industry expanded with the greatest vigor. The related increase in the demand for labor more than kept pace with the growth of the labor force. Moreover, throughout the century after the Dutch Revolt, urbanization was sufficiently rapid to hold down the rate of rural population growth to the modest overall level of 0.2 percent per annum, less than half the total rate of 0.46 percent. The agricultural sector proved more than capable of accommodating that modest rate of population growth without suffering a decline in labor productivity. In sixteenth-century England, however, an overwhelming majority of the additional population had to seek employment on the land with the consequence—common to most of Europe at the time—that labor productivity fell.

The Dutch population reached a peak in the third quarter of the seventeenth century, giving way in the densely populated maritime provinces to an absolute decline that was particularly

---

21 For the experience of other European countries, see Phelps Brown and Hopkins, "Wage-Rates and Prices: Evidence for Population Pressure in the Sixteenth Century," *Economica*, XXIV (1957), 289–305; *idem*, "Builders' Wage-Rates, Prices, and Population: Some Further Evidence," *ibid.*, XXVI (1959), 18–38; Wilhelm Abel, *Agrarkrisen und Agrarkonjunktur* (Hamburg, 1966; 2nd ed.). For the Netherlands the data are not abundant, but can be summarized as follows:

| | | SPAARNDAM | | UTRECHT | |
| | PRICE | COMMON | | COMMON | |
| PERIOD | INDEX | LABOR | CRAFTSMEN | LABOR | CRAFTSMEN |
| --- | --- | --- | --- | --- | --- |
| 1500–19 | 100 | 100 | 100 | 100 | 100 |
| 1583–92 | 294 | 300 | 273 | 280 | 261 |
| % Change in Real Wage | | +2 | −7 | −5 | −11 |

For England, the Phelps Brown and Hopkins study shows the following:

| | PRICE | SOUTHERN ENGLAND |
| PERIOD | INDEX | CRAFTSMEN |
| --- | --- | --- |
| 1500–19 | 100 | 100 |
| 1583–92 | 331 | 200 |
| % Change in Real Wage | | −40 |

severe in centers of industrial production (Leiden, Haarlem, Delft, and Gouda) and in the commercial agricultural zones of North Holland and Friesland. Holland, the hardest hit province, lost about 10 percent of its peak population in the late-seventeenth and early eighteenth centuries. This demographic retreat has generally been interpreted as a reflection of the severe economic problems that the Dutch Republic began to face after 1650, problems that brought its "Golden Age" to an irrevocable close.[22]

Restoration England, with an economy waxing fat on the contemporary misfortunes of the Dutch, also experienced an absolute decline in population of no less than 7 percent between 1655 and 1690. Once again, contrasting economic environments were accompanied by similar movements of total population.

*1700–1820.* During the eighteenth century the trends of real wages in the two countries were in close agreement. They differed in that English nominal wages rose at intervals throughout the century to catch up with the unchanging nominal wage level of the Republic.[23] But movements in the price level dominated the course of eighteenth-century real wages, so that, in contrast to the sixteenth and seventeenth centuries, the trends and turning points in the two countries were essentially the same (see Figure 2).

No such correspondence is evident in the demographic histories of the two societies in the eighteenth century. Whereas the Dutch population was 37 percent of the English in 1700, it amounted to only a quarter of the English total by 1800 and fell further to a sixth of the English level by 1870. (Thereafter the relative growth rates changed; today the Dutch population equals 30 percent of the English.)

Just as the Dutch economy had been exceptional in the first period, so the Dutch population was the exception in the eighteenth century; it failed to participate in the general European growth of population. The acceleration of population growth that began between 1730 and 1750 in most of Europe was delayed until after 1815 in the Netherlands.

22 This position is defended and elaborated in Van der Woude, *Het Noorderkwartier,* II, 608; Faber, *Drie eeuwen Friesland* (Wageningen, 1972), I, 391–393.
23 To be more precise, this statement should probably be confined to southern England. The more rapid growth of wages in northern England, particularly after 1750 (see Wrigley and Schofield, *Population History,* 432), calls for a separate analysis.

As noted earlier, the demographic explanation for this long era of population stagnation (c. 1650 to c. 1815) remains a topic for debate. The level of mortality was probably high in comparison with surrounding countries. But the fragmentary evidence of low fertility in the eighteenth century and the observation that the post-1815 growth of population was chiefly the product of increased fertility support the position that fertility changes were likely to have dominated Dutch population change in this era. If that is so, then it might seem that the Dutch population was controlling fertility from the mid-seventeenth century onward in an effort to protect living standards in an economy that was no longer expanding and, in some sectors, was absolutely declining. Yet, real wages reached their peak in the period from 1680 to 1740, after the population had peaked and begun to subside, and during two generations in which it is believed that the Dutch were marrying later and taking other steps to reduce fertility to or below the replacement level.

The rise in fertility after 1815 is no less puzzling, for the real wage evidence showed no sign of any sustained improvement in the preceding decades (the trend had been downward for seventy years).

The point of these last ruminations is simple: the reversals of trend in real wages do not appear to stand in any consistent relationship to the reversals of trend in fertility that are suggested by the available data.

|  | TROUGH | PEAK | TROUGH |
|---|---|---|---|
| Real Wage | 1570s | 1680–1740 | 1810s |
| Total Fertility (speculative) |  | 1610–1630 | 1750–1800 |

A MODEL    In light of the anomalous character of much of the evidence and conjecture reviewed here, is it possible to develop a model of the relationship between population and the economic setting in the Netherlands?

The model proposed by Wrigley and Schofield for early nineteenth-century England, suitably modified (Figure 4), seems an appropriate starting point, for it captures certain features of Dutch society throughout the period under discussion. We have already observed that net migration (immigration less emigration) was always important in the Netherlands and that the high level

*Fig. 4* The Netherlands in the Seventeenth and Eighteenth Centuries.[a]

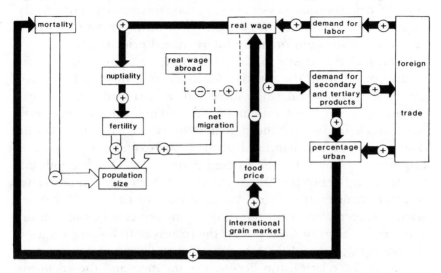

[a]Adaptation of Wrigley and Schofield, *Population History,* Fig. 11.8.

of urbanization attained by the mid-seventeenth century probably affected population size because of its impact on mortality. The strong negative relationship between population size and food prices characteristic of preindustrial populations generally, and an integral part of the Malthusian positive and preventive checks, was broken in England by the early nineteenth century. In the Netherlands this relationship had been weak, if not altogether absent, since the sixteenth century, because the growth of the international grain trade permitted the Dutch economy to depend for its food supply on the international market, and hence on prices determined by conditions outside the Netherlands.[24]

I have portrayed the Dutch economy as one in which the Malthusian checks had been lifted. Only the mortality consequences of urbanization remained to limit the pace of population growth. To be more precise, only urbanization remained among *domestic* limitations on the growth of population. Food prices, the influence of which on the real wage remained great, were now received as an exogenous force in the Dutch economy. Rapid

24  *Ibid.,* Fig. 11.8.

Dutch population growth (in the sixteenth century) did not necessarily bring about sky-rocketing food prices but, conversely, population stagnation (in the eighteenth century) could not prevent the importation of rising international price levels.

This characteristic of a small, open economy is of even greater moment in the positive feedback loop of industrial activity. A rise in the real wage increased the demand for non-agricultural products, but this increased demand did not necessarily have much impact on the demand for labor, since the product demand could be channeled abroad, increasing the volume of imports. Analogously, the foreign demand for Dutch goods and services, and hence for Dutch labor, may have been uncorrelated to prior changes in the real wage. Indeed, to the extent that real wage changes were a consequence of movements of the nominal wage rather than of food prices, the relationship linking wages to the (foreign) demand for labor might have been negative. In my model of the relationship between population and the economic setting modified to reflect Dutch conditions, there are no wholly domestic feedback loops, whether negative or positive.

Wrigley and Schofield applied the term "dilatory homeostasis" to the English pattern of gradual, delayed compensatory fertility responses to changing economic conditions. The open character of the Dutch economy had the effect of further complicating the adjustment process. The link between domestic demographic behavior and the supply of labor was pervasively influenced by internal (rural-urban) migration and external migration, both temporary and permanent. At the same time, the proximate determinants of the real wage level—food prices and the demand for labor—both acted as carriers of exogenous shocks to the domestic economy. Viewed from this perspective, it is puzzling that the society sought to adjust to its rapidly changing economic environment—brought about by volatile international prices, shifts in the demand for labor, and exogenous shocks induced by diplomacy and trade policy—by relying on the slow-moving and blunt instrument of nuptiality and related fertility behavior. Dutch society, deeply involved in foreign trade and with a large proportion of its labor force dependent on wages, had at its disposal economic policy instruments that could have offered faster, more effective adjustments to changes in the economic environment. But these were left untouched.

When an economy is predominantly agrarian and is treated as a world unto itself, as Wrigley and Schofield's series of models treat England, the economic and demographic variables can be linked to each other in slow-moving feedback relationships. But for the more diversified and open Dutch economy this approach is unrealistic. Today the relations between a national economy and the rest of the world are mediated, however imperfectly, by tariffs and other trade controls, currency exchange rates, and tax and subsidy structures. These measures allow for a much quicker response to changes in the international environment than do demographic adjustments. Although eighteenth-century governments did not manipulate these policy instruments with the alacrity of modern states, they were all known and used. However, the governments of the Republic never used, or, more correctly, never altered significantly their policy with respect to these measures.

For this reason the Dutch Republic can be treated as a region of a larger international economy. Its demographic behavior bore the brunt of absorbing both external and internal economic changes. This situation, in turn, required that nuptiality, the slow-moving variable, needed to be supplemented by migration, the faster-moving variable. The large-scale immigration of foreigners, both temporary and permanent, the emigration (to sea) of Dutchmen, and rural-urban migration, in turn, directly affected nuptiality and mortality levels. That is, the demographic process was governed by two pre-eminently social, consciously made acts: marriage and migration.

The value of generalized models of the type shown in Figure 4 is not that they encapsulate reality so much as that they serve as a useful point of departure for further reflection and research. By identifying relationships which probably existed, they encourage attempts to measure their relative strengths at a point in time or as they changed over time. They represent a set of interconnected hypotheses which can be tested and examined with regard to their logical structure and implications. Inasmuch as they can be used in the study of different countries, with or without modification, they advance comparative knowledge, always a *desideratum* in economic, demographic, and social history.

The factual basis for the analysis of Dutch historical demographic processes still leaves much to be desired. But, in comparing what little we now know with the better documented experience of neighboring societies, fruitful questions arise about both the Dutch and their neighbors. In view of the apparent importance of migration for Dutch demographic adjustment mechanisms, it is worth considering the role that interregional migration played in England. The "national" demographic pattern projected by the work of Wrigley and Schofield may obscure a series of distinctive regional demographic processes that were linked together by migration.

The Dutch experience, when viewed in an international context, suggests that a modern, urban, commercial economy was continuing to rely on premodern, rural-agrarian techniques to adjust its population to its economic environment. The proto-modernity of the Dutch Republic has long intrigued historians at the same time that it has puzzled them. This inquiry into Dutch historical demography has revealed yet another dimension of the puzzle. But historical demography is one of the few branches of historical inquiry where recent developments hold out the promise of progress in understanding past social behavior.

E. *Anthony Wrigley*

## Urban Growth and Agricultural Change: England and the Continent in the Early Modern Period

The complexity and contingency of any relationship between economic growth and urban growth should need no stressing. It is clearly hazardous to undervalue, still more to ignore, the difficulties attending any examination of this topic. In the early part of this article I prefer to sketch out an initial thesis rather starkly at the risk of oversimplifying "reality." Later the limitations of the initial formulation become clear.

A rising level of real income per head and a rising proportion of urban dwellers, other things being equal, are likely to be linked phenomena in a preindustrial economy. If income elasticity of demand for food is less than unity, then, with rising real incomes, demand for secondary and tertiary products will grow more rapidly than that for primary products, and will therefore cause employment in secondary and tertiary industries to rise more rapidly than in agriculture. Such employment is likely to be higher in towns, especially in the case of tertiary employment, and will result in an increase in the proportion of the total population living in towns. There may be an important feedback element in this relationship, since the growth of towns may help to further agricultural investment and specialization and so carry forward the rising trend in real incomes. Declining real incomes will have an opposite effect.[1]

In an economy which meets its own food needs, urban growth may not only be a symptom of rising real incomes: it

E. Anthony Wrigley is Professor of Population Studies at the London School of Economics and Associate Director of the Economic and Social Research Council Cambridge Group for the History of Population and Social Structure.

The author is grateful to Penelope Corfield, Jack Goldstone, and Tony Sutcliffe for comments on an earlier version of this article.

1  Adam Smith stressed the mutual stimulus which urban growth and agricultural improvement might afford each other in *An Enquiry into the Nature and Causes of the Wealth of Nations* (Edinburgh, 1863), 181–187. He included a chapter entitled, "How the commerce of towns contributed to the improvement of the country."

may also be a rough measure of the level of productivity per worker in the agricultural sector of the economy. If productivity per head in agriculture is sufficiently low, the surplus of food available after meeting the needs of the agricultural population may be enough to sustain only a tiny urban sector. At the other extreme, if agricultural productivity is high, the economy may be able to support a third or a half of the population in towns without prejudicing nutritional levels elsewhere. In a closed economy, therefore, a substantial rise in the proportion of the population living in towns is strong presumptive evidence of a significant improvement in production per head in agriculture, and may provide an indication of the scale of the change.

Sufficient information is now available to justify an initial application of this line of thought to early modern England.

THE PACE OF URBAN GROWTH IN ENGLAND    Table 1 sets out some estimates of the size of the populations of leading English towns in about 1520, 1600, 1700, 1750, and 1800. Table 2 provides estimates of the total population of England at each of these dates and of the population of London and other urban centers with 5,000 or more inhabitants.

As the notes to the tables make clear, all of the data given are subject to a substantial measure of uncertainty. Their sources are various and, apart from those taken from the 1851 census, most have been obtained by inflating and adjusting the raw data because the latter cover only a proportion of the total population. Some figures were originally suspiciously rounded and many incorporate alterations made in the light of subjective assessments of their deficiencies. Moreover, it is entirely arbitrary to draw a dividing line between urban and non-urban at 5,000. It was done on the supposition that only a tiny fraction of the inhabitants of towns larger than 5,000 would have been principally engaged in agriculture, but a plausible case might be made for a significantly lower dividing line.

To add still further to the crudity of the exercise, it is questionable whether the same dividing line should be used over a long period of time, during which the population increased greatly. For example, a moderate-sized market town with a population of, say, 3,000 at the start of the period, serving a hinterland in which the population doubled, would itself grow in size and at some point exceed 5,000 in population even though the functions it discharged did not alter. If this pattern were widely repeated, it would result in an upward drift in the overall urban percentage, but such movement would have occurred only because the total population had risen. It would not imply any structural change in the economy. Nevertheless, certain features of change over time are so prominent that they would remain clear cut, or might even be more pronounced, if less crude information were available.

During the sixteenth century, urban growth, relative to national population trends, was largely confined to London, the population of which quadrupled. London's share of the national total rose from 2.25 to 5 percent. The percentage of the population living in other towns, however, rose only modestly from 3 to 3.25 percent. Even this rise was largely because ten towns crept over the 5,000 mark (Plymouth, King's Lynn, Gloucester, Chester, Hull, Great Yarmouth, Ipswich, Cambridge, Worcester, and Oxford). Most large provincial centers were growing *less* quickly than the national population as a whole, as appears to have been true of Norwich, Bristol, Exeter, Canterbury, Coventry, Colchester, and Salisbury. Of the initial list of towns above 5,000 in population, excluding London, only Newcastle increased its share of the national total (Table 1). Its surge in growth was no doubt partly due to London's extraordinary rise, since the coal trade down the east coast flourished as London grew and brought with it prosperity to Newcastle.[2]

The effect of the artificial boost given to urban growth outside London by the inclusion of several new towns which had reached 5,000 in population between 1520 and 1600 can be estimated either by ignoring the new entrants on the 1600 list, or by basing the calculation on the full 1600 list. The group of nine provincial towns on the 1520 list displayed a collective growth of

[2]  The modesty of urban growth outside London may be overstated by concentrating on places with 5,000 or more inhabitants. There is evidence to suggest that the smaller towns were growing more rapidly than the provincial centers. Using a total of 2,000 rather than 5,000 inhabitants to divide urban populations from the remainder would probably have resulted in an impression of greater buoyancy for the urban population in the sixteenth century. Charles Phythian-Adams, "Urban Decay in Late Medieval England," in Philip Abrams and Wrigley (eds.), *Towns in Societies. Essays in Economic History and Historical Sociology* (Cambridge, 1978), 171–172.

Table 1  Urban Populations ('000s)

| c. 1520 | c. 1600 | c. 1670 | c. 1700 | c. 1750 | 1801 |
|---|---|---|---|---|---|
| London 55 | London 200 | London 475 | London 575 | London 675 | London 959 |
| Norwich 12 | Norwich 15 | Norwich 20 | Norwich 30 | Bristol 50 | Manchester 89[a] |
| Bristol 10 | York 12 | Bristol 20 | Bristol 21 | Norwich 36 | Liverpool 83 |
| York 8 | Bristol 12 | York 12 | Newcastle 16 | Newcastle 29 | Birmingham 74 |
| Salisbury 8 | Newcastle 10 | Newcastle 12 | Exeter 14 | Birmingham 24 | Bristol 60 |
| Exeter 8 | Exeter 9 | Colchester 9 | York 12 | Liverpool 22 | Leeds 53 |
| Colchester 7 | Plymouth 8 | Exeter 9 | Gt Yarmouth 10 | Manchester 18 | Sheffield 46 |
| Coventry 7 | Salisbury 6 | Chester 8 | Birmingham | Leeds 16 | Plymouth 43[b] |
| Newcastle 5 | King's Lynn 6 | Ipswich 8 | Chester | Exeter 16 | Newcastle 42[c] |
| Canterbury 5 | Gloucester 6 | Gt Yarmouth 8 | Colchester | Plymouth 15 | Norwich 36 |
|  | Chester 6 | Plymouth 8 | Ipswich | Chester 13 | Portsmouth 33 |
|  | Coventry 6 | Worcester 8 | Manchester | Coventry 13 | Bath 33 |
|  | Hull 6 | Coventry 7 | Plymouth | Nottingham 12 | Hull 30 |
|  | Gt Yarmouth 5 | King's Lynn 7 | Worcester | Sheffield 12 | Nottingham 29 |
|  | Ipswich 5 | Manchester 6 | Bury St Edmunds | York 11 | Sunderland 26 |
|  | Cambridge 5 | Canterbury 6 | Cambridge | Chatham 10 | Stoke 23[d] |
|  | Worcester 5 | Leeds 6 | Canterbury | Gt Yarmouth 10 | Chatham 23[e] |
|  | Canterbury 5 | Birmingham 6 | Chatham | Portsmouth 10 | Wolverhampton 21[f] |
|  | Oxford 5 | Cambridge 6 | Coventry | Sunderland 10 | Bolton 17 |
|  | Colchester 5 | Hull 6 | Gloucester | Worcester 10 | Exeter 17 |
|  |  | Salisbury 6 | Hull |  | Leicester 17 |
|  |  | Bury St Edmunds 5 | King's Lynn |  | Great Yarmouth 17 |
|  |  | Leicester 5 | Leeds |  | Stockport 17 |
|  |  | Oxford 5 | Leicester |  | York 16 |
|  |  | Shrewsbury 5 | Liverpool |  | Coventry 16 |
|  |  | Gloucester 5 | Nottingham |  | Chester 16 |
|  |  |  | Oxford |  | Shrewsbury 15 |
|  |  |  | Portsmouth |  |  |
|  |  |  | Salisbury |  |  |
|  |  |  | Shrewsbury |  |  |
|  |  |  | Sunderland |  |  |
|  |  |  | Tiverton |  |  |

In the c. 1700 column, the entries from Birmingham through Worcester are bracketed as 8–9, and the entries from Bury St Edmunds through Tiverton are bracketed as 5–7.

NOTES:

a  Including Salford.
b  Including Devonport
c  Including Gateshead
d  Stoke and Burslem
e  The Medway towns: Chatham, Rochester, and Gillingham
f  Wolverhampton, Willenhall, Bilston, and Wednesfield

SOURCES: The following sources were used in compiling the table. (1) Penelope J. Corfield, "Urban Development in England and Wales in the Sixteenth and Seventeenth Centuries," in Donald C. Coleman and Arthur H. John (eds.), *Trade, Government and Economy in Pre-industrial England* (London, 1976), 214–247; (2) Corfield, *The Impact of English Towns, 1700–1800* (Oxford, 1982); (3) Frank V. Emery, "England circa 1600," in H. Clifford Darby (ed.), *A New Historical Geography of England before 1600* (Cambridge, 1976), 248–301; (4) Charles Phythian-Adams, *Desolation of a City. Coventry and the Urban Crisis of the Late Middle Ages* (Cambridge, 1979); (5) John Patten, *English Towns 1500–1700* (Folkestone, 1978); (6) *idem*, "Population Distribution in Norfolk and Suffolk during the Sixteenth and Seventeenth Centuries," *Transactions of the Institute of British Geographers*, LXV (1975), 45–65; (7) 1851 Census, Population tables I, Numbers of inhabitants 1801–51, I, II, *Parliamentary Papers* (1852–3), LXXXV, LXXXVI; (8) C. M. Law, "Some Notes on the Urban Population of England and Wales in the Eighteenth Century," *The Local Historian*, X (1972), 142–147; (9) Roger Finlay, *Population and Metropolis. The Demography of London, 1580–1650* (Cambridge, 1981); (10) 1801 Census, Enumeration, *Parliamentary Papers* (1802), VII.

The data were abstracted as follows with the numbers given in brackets relating to the sources listed above. London 1520, 1600: (1), 217. London 1660: (9), 60. London 1700, 1750: (2). 8. Other towns 1520: (4), 12 and (1), 222. Other towns 1600: (3), 294–298 and (5), 115. Other towns 1670: (5), 106; 109–110; 114, 116, 120 and (1), 239, 241. Other towns 1700: (1), 223. Other towns 1750: (8), 22–26. All towns 1801: (7).

Some of the estimates may refer to dates a dozen or more years away from the date at the head of the column, except in 1750 and 1801. Often different scholars suggest different totals, or the same scholar may present more than one estimate for the same place and period. An element of judgment and selection is therefore unavoidable in compiling a table of this type. In one instance a quoted estimate seemed improbable and has been changed: (5), Table 9, 109 gives a figure of 9,000 for Cambridge in the 1670s, which seems implausibly high in view of the estimates for 1600 and 1700. In one or two cases (for example, Plymouth, 1670), I could find no figure for a year close to the target year and the total was therefore estimated.

*Table 2* National, London, and Other Urban Population Estimates (thousands)

| | C. 1520 | C. 1600 | C. 1670 | C. 1700 | C. 1750 | 1801 |
|---|---|---|---|---|---|---|
| Population of England | 2400 | 4110 | 4980 | 5060 | 5770 | 8660 |
| London | 55 | 200 | 475 | 575 | 675 | 960 |
| Other urban population in towns with 5,000 or more inhabitants | 70 | 135 | 205 | 275 | 540 | 1420 |
| Total urban | 125 | 335 | 680 | 850 | 1215 | 2380 |
| Urban populations as a percentage of the national total | | | | | | |
| London | 2.25 | 5.0 | 9.5 | 11.5 | 11.5 | 11.0 |
| Other urban | 3.0 | 3.25 | 4.0 | 5.5 | 9.5 | 16.5 |
| Total urban | 5.25 | 8.25 | 13.5 | 17.0 | 21.0 | 27.5 |

NOTES: The population totals and percentages have been rounded to emphasize the approximate nature of the calculations. National population totals refer to England, excluding Monmouth, and those for c. 1600, c. 1670, c. 1700, and c. 1750 relate to the years 1601, 1671, 1701, and 1751.

All the estimates of urban populations given in this table are subject to substantial margins of error. This is true even for those for 1801 derived from the 1801 census. For example, Law's careful examination of the 1801 material in the general context of nineteenth-century censuses led him to suggest a total urban population in England and Wales of 3,009,260 (in towns of 2,500 inhabitants or more) compared with Corfield's estimate of 2,725,171, using the same definition of urban. The former figure is 10% larger than the latter. All earlier totals are subject to far wider margins of error. Law, "The Growth of Urban Population in England and Wales, 1801–1911," *Transactions of the Institute of British Geographers,* XLI (1976), 141; Corfield, *Impact of English Towns,* 8.

SOURCES: English population totals 1600 to 1801: Wrigley and Roger S. Schofield, *The Population History of England, 1541–1871: A Reconstruction* (Cambridge, Mass., 1981), 208–209. The figure for 1520 is an estimate based on the discussions in *ibid.,* 565–568,

London totals: Table 1.

Other urban totals: 1520, 1600, 1670, Table 1; 1700, 1750, and 1801, Corfield, *Impact of English Towns,* 8. The totals have been rounded and, in the case of the 1801 total, slightly reduced to reflect the fact that Corfield's estimates refer to England and Wales (by this date 3 Welsh towns exceeded 5,000 in population).

only about 15 percent, sluggish growth during a period when the national total population rose by about 70 percent. If, alternatively, the list of nineteen large provincial towns in 1600 is made the basis of measurement, a rather higher percentage growth figure results. In 1520 these towns housed a total population of about 107,000 (see Table 1, sources). By 1600 the total had risen to about 137,000, a rise of 28 percent. Both calculations underline the point that the doubling of the population living in provincial towns shown in Table 2 is misleading, since it was preponderantly due to the recruitment of new towns into the category, and not to growth within the individual towns.

If London's growth is ignored, the urban growth pattern elsewhere conforms well to expectation. In the course of the sixteenth century, real incomes in England fell substantially. If the Phelps Brown and Hopkins index of real wages is used as a guide to the extent of the fall in living standards, it suggests a decline between 1520 and 1600 of over 40 percent. Even if the index overstates the change, a significant deterioration is nonetheless probable and ought, in conformity with the model sketched earlier, to have acted as a brake on urban growth and to have reduced urban population in percentage terms. London remains an exception so important as to outweigh in aggregate faltering urban growth elsewhere, but its overall dominance should not be allowed to obscure the significance of trends in the provinces.[3]

In the seventeenth century circumstances changed greatly. England's population grew by less than a quarter over the century as a whole and was falling gently during its third quarter. The Phelps Brown and Hopkins index suggests that real wages bottomed out early in the century and had risen substantially by its end.[4] Urban growth went on apace whether judged in absolute or percentage terms. London continued to dominate the picture. By 1700 the capital housed about 11 percent of the total national population, more than double the percentage of a century earlier. It had become the largest city in Western Europe and continued to dwarf all local rivals. But other towns also began to grow vigorously. They grew rather slowly in the first half of the cen-

3  E. Henry Phelps Brown and Sheila V. Hopkins, "Seven Centuries of the Price of Consumables, Compared with Builders' Wages," *Economica*, XXIII (1956), 296–314. The construction of a slightly modified version of the Phelps Brown and Hopkins index is described in Wrigley and Schofield, *Population History*, Appendix 9. The 25-year centered moving average of the annual figures given in Table A9.2 fell by 44% between 1520 and 1600. David M. Palliser, "Tawney's Century: Brave New World or Malthusian Trap?" *Economic History Review*, XXXV (1982), 349–351. Palliser suggests reasons to suspect that the Phelps Brown and Hopkins index overstates the extent of the fall in real incomes.
4  The centered 25-year moving average suggests a rise of 27% between 1600 and 1700. Both the extent of the rise and the timing of the end of the long fall in Tudor and early Stuart times are debatable. Bowden's index of the purchasing power of agricultural wages in southern England suggests that the beginning of a recovery may have been as late as the 1640s. From a stable plateau in the 1520s and 1530s (the index figure is 80 in both decades where 1460–9 = 100), his index falls by 35–40% by the 1590s and shows no subsequent decisive trend until the series ends in 1640–9. Peter Bowden, "Statistical Appendix," in Joan Thirsk (ed.), *The Agrarian History of England and Wales: IV, 1500–1640* (Cambridge, 1967), 865.

tury, but after 1670 their relative growth was at least as rapid as that of London. The smaller urban centers were now increasing far faster than the country as a whole. Their population more than doubled during the century, a rate of growth more than four times that of the national aggregate.

Measurement of urban growth is less bedevilled in the seventeenth century than it was in the previous century by the problem of 'drift' across the arbitrary 5,000 dividing line between urban and rural. In the sixteenth century, the increase of population in towns of 5,000 or more was about 95 percent, judged crudely, but the increase in the towns on the 1600 list was only 28 percent and only 15 percent on the 1520 list. The comparable figures for the seventeenth century were more closely bunched at about 105, 60, and 46 percent respectively.[5] Several major provincial centers, notably Norwich, Bristol, Newcastle, and Exeter, increased by between 50 and 100 percent. A striking portent for the future was the appearance on the list for the first time of towns never previously of much note but later to herald a new age. In 1670 Birmingham, Manchester, and Leeds appear for the first time, and in 1700 Liverpool.

If the seventeenth century saw a notable acceleration of growth within an urban system still consisting largely of towns with long-familiar names, the eighteenth brought radical reordering of the urban hierarchy and further rapid urban growth. London, moreover, although still vastly larger than any other city, no longer stood out because of its rate of growth. In 1800 it comprised much the same proportion of the national population as it had 100 years before. Meanwhile, the share of other towns larger than 5,000 in population increased dramatically, rising from 6 to 17 percent of the national total, and for the first time surpassing London's share.

Growth was widely but very unevenly spread. London's old rivals fared less well than London in the main. Bristol grew rapidly, riding on the back of buoyant Atlantic trade, but several cities which had once figured prominently in the English urban hierarchy, including Norwich, Exeter, and York, grew less quickly than the population overall and ended the century with

5 In order to calculate the 60% figure some town populations had to be estimated (i.e. for some of the towns appearing on the 1700 list but not the 1600 list in Table 1).

smaller fractions of the national total than at the beginning. For many centuries such towns had exchanged places in the premier urban league, but the league's membership had not greatly altered. By 1800, however, only Bristol, Newcastle, and Norwich of the old major regional centers remained among the country's ten largest towns. Manchester, Liverpool, and Birmingham stood second, third, and fourth after London. They ranged between 70,000 and 90,000 in population, having grown fiftyfold or more since the early sixteenth century.

Lower down the list a host of new names appeared. Several were the seats of new industry—Leeds, Sheffield, Stoke, Wolverhampton, Bolton, and Stockport; but others reflected changing social customs and new forms of expenditure. Bath, for example, with 33,000 inhabitants, was the twelfth largest town in England, a gracious monument to the new ways in which the wealthy and well born found it convenient to make or maintain contacts with each other or to pass their hours of leisure. Ports and dockyard towns also enjoyed vigorous growth. Plymouth and Portsmouth were among the country's largest towns, and Hull, Sunderland, Chatham, and Great Yarmouth all exceeded 15,000 in population at the time of the 1801 census (although not all of the towns in this category were new names).

The simplest model connecting real income and urban growth will no longer "save the phenomena" for the eighteenth century. The sustained momentum of urban growth, accelerating toward the century's end, would suggest a parallel rise in real incomes, but in some parts of England the long-sustained rise in real wages had ceased before the middle of the eighteenth century. It had probably halted nationally by 1780, to be succeeded by a substantial fall lasting about thirty years.[6]

By the eighteenth century the assumption of a closed economy is even more unrealistic than for the sixteenth. External

6 The behavior of wages and prices and, *a fortiori*, of real wages, both regionally and nationally between 1700 and 1850 has been the subject of much controversy. There have been several valuable surveys of the issues recently, and also some new empirical work. Michael W. Flinn, "Trends in Real Wages, 1750–1850," *Economic History Review,* XXVII (1974), 395–411. G. Nicholas von Tunzelmann, "Trends in Real Wages, 1750–1850, Revisited," *ibid.,* XXXII (1979), 33–49. Peter H. Lindert and Jeffrey G. Williamson, "English Workers' Living Standards during the Industrial Revolution: A New Look," *ibid.,* XXXVI (1983), 1–25.

demand represented a substantial fraction of total demand in many industries, although it is easy to exaggerate the importance of overseas markets. Any increase in the relative importance of overseas trade, however, would stimulate urban growth, conspicuously in the case of ports like Bristol and Liverpool, but in a lesser degree also elsewhere. Equally, transport improvements within England increased the scale of internal trade. The average distance travelled by goods between producer and consumer probably also increased. Both trends must have stimulated employment in the urban centers through which goods passed.[7] The pattern of urban growth suggests that the deceleration in urban growth which might have been expected on the simplest possible view of the link between real incomes and urban growth affected the older centers in the expected fashion, but that the new features of the English economy imparted impetus to those towns most caught up in the new developments. London, affected by all of the various and conflicting influences on urban growth, occupied an intermediate position.

The extent of the contrast among the fortunes of different types of towns in the course of the early modern period is illustrated in Table 3. The choice of towns in each group is inevitably arbitrary, both in the sense that other sets might have been made up to represent the type in question, and in the sense that 'pure' types are rare in large towns since size and complexity of function are closely linked. The balance of market functions, craft industry, administrative services, and professional employment varied considerably among the set of ten historic regional centers, and two of them, Chester and Exeter, also had important port functions. Nevertheless, the contrast among the groups is sufficiently marked to make it unlikely that other choices made with the same distinction in mind would have produced a very different result.

The historic regional centers did not keep pace with national population growth over the early modern period as a whole. In the two middle periods, when real wages were rising, they experienced a faster population growth than the national average;

7 On overseas trade see, e.g., R. P. Thomas and Donald N. McCloskey, "Overseas Trade and Empire, 1700–1860," in Roderick Floud and McCloskey (eds.), *The Economic History of Britain since 1700* (Cambridge, 1981), I, 87–102. An excellent summary of knowledge about inland transport may be found in John A. Chartres, *Internal Trade in England, 1500–1700* (London, 1977), 13–46.

*Table 3*  Patterns of Growth. Urban Growth in Early Modern England (thousands)

| | POPULATION TOTALS | | | | | PERCENTAGE GROWTH | | | |
| --- | --- | --- | --- | --- | --- | --- | --- | --- | --- |
| | C. 1520 | C. 1600 | C. 1700 | C. 1750 | 1801 | 1600/1520 | 1700/1600 | 1750/1700 | 1801/1750 |
| England | 2400 | 4110 | 5060 | 5770 | 8660 | 71 | 23 | 14 | 50 |
| London | 55 | 200 | 575 | 675 | 960 | 264 | 188 | 17 | 42 |
| 10 historic regional centers[a] | 62 | 73 | 107 | 126 | 153 | 18 | 47 | 18 | 21 |
| 8 established ports[b] | 38 | 53 | 81 | 128 | 190 | 39 | 53 | 58 | 48 |
| 4 'new' manufacturing towns[c] | 6 | 11 | 27 | 70 | 262 | 83 | 145 | 159 | 274 |

NOTES:

a  Norwich, York, Salisbury, Chester, Worcester, Exeter, Cambridge, Coventry, Shrewsbury, Gloucester.

b  Bristol, Hull, Colchester, Newcastle, Ipswich, Great Yarmouth, King's Lynn, Southampton.

c  Birmingham, Manchester, Leeds, Sheffield.

SOURES: See source note to Table 1.

in the sixteenth and later eighteenth centuries, however, when real wages were probably declining, their rate of growth fell well below the national average. Thus they exhibited what might be termed the classic pattern of relative growth in terms of the model of the relationship between income and urban growth described earlier.

At the other extreme, the four towns which in 1801 were the largest manufacturing towns in England were always growing faster than any other groups in the table, apart from London until 1700. Their rate of growth accelerated steadily throughout the three centuries, becoming so hectic in the last half-century that their population almost quadrupled in fifty years.

The established ports also grew with increasing speed, except in the last period, outstripping the national growth rate, except in the first and last periods. The slight fall in growth rate in this group in the later eighteenth century was due in part to the extraordinarily rapid growth of Liverpool. If Liverpool were included in the group, the percentage growth of population in the group would rise to 72 between 1700 and 1750 and to 82 between 1750 and 1801.

London contrasts sharply with each of the other three groups, growing far more quickly until the end of the seventeenth century. It became so large that in 1700 it housed more than two-and-a-half times as many people as the other three groups combined. Thereafter, however, London was outpaced by both the ports and the new manufacturing towns, and did not even match the national average growth rate.

The foregoing is both compressed and simplistic. Uncertainties of definition, estimation, and periodization have been dealt with summarily or ignored. Nor has the nature as opposed to the quantity of urban growth been explored. It is possible, for example, that much of the growth of sixteenth-century London was a "push" phenomenon linked to the scale and depth of rural poverty, and due to what Clark termed "subsistence" migration. Later, in contrast, movement to the capital may have had a greater "pull" element as living standards rose and "betterment" migration came to predominate.[8]

---

8  Peter Clark, "The Migrant in Kentish Towns, 1580–1640," in *idem* and Paul Slack (eds.), *Crisis and Order in English Towns, 1500–1700* (London, 1972), 117–163.

It remains reasonable to argue, however, that there were important links between some types of urban growth and real income trends in early modern England, although urban growth is not to be explained solely in this way. Neither the headlong growth of London in the sixteenth and early seventeenth centuries, nor the acceleration of urban growth in the new manufacturing towns in the later eighteenth century, is easily explicable in terms of the behavior of domestic real income per head, yet both were developments of massive importance.

URBAN GROWTH AND AGRICULTURE     Even if the causes of urban growth are elusive, the fact of growth remains, and some of its implications can be examined. In any preindustrial community, agriculture is the dominant form of economic activity and the levels of productivity per head achieved in agriculture necessarily govern the growth opportunities of other industries. This point was so well known to those living in preindustrial economies as scarcely to warrant remark, and, when political economy reached its first great statement in the *Wealth of Nations,* Smith made the examination of this issue one of his chief concerns.[9]

But agricultural productivity has proved difficult to measure directly. One way of measuring it indirectly is to consider the extent of the rise in agricultural productivity suggested by the course of urban growth in England, while also taking into account changes in the occupational structure of the rural component of the total population.

To simplify calculations I have assumed that consumption of food per head did not vary between 1520 and 1800 and that England was neither a net importer nor a net exporter of food. The first assumption is doubtful and the second is demonstrably false, especially during the eighteenth century. In its early decades England was a substantial net exporter of grain, and toward the century's end large quantities of meat and grain reached the En-

9 Smith's chapter, "Of the Different Employment of Capitals," includes a strong plea for agricultural investment as the ultimate basis of national productive capacity. "The capital employed in agriculture, therefore, not only puts into motion a greater quantity of productive labour than any capital employed in manufactures, but in proportion, too, to the quantity of productive labour which it employs it adds a much greater value to the annual produce of the land and labour of the country, to the real wealth and revenue of its inhabitants. Of all the ways in which a capital can be employed, it is by far the most advantageous to the society." Smith, *Wealth of Nations,* 161–162.

glish market from Ireland. Yet it is convenient to begin with such simple assumptions.[10]

In 1520 the urban percentage was 5.25: in 1801, 27.5 (Table 2). This movement in itself suggests a useful gain in agricultural productivity. In 1520, 100 rural families fed 106 families in all; in 1801, 138 ($100 \times 100/[100 - 5.25] = 106$: $100 \times 100/[100 - 27.5] = 138$). The level of productivity in 1800 was 30 percent higher than in 1520, far from a negligible increase, even if scarcely sensational. But any such exercise must understate the extent of the increase in agricultural productivity if there also is a decline in the proportion of the rural labor force engaged in agriculture.

There can be no reasonable doubt that such a decline occurred. In certain rural areas in the eighteenth century the growth in non-agricultural employment was so great as to dwarf the remaining agricultural population. Framework knitting became the dominant source of employment in many Leicestershire villages. In parts of Warwickshire and Staffordshire there was very rapid growth in the manufacture of small metal wares—nails, chains, buckets, etc. In much of south Lancashire and the West Riding of Yorkshire, the textile industry, whether cotton or wool, provided income for many more men and women than did agriculture. The steady growth of coal production in Northumberland and Durham produced the same result in substantial tracts of these counties. Even in more strongly agricultural counties in the south, lace making, straw plaiting, and the like provided much employment for women.

Moreover, in areas which attracted little industry there was often a growth in employment in service industries. In the rare

10  Brinley Thomas has recently estimated the relationship between the value of imports of grain, meat, and butter and the income of British agriculture. From 1814 to 1816, total imports of the three commodities represented 6.4% of British agricultural income and of these imports 70% came from Ireland. See his article in this issue, "Escaping from Constraints: The Industrial Revolution in a Malthusian Context," Table 2. Jones recently estimated that 90% of the population of Great Britain was fed from domestic agricultural production in 1800. Eric L. Jones, "Agriculture, 1700–80," in Floud and McCloskey (eds.), *Economic History of Britain*, I, 68. In contrast, in the first half of the eighteenth century, English net grain exports were a substantial fraction of total production, reaching perhaps 6% of gross domestic grain output about the mid-century. Phyllis Deane and W. A. Cole, *British Economic Growth, 1688–1959* (Cambridge, 1962), 65; David Ormrod, "Dutch Commercial and Industrial Decline and British Growth in the Late Seventeenth and Early Eighteenth Centuries," in Frederick Krantz and Paul M. Hohenberg (eds.), *Failed Transitions to Modern Industrial Society: Renaissance Italy and Seventeenth-Century Holland* (Montreal, 1975), 36–43.

cases where parish registers provide data on occupation over long periods of time, it is a commonplace to note a growth in specialist employments not previously encountered, especially during the eighteenth century. A small town like Colyton, for instance, even provided a living for a peruke maker in the 1760s.

Almost everywhere the proportion of men described as laborers, husbandmen, yeomen, or farmers declined as a proportion of all the occupations mentioned. Many craftsmen also owned scraps of land and their produce was of crucial significance in their domestic economy. Even those who worked no land might nevertheless have been drawn into the labor of harvest. However, the reverse was often also true. Those to whom an agricultural occupation was attributed might turn their hands to craftwork during the seasonal slack periods on the farms.

Ideally, it would be preferable to measure hours worked in different forms of employment rather than to treat each member of the work force as uniquely engaged in a single occupation, but for the present purpose it is enough to show that there was a major fall in the proportion of the rural labor force in agricultural occupations.

By 1800 a tolerably accurate picture of rural employment structure can be drawn. Deane and Cole estimated that 35.9 percent of the labor force in 1801 was engaged in agriculture, forestry, and fishing. If we assume for simplicity's sake that none of these workers was living in towns, then it follows that only some 50 percent of the rural population were engaged in agriculture, given that the rural population comprised 72.5 percent of the whole ($35.9/72.5 \times 100 = 49.5$). The comparable figure at earlier periods is difficult to establish, although useful clues may be found in the work of King and Massie. In order to make revised estimates of the changes in agricultural productivity, I have assumed that 80 percent of the rural labor force was in agriculture in 1520; that this figure declined very slowly to 70 percent by 1670, with the bulk of the fall occurring after 1600; that it fell more quickly to 66 percent in 1700; and then moved linearly in the eighteenth century to 50 percent in 1801.[11]

11  Deane and Cole's estimate of the percentage of the labor force, quoted above, may be found in their *British Economic Growth*, 142. The first serious attempt to quantify the occupational and social structure of England before 1801 was that carried out by Gregory King in 1688. King, *Natural and Political Observations and Conclusions upon the State and Condition of England, 1696*, reprinted in *The Earliest Classics*, with an introduction by Peter

These assumptions allow the population to be subdivided into three groups rather than two: the urban population, the rural population engaged in agriculture, and the rural population dependent on employment other than in agriculture. At the same time, changes in output per head can be calculated. The results are set out in Table 4.

The table suggests that the rural agricultural population scarcely changed in size for a century and a half between 1600 and 1750 and that even in 1800 it was only a tenth larger than 200 years earlier. It is not surprising, therefore, that the table should show a striking rise in agricultural productivity, and indeed, to the degree that the assumptions which have been made in constructing the table are justified, the conclusions are inescapable. The crucial assumptions are that England was not a signficant net importer or exporter of food; that the growth of the percentage of the population living in towns followed the pattern set out in Table 2; and that the proportion of the rural population engaged in non-agricultural production rose from 20 to 50 percent between 1520 and 1800. For the second and third assumptions the central issue is the extent of change over the period as a whole; the question of its timing, although fascinating, is of lesser importance.[12]

---

Laslett (London, 1973), 48–49. When Deane and Cole considered King's estimates they suggested that "between 75 and 80 percent of the occupied population was primarily engaged in agriculture." Deane and Cole, *British Economic Growth,* 3. This figure is implausibly high. Having regard to the total national populations in 1688 and 1801 (4.90 and 8.66 millions) and the proportions in agriculture (say 75% and 35.9%), such a high proportion in 1688 would imply a fall in the absolute scale of agricultural employment of more than 15% over the intervening century.

Lindert has recently reexamined changes in English occupational structure in the eighteenth century, but the results, at least for agriculture, do not appear convincing. The percentage of the male labor force employed in agriculture is estimated at 22.3 in 1700, 26.1 in 1740, and 13.7 in 1811. Lindert, *English Occupations, 1670–1811* (Davis, 1980), 46–47. See also note 13 below.

12  In connection with the argument of this paragraph it may be noted that Jones estimated that the agricultural population of England and Wales increased by 8.5% in the eighteenth century. Jones, "Agriculture, 1700–80," 71. Crafts' recent calculations produce results broadly similar to those implied by Table 4 in relation to agricultural productivity. He estimated that agricultural output rose at the following percentage rates per annum over the periods 1710–1740, 1740–1780, and 1780–1800: 0.9, 0.5, and 0.6. This change implies a total increase in output of almost exactly 80% over the 90-year period as a whole. Assuming that the agricultural labor force grew by 13% over the century, as Table 4 suggests, the increase in output per man, at 59%, is closely similar to that which may be calculated from column 7 of Table 4 (52%). Nicholas F. R. Crafts, "The Eighteenth

Precision about any of the three basic assumptions is beyond reach. Regarding the first, it is worth noting that because England was a substantial food exporter in the early eighteenth century, agricultural productivity was probably understated at that period. Equally, by the end of the century, England had become a net importer, especially from Ireland, which implies the opposite. The second set of assumptions concerning urban growth is probably sufficiently accurate to avoid significant error. The third assumption relates to the agricultural proportion of the rural population. The figure for 1800 is fairly firmly grounded in the evidence of the early censuses, but earlier estimates become increasingly fallible. Any figure for the early sixteenth century must be largely guesswork. A lower figure would reduce the apparent gain in agricultural productivity, but only a radically lower figure would greatly change the general picture.[13]

---

Century: A Survey," in Floud and McCloskey (eds.), *Economic History of Britain*, I, Tables 1.1, 1.2, 2–3.

13  It is possible to use the work of King and of Joseph Massie to test how far the estimates made by contemporaries agree with those in Table 4. In 1760, out of a total of 1,472,000 families, Massie supposed that 210,000 were freeholders, 155,000 farmers, and 200,000 husbandmen, making a total of 565,000 clearly engaged in agriculture. In addition he estimated that there were 200,000 families of laborers outside London. Not all of these would be agricultural laborers. Massie reckoned that there were 20,000 laborers in London, only slightly short of the number to be expected on the assumption that laborers were as numerous per 1,000 population inside cities as in the countryside. We may assume, therefore, that a further 15,000–20,000 were to be found in other urban centers, and it is probable that a further group, although living in the countryside, were employed outside agriculture, especially in the building trades (which were not separately itemized by Massie). Assume that these, too, were about 20,000 in number; then the overall total of those families engaged in agriculture would be c.730,000, or fractionally less than one half of the national total. The comparable figure in Table 4, that for 1750, is 46%, a broadly similar figure.

A comparison with King (1688) is more difficult to make because of the form in which he drew up his famous table. King's totals for families of freeholders and farmers are not greatly different from Massie's (180,000 and 150,000 respectively), but he gave no separate figure for husbandmen. Instead, all other families which might be engaged in agriculture appear in two categories: laboring people and outservants (364,000); and cottagers and paupers (400,000). Most of those engaged in industrial crafts—weavers, glovers, knitters, tanners, carpenters, coopers, sawyers, thatchers, smiths, wrights, cordwainers, and so on—must have been included in one of these two categories (King lists only 60,000 families of artisans or handicraft workers in the entire country), together with all laboring families living in London or other towns. Assuming that half of the cottars were what Massie would have termed husbandmen and half were engaged in industrial crafts, a split similar to that found in Massie's separate tabulation of the two categories; that 15% of all laborers were in towns (where at this date about 15% of the population lived); and that of the remaining 309,000 laborers, 25,000 were employed outside agriculture—the total

Table 4  Urban, Rural Agricultural, and Rural Non-Agricultural Populations (millions)

| | (1) TOTAL POPULATION | (2) URBAN POPULATION | (3) RURAL POPULATION | (4) PROPORTION OF RURAL POPULATION IN AGRICULTURE | (5) RURAL AGRICULTURAL POPULATION $(3) \times (4)$ | (6) RURAL NON-AGRICULTURAL POPULATION $(3) - (5)$ | (7) TOTAL POPULATION PER 100 RURAL AGRICULTURAL $(1)/(5)$ | (8) COLUMN (7) 1520 = 100 |
|---|---|---|---|---|---|---|---|---|
| 1520 | 2.40 | 0.13 | 2.27 | 0.80 | 1.82 | 0.45 | 132 | 100 |
| 1600 | 4.11 | 0.34 | 3.77 | 0.76 | 2.87 | 0.90 | 143 | 108 |
| 1670 | 4.98 | 0.68 | 4.30 | 0.70 | 3.01 | 1.29 | 165 | 125 |
| 1700 | 5.06 | 0.85 | 4.21 | 0.66 | 2.78 | 1.43 | 182 | 138 |
| 1750 | 5.77 | 1.22 | 4.55 | 0.58 | 2.64 | 1.91 | 219 | 166 |
| 1801 | 8.66 | 2.38 | 6.28 | 0.50 | 3.14 | 3.14 | 276 | 209 |

Percentages of total population in major categories

| | (1) URBAN | (2) RURAL AGRICULTURAL | (3) RURAL NON-AGRICULTURAL | (4) TOTAL |
|---|---|---|---|---|
| 1520 | 5.5 | 76.0 | 18.5 | 100 |
| 1600 | 8.0 | 70.0 | 22.0 | 100 |
| 1670 | 13.5 | 60.5 | 26.0 | 100 |
| 1700 | 17.0 | 55.0 | 28.0 | 100 |
| 1750 | 21.0 | 46.0 | 33.0 | 100 |
| 1801 | 27.5 | 36.25 | 36.25 | 100 |

Populations relative to 1800 total (1800 = 100)

| | | | | |
|---|---|---|---|---|
| 1520 | 5.5 | 58 | 14 | 28 |
| 1600 | 14 | 91 | 29 | 47 |
| 1670 | 29 | 96 | 41 | 58 |
| 1700 | 36 | 89 | 46 | 58 |
| 1750 | 51 | 84 | 61 | 67 |
| 1801 | 100 | 100 | 100 | 100 |

Relative population growth by period (100 × total at later date/total at earlier date)

| | | | | |
|---|---|---|---|---|
| 1600/1520 | 262 | 158 | 200 | 171 |
| 1670/1600 | 197 | 105 | 143 | 121 |
| 1700/1670 | 127 | 92 | 111 | 102 |
| 1750/1700 | 144 | 95 | 134 | 114 |
| 1801/1750 | 195 | 119 | 164 | 150 |

SOURCE: For population totals in top panel see Table 3 and discussion in text.

Other assumptions could be used to construct Table 4. For example, if one were to assume that 15 percent of English food requirements were met by imports in 1800, and that agriculture employed 55 percent of the rural labor force rather than 50 percent, while other assumptions were unchanged, the estimated overall rise in agricultural productivity would be reduced from 109 to 61 percent. If one were to go still further, reducing the 1520 figure in column 4 from 0.80 to 0.70 and retaining the modified assumptions for 1801, the figure would drop even more to 41 percent, but this figure is improbably low. On present evidence, therefore, although the particular figure given in Table 4 is arbitrary, there is a strong likelihood that the true figure lies between 60 and 100 percent.[14]

The phasing of changes in the proportion of the rural labor force engaged in agriculture, no less than their scale, is also largely a matter of judgment, rather than a demonstrable pattern. The same pressures which kept urban growth outside London at such modest proportions in the sixteenth century are likely to have restricted employment opportunities outside agriculture. It therefore seems appropriate to make only a small reduction in the proportion of the rural population in agriculture between 1520 and 1600. Thereafter the pace of change probably accelerated.

---

of families employed in agriculture is 814,000 or 60% of the national total of 1,361,000 families. The comparable figure in Table 4 is about 58% (1670, 60.5%; 1700, 55.0%). There is a convenient reproduction of both King's and Massie's tables and a discussion of the difficulties in comparing them in Peter Mathias, "The Social Structure in the Eighteenth Century: A Calculation by Joseph Massie," in idem, The Transformation of England. Essays in the Economic and Social History of England in the Eighteenth Century (London, 1979), 171–189. See note 11 for the provenance of King's table. Massie's table is derived from a broadsheet dated Jan. 10, 1760, entitled A computation of the money that hath been exorbitantly raised upon the people of Great Britain by the sugar planters in one year from January 1759 to January 1760; shewing how much money a family of each rank, degree or class hath lost by that rapacious monopoly.

14 Sixteenth-century estimates of occupational structure are inevitably insecurely based, and the dominance of agriculture is probably overstated. The muster roll taken in 1608 for Gloucestershire, excluding Bristol, for example, suggests that only 46.2% of the adult male population between the ages of 20 and 60 were engaged in agriculture. The comparable figure when the 1811 census was taken was virtually the same at 45.8%. The economic history of Gloucestershire is far from typical of the country as a whole, but Gloucestershire affords an example which should caution us against assuming too readily that rural non-agricultural employment was always very limited in Tudor or early Stuart England. A. J. and R. H. Tawney, "An Occupational Census of the Seventeenth Century," Economic History Review, V (1934), 25–46. 1811 Census, Enumeration, Parliamentary Papers (1812), XI, 121.

One further implicit assumption deserves discussion. Individual intake of food measured in calories varies within fairly narrow limits. There is little evidence of widespread malnutrition so extreme as to cause death in early modern England. With rare and usually local exceptions even severe harvest failure did not provoke heavy mortalities. It is improbable (although also undemonstrable) that mean personal daily calorie intake varied in a manner which would significantly undermine the line of argument followed above. Nevertheless, periods of rising real income must have been periods in which food consumption per head rose, with the opposite happening in times of declining living standards. In addition there were changes in the composition of individual diet as incomes rose or fell. Meat was a luxury to the pauper but a commonplace to more prosperous members of society, and there were secular shifts in the relative prices of grain and meat which reflected the long-term trends of the average real income.[15]

Since such foods as meat and dairy produce needed larger inputs of labor, as well as land and capital, to produce the same number of calories of food as grain, it might seem that an allowance should be made for the impact of secular real income trends in attempting an individual measure of agricultural productivity. This consideration in turn would imply that agricultural productivity per head was rising faster during the seventeenth and early eighteenth century than suggested by Table 4, but less quickly during the later eighteenth century. It also suggests that it may

15  On harvest fluctuations and mortality, see Wrigley and Schofield, *Population History*, 320–340, 370–382, appendix 10. The principal exception to the rule that harvest failure did not provoke big mortalities was northwestern England in the sixteenth and early seventeenth centuries. Andrew B. Appleby, *Famine in Tudor and Stuart England* (Stanford, 1978). Estimating income elasticity of demand for food in eighteenth-century England presents great difficulties because of lack of relevant data. In a recent review of the limited evidence, Crafts concluded that the most probable figure for the late eighteenth and early nineteenth centuries was 0.7. Crafts, "Income Elasticities of Demand and the Release of Labour by Agriculture during the Industrial Revolution," *Journal of European Economic History*, IX (1980), 154–159. Kussmaul provides a convenient graph of the relative prices of grain and meat. It bears a strong resemblance to an inverted graph of the Phelps Brown and Hopkins real wage series, although the match is by no means perfect, especially in the early seventeenth and late eighteenth centuries. Ann Kussmaul, *Servants in Husbandry in Early Modern England* (Cambridge, 1981), Fig. 6.3, 104. Real wage data based on Phelps Brown and Hopkins are set out in Wrigley and Schofield, *Population History*, appendix 9, and shown graphically in *ibid.*, Fig. 10.5, 414.

have been falling in the sixteenth century, a finding in keeping with common sense, since the rural agricultural population is estimated to have risen by almost 60 percent between 1520 and 1600, a scale of increase likely to have involved a falling marginal productivity of labor and much concealed or overt underemployment.

Making an explicit allowance for real income changes, however, presents problems. At present, real income data are based on slender foundations and involve wide margins of uncertainty. Little is known about any changes which may have occurred over time in the income elasticity of demand for food. The only existing real wage series covering the whole period, that of Phelps Brown and Hopkins, stood higher in 1800 than it had two centuries earlier. The apparent gains in agricultural productivity over the seventeenth and eighteen centuries as a whole are therefore unlikely to be overstated because of a failure to take real income explicitly into account.[16]

Labor released from agriculture is available to increase other forms of production. The gross changes were striking. The rural agricultural population in 1520 was 76 percent of the total population in 1520 but only 36 percent in 1800 (Table 4). Non-agricultural employment therefore grew from 24 to 64 percent of the whole. This difference may overstate the extent of the change in that some of the growth of non-agricultural employment represented jobs created by increased specialization of function. A carter, for example, making his living by moving to market goods previously taken there by local farmers, may be placed outside agriculture in an occupational breakdown, but undertakes a task previously performed by the farmer.

Yet the change was great. Smith argued that a surplus of agricultural production over the food needs of the farming population might either be consumed unproductively by, say, retinues of servants, or productively, if the surplus maintained an army of "manufacturers" whose output added to the wealth of the community as a whole. In early modern England the growth of employment in industry and commerce is a testimony to the

16 The Phelps Brown and Hopkins index stood at 409 on average for the 11 harvest years 1595–96 to 1605–06 compared with 507 in the period 1795–96 to 1805–06. *Ibid.*, 642–644.

predominantly "productive" use to which the growing relative surpluses in the agricultural sector were put. Smith considered that the scale of such growth was largely conditioned by the extent of the rise in agricultural productivity. He did not envisage the much more radical type of change which has come to be called an industrial revolution, nor is there any compelling reason to suppose that even increases in agricultural productivity as striking as those achieved in England between 1600 and 1800 must necessarily engender an industrial revolution. Yet the scale of change in early modern England bears stressing. It stands out more clearly if comparison is made with other countries.[17]

URBAN GROWTH ON THE CONTINENT    De Vries has recently published an informative analysis of urban growth patterns between 1500 and 1800 for Europe as a whole and for some major regional subdivisions. In it he makes use of an empirical relationship between the sizes of the towns and their position in a rank ordering whereby the difference in their populations is proportional to the difference in their rank orders. Thus $p_i = p_1/i$ where $p_1$ is the population of the largest town and i refers to the rank order of a town after all towns have been arranged in descending order of size. The population of the fifth largest town may therefore be expected to be a fifth of that of the largest, and so on. If logarithmic scales are used to plot the population and rank coordinates of each town, the resulting distribution in the archetypal case will fall on a straight line with a slope of 45 degrees. In practice the slope of the line may vary somewhat from the 45-degree slope suggested by the strictly proportional relationship, and the first few points plotted are sometimes aberrant, as when the largest settlement is much bigger than the second largest. But regularities in town size distributions are often impressive, and any anomalies within a data set or changes in the angle of the plotted slope over time may prove illuminating.[18]

17  On Smith's views on productive and unproductive labor, see the chapter in the *Wealth of Nations,* "Of the accumulation of capital, or of productive and unproductive labor." An attempt to clarify the contingent nature of the circumstances which preceded and accompanied the industrial revolution may be found in Wrigley, "The Process of Modernization and the Industrial Revolution in England," *Journal of Interdisciplinary History,* III (1972), 225–259.
18  Jan de Vries, "Patterns of Urbanization in Preindustrial Europe, 1500–1800," in H. Schmal (ed.), *Patterns of European Urbanization since 1500* (London, 1981), 77–109.

By compiling rank-size data for European towns at intervals over a three-century period starting in 1500, de Vries was able to establish changes in the slope and shape of the urban hierarchy sufficiently pronounced and consistent to distinguish three major periods, as shown in Figure 1. At the beginning of the sixteenth century the slope was gentle and there was a flat 'top' to the distribution. He attributed the latter to the still strongly regional character of the European economy, which was insufficiently articulated to produce leading urban centers of the size implied by the slope of the lower part of the distribution. During the sixteenth century the rank-size plot gradually straightened. The continent-wide economy was becoming more integrated, and cities such as London, Paris, and Amsterdam grew rapidly as they assumed urban functions over wide hinterlands.

A second period then supervened, running from about the early seventeenth to the mid-eighteenth century. In general, in this period, the larger the town, the more rapidly it grew, so that

*Fig. 1*   Urbanization in Europe

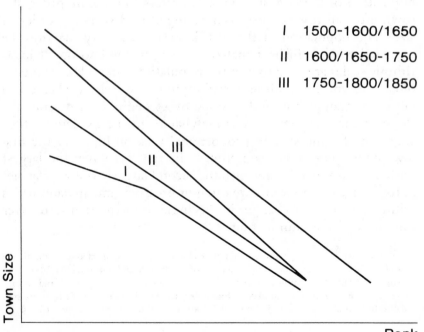

I    1500-1600/1650

II   1600/1650-1750

III  1750-1800/1850

SOURCE: de Vries, "Patterns of Urbanization."

a disproportionate part of the overall rise in urban population took place in the larger towns. The rank-size line pivoted slowly round a point close to its lowest reading and thus grew steadily steeper. After about 1750, however, urban growth changed in character again and a third period started. The rank-size line moved outward from the origin of the graph, implying a rise in the number of towns in all size categories, but there was more rapid growth in the number of smaller towns than in the number of larger ones. The slope became less steep once more. The sequence of changes was shared by the major subdivisions of Europe used by de Vries, although the timing of the changes varied somewhat. The pattern of change in England, however, was unlike that on the continent.

As Table 5 shows, England began the period with an unusually slight proportion of her population living in large towns, but passed the European average in the mid-seventeenth century and the northwest European average by 1700. By the beginning of the nineteenth century England was relatively heavily urbanized. Events there, however, were so different from those elsewhere as to distort patterns of change when England is included in some larger grouping.

It is instructive to remove England from both the urban and the overall population totals used to generate urban percentages for continental areas. The result is shown in Table 6. Urbanization

*Table 5* Urbanization in England and the Continent

Percentage of total populations in towns with 10,000 or more people

|  | 1500 | 1600 | 1650 | 1700 | 1750 | 1800 |
|---|---|---|---|---|---|---|
| England | 3.2[a] | 6.1 | 10.8[b] | 13.4 | 17.5 | 24.0 |
| North and West Europe[c] | 6.0 | 8.1 | 10.7 | 13.0 | 13.8 | 14.7 |
| Europe[d] | 6.1 | 8.0 | 9.3 | 9.5 | 9.9 | 10.6 |

NOTES:

a c. 1520

b c. 1670

c Scandinavia, Netherlands, Belgium, England, Scotland, Wales, and Ireland.

d The countries included in Europe are Germany, France, Switzerland, Italy, Spain, and Portugal together with those listed in note c.

SOURCES: For England see source notes to Tables 1 and 2. Other data from de Vries, "Patterns of Urbanization," 88.

*Table 6* Urbanization in England and the Continent (revised)

Percentage of total population in towns with 10,000 or more people

|  | 1600 | 1700 | 1750 | 1800 |
|---|---|---|---|---|
| England | 6.1 | 13.4 | 17.5 | 24.0 |
| North and West Europe minus England | 9.2 | 12.8 | 12.1 | 10.0 |
| Europe minus England | 8.1 | 9.2 | 9.4 | 9.5 |

NOTES: De Vries provides estimates of population totals for north and west Europe and for Europe as a whole for 1600, 1700, 1750, and 1800 in the work listed below (although not for the other dates in Table 5). This information and the urban percentages given in Table 5 make it possible to calculate the size of the urban populations. The English totals can then be removed from both the urban and total populations and the percentages recalculated.

SOURCES: For England see source notes to Tables 1 and 2. For other data see source notes to Table 5; de Vries, *The Economy of Europe in an Age of Crisis* (Cambridge, 1976), 5.

in northern and western Europe recedes rather than advancing substantially in the eighteenth century, although the scale of advance in the seventeenth century is little altered. In Europe as a whole the exclusion of England slows the increase in urbanization in the seventeenth century and brings it almost to a halt in the eighteenth.[19] Over the full 200-year period the urban percentage quadrupled in England, scarcely changed in the rest of north-western Europe, and advanced rather modestly on the continent as a whole. The English experience appears to be unique.

The extent of the contrast also comes home forcefully if de Vries' estimates are reworked to permit another comparison to be made, as in Table 7. The urban population of Europe more than doubled between 1600 and 1800, but the total population rose by almost 60 percent, so that much of the rise in urban population was caused by the rise in overall numbers rather than by an increase in the proportion of the population living in towns. Column 4 shows how the urban population would have grown if the urban percentage had stayed at the level prevailing in 1600. The totals in column 5 show the net gain in urban population at

19  This finding might be thought spurious if de Vries' estimates of the population of English towns and those shown in Table 1 were widely divergent. But a detailed comparison of his data with those of Table 1 suggests that this is a groundless fear.

*Table 7*  The English Share of European Urban Growth, 1600–1800 (populations in millions)

| | (1)<br>TOTAL POPULATION | (2)<br>URBAN PROPORTION | (3)<br>URBAN TOTAL (1) × (2) | (4)<br>URBAN TOTAL AT 1600 PROPORTION | (5)<br>NET GAIN ON 1600 (3) − (4) | (6)<br>NET GAIN ON LAST DATE (DIFFERENCE BETWEEN SUCCESSIVE TOTALS IN (5)) |
|---|---|---|---|---|---|---|
| EUROPE[a] | | | | | | |
| 1600 | 70.6 | 0.080 | 5.65 | 5.65 | 0.00 | |
| 1700 | 75.0 | 0.095 | 7.13 | 6.00 | 1.13 | 1.13 |
| 1750 | 86.6 | 0.099 | 8.57 | 6.93 | 1.64 | 0.51 |
| 1800 | 111.8 | 0.106 | 11.85 | 8.94 | 2.91 | 1.27 |
| ENGLAND | | | | | | |
| 1600 | 4.11 | 0.061[b] | 0.249 | 0.249 | 0.000 | |
| 1700 | 5.06 | 0.134[b] | 0.680 | 0.309 | 0.371 | 0.371 |
| 1750 | 5.77 | 0.175[b] | 1.012 | 0.352 | 0.661 | 0.290 |
| 1800 | 8.66 | 0.240[b] | 2.079 | 0.528 | 1.551 | 0.890 |

English Percentage of Total European Net Urban Gain

1600/1700   100(0.371/1.13) = 33
1700/1750   100(0.290/0.51) = 57
1750/1800   100(0.890/1.27) = 70
1600/1800   100(1.551/2.91) = 53

NOTES: a  For a list of the countries comprising "Europe," see notes to Table 5.

b  These proportions are derived from the column (3) totals rather than vice-versa as in the top panel.

SOURCES: For England see source notes to Tables 1 and 2.

For Europe see source notes to Table 5.

each later date compared with 1600: that is, the number by which the urban population exceeded what would have obtained had the urban percentage not changed in the interim. The second panel of the table repeats the calculation for England.

By combining information from the two upper panels, the proportion of total European urban growth that occurred in England can be calculated for the periods 1600 to 1700, 1700 to 1750, and 1750 to 1800. The proportion rises steadily from a third in the seventeenth century to 70 percent in the second half of the eighteenth. Over the two-century period as a whole the proportion exceeded one half. Since England contained only 5.8 percent of the population of Europe in 1600 and only 7.7 percent even in 1800, these proportions are an extraordinary testimony to the extent of the difference in urban growth between the island and the continent.

De Vries placed particular emphasis on the absence of growth in the smaller towns between 1600 and 1750, a period which he defined as the age of the rural proletariat. He argued that urban growth was almost entirely confined to very large cities, with 80 percent of all growth taking place in towns with 40,000 inhabitants or more. These towns were almost all capital cities or large ports, the development of which was stimulated by the growth in administrative, military, and legal employment in both absolutist and constitutional states, or by the development of long-distance, often extra-European trade. Smaller towns stagnated or lost population, afflicted by loss of political autonomy and by the "abandonment of cities as locations for many of the most labour-absorbing industries."[20] The balance of advantage favored protoindustrial development in the countryside.

There was unquestionably much growth in industrial employment in rural England during this period. At the same time London, combining administrative, commercial, and trading dominance, enjoyed an astonishing expansion. But neither the development of rural industry nor the growth of London precluded an equally remarkable surge of urban growth elsewhere in England. Other towns grew by much the same absolute amount as London between 1600 and 1750 and proportionally were grow-

20  De Vries, "Patterns of Urbanization," 101.

ing even faster than London (Table 2). Towns with between 5,000 and 10,000 inhabitants doubled in number from fifteen to thirty-one, while over the same period the number in Europe minus England fell from 372 to 331. Figure 2 shows rank-size plots for England. Like Figure 1 it is schematically drawn: empirical data plots would show points falling on either side of the straight lines for each date. Although the number of towns is small and the presence of London severely distorts the top of the distribution,

*Fig. 2*   Urbanization in England

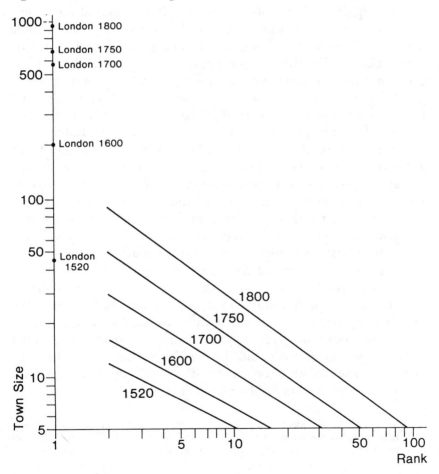

the lines emphasize how different England was from the continent (compare Figure 1).[21]

De Vries' study has the admirable virtue of providing a framework of comparison for smaller units by epitomizing the characteristics of Europe as a whole. This framework helps to bring out the distinctiveness of English history, and it may be further examined by considering comparative data about England's two greatest rivals, Holland and France.

HOLLAND AND FRANCE     Even in 1800 England was a less urbanized country than Holland. Already in the early sixteenth century many Dutch people were town dwellers and their numbers increased rapidly as the century wore on. In this period the course of real wages in Holland was almost the reverse of the comparable pattern in England: real wages rose to a peak around 1610, the date when the English series approached its nadir, and urbanization continued. The percentage of the population living in towns grew from about 21 to about 29 percent, and since the total population of Holland was rising moderately quickly at the time, the absolute number of town dwellers rose even faster, from about 260,000 to about 435,000. There followed a period of half a century during which Dutch real wages fell back somewhat, just as a recovery was starting in England, maintaining the inverse movement in the two countries for a full century. After the 1650s, however, Dutch real wages rose rapidly once more to a new and substantially higher peak in the 1690s, after which they fell, uncertainly at first, but more quickly and without interruption from the 1740s until the end of the century. The trend of urban percentages moved broadly in sympathy with real wage movements, reaching a high point around 1700, when about 39 percent of the Dutch population was urban. It then declined slowly until, by 1800, it was not much higher than the English figure. Some Dutch towns experienced severe falls in population, and, since the population as a whole grew only modestly in the eighteenth century, the total number of town dwellers fell slightly.[22]

21  On the growth of London, see Wrigley, "A Simple Model of London's Importance in Changing English Society and Economy," *Past & Present,* 37 (1967), 44–70. The totals of towns with between 5,000 and 10,000 inhabitants are taken from de Vries, "Patterns of Urbanization," 93. For sources of data about English towns see source notes to Table 1.
22  For Dutch real wages, see de Vries, "The Population and Economy of the Preindustrial

Dutch rural population trends also warrant notice. During the long period of urban growth from 1550 to 1700 the rural population grew only modestly. It was 17 percent larger at the latter than the former date. In the eighteenth century, however, when there was urban decline and real wages languished, rural population numbers rose by 20 percent. In England in the eighteenth century the rural population grew by 49 percent overall, but the rural agricultural population by only 13 percent, even though the overall population growth in England during the century reached 71 percent compared with a Dutch figure of only 11 percent. If, therefore, it is safe to assume that the Dutch rural agricultural population was rising as fast as the rural population as a whole—a plausible supposition at a time of falling real wages—rural agricultural population totals in the two countries must have moved almost exactly in step in the eighteenth century, even though their overall rates of population growth diverged so markedly. Conversely, in the sixteenth century, while impoverishment increased in England and its rural agricultural population grew fast (by 58 percent between 1520 and 1600), in Holland there can have been little comparable increase, although the population of Holland was rising fairly rapidly. In columns 5 to 7 of Table 8 the rural population is subdivided between agricultural and other employment in conformity with arbitrary assumptions, the basis of which is explained in the notes to the table. To the degree that the figures mirror reality, they underline the points just made. The golden age of the Dutch rural economy was clearly one free from increasing pressure on the land, but it was succeeded by more trying times.[23]

A comparison of the urban sectors in England and Holland should not be pressed too far. It would make no sense, for example, to use estimates of urban percentages in Holland as an indirect measure of agricultural productivity, since Holland was a large importer of agricultural products, especially Baltic grain,

---

Netherlands," in this issue, Fig. 2. See Table 8 notes for sources for the estimates of Dutch urban populations. A. van der Woude provides much detail of urban fortunes in Holland betwen 1525 and 1795 in "Demografische ontwikkeling van de Noordelijke Nederlanden 1500–1800," in *Algemene Geschiedenis der Nederlanden,* V (1980), 134–139.

23 De Vries, "Population and Economy of Preindustrial Netherlands," Fig. 2, charts the fall in real wages from a late-seventeenth-century peak which, in a period of static or falling population, was eloquent testimony to Dutch difficulties.

*Table 8* Dutch Urban and Rural Population Estimates (thousands)

| | (1)<br>TOTAL<br>POPULATION | (2)<br>PROPORTION<br>URBAN | (3)<br>POPULATION<br>(1) × (2) | (4)<br>RURAL<br>POPULATION<br>(1) − (3) | (5)<br>RURAL<br>AGRICULTURAL<br>PROPORTION | (6)<br>RURAL<br>AGRICULTURAL<br>POPULATION<br>(4) × (5) | (7)<br>RURAL<br>NON-AGRICULTURAL<br>POPULATION<br>(4) − (6) |
|---|---|---|---|---|---|---|---|
| 1550 | 1250 | 0.21 | 260 | 990 | 0.75 | 745 | 245 |
| 1600 | 1500 | 0.29 | 435 | 1065 | 0.705 | 750 | 315 |
| 1650 | 1875 | 0.37 | 700 | 1175 | 0.66 | 775 | 400 |
| 1700 | 1900 | 0.39 | 740 | 1160 | 0.66 | 768 | 395 |
| 1750 | 1925 | 0.35 | 675 | 1250 | 0.66 | 825 | 425 |
| 1800 | 2100 | 0.33 | 700 | 1400 | 0.66 | 925 | 475 |

NOTES: Urban is defined as relating to towns of 5,000 inhabitants or more.

The population totals in columns (3) and (6) have been rounded to emphasize the approximate and arbitrary nature of the calculation.

The proportion urban in column (2) was estimated from data given by de Vries. His data refer to the percentages of the population living in towns containing 2,500 inhabitants or more, and in towns containing 10,000 inhabitants or more. I assumed that half of those living in towns with 2,500 to 9,999 inhabitants were living in towns of 5,000 to 9,999 inhabitants. For some dates de Vries provides data only for the urban percentage in towns of 10,000 or more inhabitants, but sufficient paired estimates are given for other dates to make it feasible to provide plausible estimates at half-century intervals.

The rural agricultural proportions (column 5) stem from the following observations and assumptions. Mitchell provides data which show that 44.1% of the total Dutch labor force in 1849 was in agriculture. At that date the urban proportion was the same as in 1800 (de Vries, Table 1), and therefore the proportion of the *rural* labor force engaged in agriculture was 66% (0.441/0.67 = 0.66). I have assumed arbitrarily that in Holland in the mid-sixteenth century the comparable figure was 75%, a slightly lower figure than that used in the parallel calculation for England, because Holland was far more urbanized than England in the sixteenth century and non-agricultural rural employment was probably more common. I have assumed that it fell to 0.66 linearly over the next century but did not change thereafter as the great Dutch growth spurt ended.

SOURCES:

Column 1: J. A. Faber, H. K. Roessingh, B. H. Slicher Van Bath, Van der Woude, and H. J. van Xanten, "Population Changes and Economic Developments in the Netherlands: A Historical Survey," *A. A. G. Bijdragen,* XII (1965), 110.

Column 2: de Vries, "Population and the Labor Market in the Netherlands, 1500–1850," paper given at the Conference on British Demographic History (1982), Table 1.

Column 5: Brian R. Mitchell, *European Historical Statistics, 1750–1975* (Cambridge, 1981; 2nd rev. ed.), 167 (see also notes above).

and was not broadly self-sufficient as was England in the early modern period. Yet the beneficial effects of urban growth on Dutch agriculture in promoting specialization and making it easier to achieve higher production per man and per farm reflect the same processes at work in Holland as London's growth produced in England. Again, the Dutch passenger canal network was the transport wonder of its age, a response to urban growth and the closely associated rise in living standards, just as similar developments in eighteenth-century England promoted the investment of capital in turnpike roads and the construction of a new canal network.[24]

Both Holland and England, therefore, vividly illustrate the beneficial interactions among urban growth, rising living standards, and a surge in agricultural productivity which was possible within the context of an early modern economy. The food needs of towns were met through the operation of a commercial market in foodstuffs. Farming units benefited from specialization and avoided the subdivision and fragmentation of holdings which were commonly the bane of peasant societies when population increased. By the late eighteenth century yields per acre were substantially higher in England and the Netherlands than elsewhere in Europe, having roughly doubled over the previous two centuries. Yet in neither country was the agriculturally employed population much larger in 1800 than in 1600.[25]

The example of Holland also shows, however, that such progress was not necessarily a passport to further success. Smith, aware like so many of his contemporaries of the exceptional economic achievements of Holland, used it as an example of the limits to growth which must beset any country at some stage, making it difficult to sustain the gains of the past, much less secure further advances. The tide began to ebb in eighteenth-century Holland. Urban population fell slightly, even though numbers rose modestly overall. Real wages sagged. Far from forming part of the vanguard of the industrial revolution, Holland moved into the industrial era later than most of Western Europe,

24 *Idem,* "Barges and Capitalism. Passenger Transportation in the Dutch Economy, 1632–1839," *A. A. G. Bijdragen,* XXI (1978), 33–398.
25 For yield data, see Slicher van Bath, *The Agrarian History of Western Europe, A.D. 500–1850* (London, 1963), 280–282.

and even as late as 1850 was no more urbanized than it had been in the later seventeenth century.[26]

France provides a very different contrast to the case of England. Some relevant data are given in Table 9. The steps leading to the estimates given in the table are explained in the table notes. As with the English and Dutch estimates, they are subject to a margin of error which in some cases may be substantial because the empirical data base is insecure or inconsistent, because some of the assumptions are questionable, or because the chains of reasoning used to produce some of the estimates were long and there may have been a compounding of errors. Despite such uncertainties, the contrast between France and England stands out so strongly that no reasonable change in the assumptions used would significantly change the picture.

In 1500 France was not only a far more populous country than England, but it was also more urbanized. Within the present borders of France there were already fourteen towns with a population of more than 20,000 and twenty-one with populations between 10,000 and 20,000, while in England only London exceeded 20,000, and probably only two other towns, Norwich and Bristol, had 10,000 or more inhabitants. London was not only smaller than Paris but was also smaller than Lyon. Overall France was almost twice as urban as England, although much less urban than Holland, but, in the next three centuries, French towns grew hardly more quickly than the French population as a whole. France closely resembled de Vries' 'Europe' both in level of urbanization and in its change over time (Table 5). By 1800 the degree of urbanization reached in England was approaching three times the French level. Moreover, the proportion of the English rural population employed outside agriculture grew much faster than in France, and agricultural productivity, using the rough measure employed *faute de mieux* in this article, progressed far more rapidly in England than in France.[27]

26 Smith makes the general observation that, "In a country which had acquired that full complement of riches which the nature of its soil and climate, and its situation with respect to other countries allowed it to acquire, which could, therefore, advance no further, and which was not going backwards, both the wages of labour and the profits of stock would, probably, be very low." He subsequently suggested that Holland was approaching this state. Smith, *Wealth of Nations*, 43–44.

27 The French town population estimates are taken from de Vries, "Patterns of Urbanization," 82–85. In some instances the effects of revolution and war caused a sharp drop in French city populations in the last decade of the eighteenth century. Jacques Dupâquier, *La population française aux XVII<sup>e</sup> et XVIII<sup>e</sup> siècles* (Paris, 1979), 91–92.

Population always grew faster in England than in France, at times dramatically so (Tables 2 and 9), yet, because of the far faster urban growth in England and the swifter rise in the proportion of the rural population employed outside agriculture, the growth of rural agricultural employment was actually slower in England than in France, except in the sixteenth century. Between 1600 and 1800 the number of those dependent upon agriculture for a living in France grew by 30 percent, whereas in England the comparable figure was 9 percent. (Over the same period the national population growth rates were 53 and 111 percent respectively.) These apparently exact percentages should be viewed with reserve, but it is probably safe to assert that the rural agricultural population in England grew no faster than its counterpart in France. If the data used are taken on trust, inferences about comparative trends in agricultural productivity in the two countries are possible.

The upper panel of Table 10 sets out information for England and France in an indexed form to make it easier to appreciate the divergent course of development which characterized them. The value for 1600 has in each case been made equal to 100. In the sixteenth century, the differences between the two countries were chiefly related to the much higher rate of growth of the English population rather than to differences in the relative proportions of the populations falling into the urban, rural agricultural, and rural non-agricultural categories. After 1600, the contrasts between the two countries grew more pronounced. England continued to grow more quickly overall, but the rural agricultural element in its population grew little over the next two centuries. Indeed, it appears to have been falling for much of the time, whereas urban growth was meteoric; the rise in the rural non-agricultural component was also pronounced. Growth in France was much more balanced and, as a result, although the total population grew less than in England, the rural agricultural population grew appreciably faster.

If it were safe to assume that the level of food consumption per head was much the same in the two countries, that the estimates of rural agricultural population are accurate, and that each country may be regarded as having supplied its own food needs (except that in this table imports were assumed to meet 10 percent of English food requirements in 1800), then it is a simple matter to compare both levels of productivity in agriculture and their

Table 9 French Urban and Rural Population Estimates (thousands)

| | (1) TOTAL POPULATION | (2) URBAN POPULATION | (3) PERCENTAGE URBAN | (4) RURAL POPULATION | (5) RURAL AGRICULTURAL PROPORTION | (6) RURAL AGRICULTURAL POPULATION (4) × (5) | (7) RURAL NON-AGRICULTURAL POPULATION (4) − (6) |
|---|---|---|---|---|---|---|---|
| 1500 | 15,500 | 1,410 | 9.1 | 14,090 | 0.80 | 11,270 | 2,820 |
| 1600 | 19,000 | 1,660 | 8.7 | 17,340 | 0.755 | 13,100 | 4,240 |
| 1700 | 21,500 | 2,350 | 10.9 | 19,150 | 0.71 | 13,600 | 5,550 |
| 1750 | 24,500 | 2,530 | 10.3 | 21,970 | 0.685 | 15,050 | 6,920 |
| 1800 | 29,100 | 3,220 | 11.1 | 25,880 | 0.66 | 17,080 | 8,800 |

NOTES: Urban is defined as relating to towns of 5,000 inhabitants or more. France was treated as if it occupied its present territory; therefore towns such as Lille were included in urban population totals. The urban population in column (2) was estimated in several stages. Chandler and Fox provide estimates of urban populations of towns of 20,000 inhabitants or more for the dates shown. De Vries gives totals of towns in several size categories ('000s) 20–29, 30–39, 40–49, 50–99, and 100 and over. Where the total for a town given by Chandler and Fox falls into the size category given by de Vries, this total was used. Otherwise de Vries' calculations were preferred and a town population was assumed to be at the centrepoint of the size range (none fell into the open-ended top category). The discrepancies between the two sources, as might be expected, were much more marked at the earlier than the later dates. The number of towns of 20,000 or more inhabitants in the two sources were as follows at five successive dates, Chandler and Fox in parentheses: 14 (20), 20 (15), 24 (26), 31 (32), 32 (36). De Vries' totals of towns with populations of 10,000 or more, multiplied by 13,500 to give a population total for this size range of towns. These two operations provide a figure for all towns with populations of 10,000 or more, leaving the problem of estimating a figure for towns of between 5,000 and 10,000 people. De Vries provides estimates of the number of towns in this size range in Europe as a whole by extrapolating from the rank-size distributions of towns of 10,000 inhabitants and above. It can be shown that the rank-size distribution of French towns was similar to that for Europe as measured by the ratio of the number of all towns above 10,000 in population to the number of towns in this size range between 10,000 and 20,000. The ratio of the number of towns in the size range between 5,000 and 10,000 to the number of towns larger than 10,000 derived from de Vries' data was used to estimate the total of smaller towns in France. (The ratios in question at the five successive dates are 2.15, 1.76, 1.60, 1.43, and 1.56; of these the third is interpolated from the second and fourth since de Vries provides no data for 1700.) The total of towns in the size range between 5,000 and 10,000 estimated in this fashion was multiplied by 6,500 to give a population total for each date. The breakdown of the individual totals was as follows ('000s):

Population totals by town size class

| | 20 and over | 10–19 | 5–9 | Total |
|---|---|---|---|---|
| 1500 | 637 | 284 | 488 | 1,409 |
| 1600 | 866 | 311 | 481 | 1,658 |
| 1700 | 1,389 | 405 | 559 | 2,353 |
| 1750 | 1,691 | 324 | 514 | 2,529 |
| 1800 | 1,810 | 621 | 793 | 3,224 |

The proportion of the rural population engaged in agriculture is based on the following data and assumptions. In 1851 the proportion of the population living in towns of 5,000 or more inhabitants was 17.9% (Pouthas, 22, 76). In 1856 the proportion of the total French labor force engaged in agriculture was 51.7%. In the mid-nineteenth century, therefore, about 63% of the rural labor force worked on the land ($100 \times (0.517/0.821) = 63$). I have assumed that the comparable figure in 1800 was 66%. As in the case of England, I assumed that in France the comparable figure in the early sixteenth century was 80%. The proportions at intermediate dates were obtained by rough linear interpolation.

SOURCES:
Column (1): Jacques Dupâquier, *La population française aux XVII<sup>e</sup> et XVIII<sup>e</sup> siècles* (Paris, 1979), 11, 34, 81; M. Reinhard, A. Armengaud, and Dupâquier, *Histoire générale de la population mondiale* (Paris, 1968; 3rd ed.), 108, 119–120; C. McEvedy and Richard Jones, *Atlas of World Population History* (London, 1978), 55–60.
Column (2): T. Chandler and G. Fox, *3000 Years of Urban Growth* (New York, 1974), 15–19, 21; de Vries, "Patterns of Urbanization," Tables 3.2, 3.4, 3.7.
Column (5): C. H. Pouthas, *La population française pendant la première moitié du XIX<sup>e</sup> siècle* (Paris, 1965); Mitchell, *European Historical Statistics*, 163.

Table 10 English and French Growth Patterns Compared

POPULATIONS RELATIVE TO 100 TOTAL (1600 = 100)

ENGLAND

| | URBAN | RURAL AGRICULTURAL | RURAL NON-AGRICULTURAL | TOTAL |
|---|---|---|---|---|
| 1520 | 38 | 63 | 50 | 58 |
| 1600 | 100 | 100 | 100 | 100 |
| 1700 | 250 | 97 | 159 | 123 |
| 1750 | 359 | 92 | 212 | 140 |
| 1801 | 700 | 109 | 349 | 211 |

FRANCE

| | URBAN | RURAL AGRICULTURAL | RURAL NON-AGRICULTURAL | TOTAL |
|---|---|---|---|---|
| 1500 | 85 | 86 | 67 | 82 |
| 1600 | 100 | 100 | 100 | 100 |
| 1700 | 142 | 104 | 131 | 113 |
| 1750 | 152 | 115 | 163 | 129 |
| 1800 | 194 | 130 | 208 | 153 |

TOTAL POPULATION PER 100 AGRICULTURAL

| | ENGLAND (1) | FRANCE (2) | | ENGLAND COLUMN (1) 1520 = 100 (3) | FRANCE COLUMN (2) 1500 = 100 (4) |
|---|---|---|---|---|---|
| 1500 | 132 | 138 | 1520 | 100 | 100 |
| 1600 | 143 | 145 | 1600 | 108 | 105 |
| 1700 | 182 | 158 | 1700 | 138 | 114 |
| 1750 | 219 | 163 | 1750 | 166 | 118 |
| 1800 | 248 | 170 | 1801 | 188 | 123 |

NOTE: See text for modification made to 1801 figure in bottom panel, columns (1) and (3)
SOURCES: Tables 4 and 9

rates of change over time in the two countries. They are given in the lower panel of the table. The figures of columns 1 and 2 represent an absolute measure of productivity per head of the rural agricultural population whereas those in columns 3 and 4 index changes over time.

The extent of the contrast between England and France may well be understated by the table, both because it is reasonable to suppose that consumption of food per head was higher in England than in France since English real incomes appear to have been the higher of the two, and also because a higher proportion of the output of English agriculture may have been used as industrial raw material rather than food. Land and labor used for the raising of sheep for wool, for example, cannot also be used to grow corn. The effect, however, is difficult to quantify since output in such cases often consisted both of food and of industrial raw materials. Producing wool for cloth or hides for the leather industry also meant producing meat for human consumption. Pure industrial land usage, as with flax for linen, was a rarer phenomenon. The use of the land to provide "fuel" for horses or oxen also suggests that the contrast between the two countries may be greater than appears in the table, since in England, by the later eighteenth century, a substantial proportion of horses were employed outside agriculture on turnpike roads, on canal towpaths, and particularly for urban transportation of men and goods.[28]

In England, as in Holland at an earlier date, urban growth, rising productivity in agriculture, and improving real incomes were interwoven with one another, and were mutually reinforcing for long periods. The French economy did not follow the same

28  Thirsk presents good reasons to suppose that the value of industrial crops rose rapidly in the later sixteenth and seventeenth centuries, and also provides abundant evidence of the enormous increase in rural employment outside agriculture. Thirsk, *Economic Policy and Projects. The Development of a Consumer Society in Early Modern England* (Oxford, 1978). There are some guarded attempts to quantify the scale of industrial crops and new food crops in *ibid.*, 177–178.

Thompson estimates that there were almost half a million (487,000) horses in use outside agriculture in 1811 (riding horses, carriage horses, post horses, trade horses, and those in the stage coach trade). At the level of consumption of oats and hay per animal which Thompson thinks appropriate, and on reasonable asumptions about yields of oats and hay per acre, sustaining such a large population must have meant devoting about 2 million acres to their fodder. Agriculture at that date is estimated to have required about 800,000 horses. F. M. L. Thompson, "Nineteenth-Century Horse Sense," *Economic History Review*, XXIX (1976), 78, 80.

pattern. On the assumptions used in constructing Table 9, there is evidence of increased pressure on the land in the eighteenth century. In a peasant economy this pressure may provoke serious economic difficulties and increase the proportion of excessively subdivided holdings, conforming to de Vries' peasant model of a rural economy. Both England and Holland accord better with his specialization model.[29]

Arguments couched in this manner are always too simplistic. It is misleading, for example, to treat preindustrial countries as if they were homogeneous units. There were major differences among different areas, even within the smallest of the three countries considered. Sometimes even intraprovincial differences in Holland were marked: interprovincial contrasts could rival those among countries. The regional variety of a country as large as France was still more notable. It could scarcely be otherwise when it is recalled that France contained more than ten times as many people as Holland and had an area fifteen times greater. Furthermore, better knowledge would no doubt cause significant alterations to be made to many of the tables on which the arguments advanced in this article are based. Yet the contrasts and similarities between the three countries would probably remain even if perfect knowledge were available.[30]

It is not difficult to find convincing reasons why a major advance in agricultural productivity is a prerequisite of industrial growth. Only if resources can be spared from the task of ensuring an adequate supply of foodstuffs can a larger scale of industrial production be attempted. It may seem quaint that Smith should have associated the prosperity of, say, Sheffield's industry with the efficiency of agriculture in the vicinity of the town, but his remark is a parable of the circumstances needed for industrial success in a preindustrial age.[31]

England was singularly fortunate in this regard. Output per head in agriculture appears to have risen by three quarters between

---

29 De Vries, *The Dutch Rural Economy in the Golden Age, 1500–1700* (New Haven, 1974), 1–21.

30 For national population totals see Tables 8 and 9. The area of France today is 212,209 square miles; that of Holland 13,967. Their areas varied somewhat over the early modern period.

31 See Smith, *Wealth of Nations*, 180–181.

the beginning of the seventeenth and the end of the eighteenth century. The annual gain in agricultural productivity per head was modest—about 0.3 percent—yet it permitted a more rapid overall rate of population growth than that found in either France or Holland, while simultaneously releasing into secondary and tertiary employment a far higher proportion of the active population than in any other European country. By 1800 little more than a third of the English labor force was engaged in agriculture at a time when it is improbable that the comparable figure elsewhere in Europe, apart from the Netherlands, was less than 55 to 60 percent. In many countries it was substantially higher.[32]

The pace of English population growth in the early modern period was exceptional. Between the mid-sixteenth and the early nineteenth century England's population grew by about 280 percent. The population of other major European countries rose much less rapidly. Germany, France, the Netherlands, Spain, and Italy all grew by between 50 and 80 percent over the same period. The demographic mechanisms by which the growth of England came about are now fairly well understood, but at one remove the problem of explaining the contrast remains. In this connection it is important to pay heed to the probability that there was nothing unusual in the rate of growth of English *rural agricultural* population, unless it was that it grew so slowly, especially after 1600. The great bulk of the overall increase took place in that part of the population which made its living *outside* agriculture. This was what made England so distinctive.[33]

In one sense an explanation of English agricultural improvement may be sought in the relatively rapid and uninterrupted growth in the urban sector of the English economy, well able to

32 In Finland in 1754, 79% of all economically active heads of families were engaged in agriculture, forestry, or fishing; in 1805, 82%. There are data for many European countries from about the middle of the nineteenth century. In the following list the percentages refer to the proportion of the total labor force (male and female) engaged in agriculture, forestry, or fishing, unless otherwise indicated: Belgium 1846, 51%; Denmark 1850, 49% (family heads); France 1856, 52%; Ireland 1851, 48%; Netherlands 1849, 44%; Spain 1860, 70% (males only); Sweden 1860, 64%; Great Britain 1851, 22%. Mitchell, *European Historical Statistics 1750–1975*, Table C1. Half a century earlier it is virtually certain that each of the comparable percentages would have been higher, sometimes substantially so.
33 Wrigley, "The Growth of Population in Eighteenth-Century England: a Conundrum Resolved," *Past & Present*, 98 (1983), 122–125. The secular changes in fertility and morality which largely governed population growth rates in England are described in Wrigley and Schofield, *Population History*, 192–284.

afford food but producing none itself. The extraordinary stimulus to improvement afforded by the growth of London, which in 1500 was not even one of the dozen largest cities in Europe, but by 1700 was larger than any other, was probably the most important single factor in engendering agricultural improvement. The momentum first given by the growth of London was carried forward later by the more general urban growth in the later seventeenth and eighteenth centuries. It encouraged both change within agriculture itself and in a host of associated institutions and activities: transport improvement, credit facilities, capital markets, and commercial exchange. The joint effect of rising productivity and increasing urbanization also fostered a great expansion in rural employment outside agriculture. The combination of a steadily rising demand for goods and services other than food with a far more sophisticated market mechanism for exciting and satisfying such a demand was the basis of prosperity for the industries in the countryside.

Yet the reasons for the exceptional growth of London from the early sixteenth to the late seventeenth century remain imperfectly understood. Its rise both deserves and demands much more attention than it has received. Understanding of the phenomenon is likely to benefit especially from study of the connection between the development of the nation state under the Tudors and Stuarts and the growth of the capital city, and from considering London's fortunes within a wider framework of analysis of European commercial exchange.

Urban growth toward the end of the early modern period presents problems of interpretation no less difficult than those at its beginning. During the eighteenth century the urban hierarchy of England was turned upside down. The new industrial towns and port cities of the north and the midlands thrust their way past all rivals other than London. Only Bristol and Newcastle, among the traditional regional centers, matched the new challenge, and then only because they could benefit from the stimuli which had forced the pace of the growth in places like Liverpool and Sunderland. Many once-great centers were on the way to the pleasant obscurity of county rather than national fame—York, Exeter, Chester, Worcester, and Salisbury.

The upsetting of the old urban hierarchy in England was, at

the time, an event without recent precedent in European history. Elsewhere the exact ranking of major cities in each country varied from time to time, but it was rare for tiny settlements to develop into major centers. The same lists of large urban centers may be found century after century only slightly rearranged. Occasionally one of the smaller centers made progress through the ranks. Atlantic and colonial trade brought Bordeaux and Nantes rapid advancement between 1500 and 1800, for example, but revolutionary changes were rare. The progress of the new centers in England was such, however, that not merely had Liverpool and Manchester outpaced all of their English rivals other than London in 1800, but by 1850 they were the seventh and ninth largest cities in Europe, and the largest anywhere in Europe other than those which were capital cities, an extraordinary tribute to their economic vitality unassisted by the employment in government, the professions, and the arts associated with capital cities.[34]

The history of urban growth in England was distinctive. The contrast with the course of events elsewhere in Europe was especially notable between 1600 and 1750, since the paralysis which affected all but the largest towns on the continent was absent in England. The expansion of secondary employment in the countryside was not a bar to urban growth in England in the manner hypothesized by de Vries for Europe as a whole. This fact may afford an important clue to the differences between England and her continental neighbors in real income levels or trends, in relative wage levels in town and country, in the terms of trade between the two, in urban institutions, or in still other factors.

In this article, however, I have concentrated on the narrower topic of the scale and speed of urban growth and the indirect measurement of the gain in agricultural productivity per head, which roughly doubled in England between 1600 and 1800. By the standards of the recent past, a doubling in agricultural productivity over a two-century span of time is not a startling achievement, but, in terms of the preindustiral world, it is much more impressive and set England apart from the great bulk of

34  Chandler and Fox, *3,000 years of Urban Growth,* 20. The first nine in order of size were London, Paris, Constantinople, St. Petersburg, Berlin, Vienna, Liverpool, Naples, and Manchester.

continental Europe, conferring on the former advantages denied to economies unable to release more than a tiny fraction of the labor force from work with the flock or plow.[35]

*Measuring* agricultural advance through urban growth falls well short of *explaining* either phenomenon. It is easy to see how these developments might reinforce one another, but the fact that similar cases were so rare, and that when they did occur they tended to lose momentum after a while, suggests that noting the logical possbility of such a link is only a first step toward undestanding what took place. The most fundamental and intriguing question may concern the circumstances in which Ricardo's law of declining marginal returns to additional unit inputs of labor and capital may be circumvented in a land long fully settled. This law, if it had universal and invariable application, would prohibit a sustained development of the kind which took place in England.[36]

The population of England increased more than 3.5 times between the early sixteenth and the early nineteenth century without becoming dependent, other than marginally, on food imports. Some new land was taken into farming use, but the bulk of the increased output must have been obtained from land already under cultivation. Moreover, after 1600 there was little increase in the agricultural labor force.

What served to neutralize the operation of declining marginal returns? The usual answer given to this question is innovation. If other things were not equal—if new methods of farming had been introduced which significantly enhanced the productivity of labor and capital—then the operaiton of Ricardo's principle could have been postponed, indefinitely if the flow of suitable innovations were sufficiently sustained. In a sense this must be the right answer but, because it is inescapable, it may be unilluminating, for, although it may be logically necessary, it was historically contingent. Relief from such a source was not always or even commonly forthcoming. Can anything be found in the circum-

35 Grigg provides information about rates of growth in labor productivity in agriculture in Denmark, France, the United States, and the United Kingdom in the late nineteenth and early twentieth centuries, and for all major subdivisions of the world since 1960. David B. Grigg, *The Dynamics of Agricultural Change* (London, 1982), 171—172. Rates as high as 5% per annum have been commonplace in developed countries in recent years.
36 David Ricardo, *On the Principles of Political Economy and Taxation* (London, 1817).

stances of early modern England which provides an answer to this conundrum?

To attempt a full examination of this issue is beyond the scope of this article, but one of its aspects may bear a slight elaboration. There was a remarkably strong and regular positive relationship between the long-term rate of growth of population and the comparable rate of change in food prices in England throughout the early modern period until 1800. At first sight this relationship suggests a uniform and inhibiting tension between population growth and the capacity to sustain rising numbers. But, although the tension was constant, it does not follow that all the demographic and economic variables involved stood in the same relationship to each other throughout. We have seen, for example, that there were major changes in national occupational structure and in agricultural productivity per head. The relationship between population growth and food prices may prove to have been common to England and other countries, but the changing structure of the component variables was not usually found elsewhere. The tension appears to have been beneficial and dynamic in England, when so often it was static and debilitating.[37]

Innovation may be the key to overcoming Ricardian constraints, but inasmuch as what happened in England was so rarely paralleled in other preindustrial economies, it seems doubtful whether innovation could be counted upon to be forthcoming in response to need. When, as in England, events took a more favorable turn, the explanation may be found not in the urgency of human need, nor in the immediate price dynamics of the market place, nor in the accident of individual inventiveness, but in the unusual structural characteristics of the prevailing situation.

If, on the one hand, it were safe to assume that a community always exploited its knowledge of production methods to the full,

---

37  On the relationship between the rates of change in population and food prices, see Wrigley and Schofield, *Population History,* Fig. 10.2. From the mid-sixteenth to the late eighteenth centuries the relationship was strikingly linear. This in itself may be suggestive. If there had been very tight constraints upon agricultural expansion, a curvilinear relationship might have been expected, with a steeper rise in price than in population as conditions worsened. Its absence may reflect the existence of an unusual capacity to rise to the challenge of increased demand on the part of English agriculture, especially when it is remembered that the absolute rate of population growth was at times quite high, approaching 1% per annum in the late sixteenth century and exceeding it in the late eighteenth. I owe this comment to Schofield's reflections on the point.

it would follow that innovation meant the introduction of some element into the productive system which was previously unknown. If, on the other hand, there were a range of alternatives to existing practice capable of raising productivity, which were held in reserve because current circumstances did not encourage or even allow of their use, the nature of the case would be changed.[38]

It may not be sufficient to look exclusively at changes in technology to explain a rise in productivity—new crops, altered cultivation practices, improved breeding techniques, and so on; nor to turn to the gains in productivity per head arising from increasing specialization of function, the chief proximate cause of enhanced productivity in Smith's analysis of the question. Other developments need to be taken into account if they encourage the exploitation of previously untapped potential and thereby transform living standards and growth prospects. It is in this context that the exceptional scale and speed of urban growth and its particular nature were so important.[39]

38 Some years ago Boserup made effective use of one form of this argument, but her model was one in which the changed methods of agriculture adopted to meet the challenge of rising population resulted in the broad maintenance of a given level of output per head per annum at the cost of a rise in the number of hours worked per annum. I have in mind changes which substantially increase labor productivity whether measured by the hour or by the year, although a part of the latter may be achieved because the workload becomes less markedly seasonal and therefore there are fewer periods during the year when labor is intermittent. Ester Boserup, *The Conditions of Agricultural Growth* (London, 1965), 41–55.

39 Some further aspects of the gain in agricultural output per man and per acre are examined in Wrigley, "Some Reflections on Corn Yields and and Prices in Preindustrial Economies," in John Walter and Schofield (eds.), *Death and the Social Order,* forthcoming.

Brinley Thomas

# Escaping from Constraints: The Industrial Revolution in a Malthusian Context

The industrial revolution was Britain's response to an energy shortage which afflicted its economy in the second half of the eighteenth century. A population explosion intensified the need to change its energy base from wood fuel to fossilized fuel. At that time Britain was unique in having to face this problem, which manifested itself in increasingly heavy pressures on land use—for bread grains, pasture for animal products, timber for ship-building and housing, charcoal for the iron industry, oaks for the Royal Navy, and wood ash for alkalies for the bleaching process in textiles. Moreover, additional land was required to meet the needs of urban growth, manufacturing plant, and transport facilities.[1]

Shortages of timber and timber products, such as charcoal, were at the heart of the problem of imbalance; Britain was dangerously dependent on outside sources (particularly the Baltic countries) for supplies of timber, iron, and naval stores. The upsurge in construction entailed a considerable expansion in the use of timber, beyond the increase in domestic supply made possible by the canals and turnpikes. Between the long swing peaks of 1752 and 1792, imports of fir timber went up from 40,000 to 313,000 tons. Reports from all over the country indicated that

Brinley Thomas is Visiting Professor of Economics at the University of California, Davis. He is the author of *Migration and Economic Growth: A Study of Great Britain and the Atlantic Economy* (New York, 1973; 2nd ed.).

The author is grateful to Carlo Cipolla, Stanley Engerman, and Eric Kerridge for their valuable comments on an earlier version of this article.

1 See Thomas, "Toward an Energy Interpretation of the Industrial Revolution," *Atlantic Economic Journal,* VIII (1980), 1–15. Part of the inspiration for this line of argument comes from E. Anthony Wrigley's pathbreaking article, "The Supply of Raw Materials in the Industrial Revolution," *Economic History Review,* XV (1962), 1–16. John U. Nef, *The Rise of the British Coal Industry* (London, 1932), 2 v., argued that the timber shortages of the sixteenth and seventeenth centuries constituted a national crisis necessitating a large-scale switch to coal. Most economic historians now agree that the processes using coal in the sixteenth and seventeenth centuries did not alter the fundamentally agrarian character of that society and do not justify the term "first industrial revolution."

these imports were essential in the absence of adequate supplies of native timber.[2]

The solution to the energy crisis—the substitution of coal for charcoal in the making of bar iron—was not achieved until a fundamental innovation had occurred. It came in 1784, when Henry Cort's puddling and rolling process overcame all of the technical problems of using coal to refine pig iron into bar iron in a reverberatory furnace. "Without these discoveries we could never have had such fundamentally important pieces of metal as a railway iron or a ship's plate. The unaided hammer could not have achieved them. The puddle and the grooved roll closed the era of the blacksmith's supremacy and opened the era of machine production." It was the quality of the new bar iron, together with James Watt's steam engine, which made possible the modern world of machine-tools, railroads, and steamships.[3]

An important part of the argument of this article is that the discontinuity at the end of the eighteenth century is to be seen in a profound disturbance to the *structure* of the economy as a result of the new coal-iron technology. This structural change tends to be hidden if we observe only the movement of national aggregates of output or investment. In analyzing the effects of major innovations, Schumpeter emphasized that ". . . it is disharmonious or one-sided increase and shifts *within* the aggregative quantity which matter. Aggregative analysis . . . not only does not tell the whole tale but necessarily obliterates the main (and the only interesting) point of the tale."[4]

From 1760 to 1801 English agriculture was unable to keep pace with the growth of population; domestic agricultural output grew by an average of only 0.44 percent per year, while population increased by an average of 0.83 percent per year. It was a Malthusian crisis. Yet growth rates accelerated to a still higher level. The population of Great Britain doubled, from 10.7 million

2   Thomas, "The Rhythm of Growth in the Atlantic Economy of the Eighteenth Century," *Research in Economic History*, III (1978), 18. *Reports of the Commissioners appointed to inquire into the State and Condition of the Woods, Forests and Land Revenues of the Crown, Eleventh Report, Naval Timber, House of Commons Journal* (London, 1792), Appendix 11, 314–327.
3   J. Russell Smith, *The Story of Iron and Steel* (New York, 1913), 75.
4   Joseph A. Schumpeter, *Business Cycles* (New York, 1939), I, 134.

to 21 million, between 1801 and 1851, a growth rate of 1.36 percent per year.[5]

How could this unprecedented swarming of people on a small, offshore island be made consistent with a rising standard of living? It was impossible on the fixed area of English cultivable land, whatever miracles English technological progress in agriculture might accomplish. The way out was for England (through a transportation revolution and international trade) to endow itself with the equivalent of a vast extension of its own land base. Because it was the first to switch from wood fuel to fossilized fuel, it was able to become the workshop of the world and exchange the industrial fruits of its new technology for abundant cheap food from newly settled overseas countries.

Britain in the nineteenth century drew heavily on the food output of land-rich continents and paid for it with manufactured goods embodying its relatively plentiful capital, labor, and technical expertise. This exchange was in effect the equivalent of a vast importation of land; from Britain's point of view it was what the Atlantic economy of the nineteenth century entailed. It was in the second half of the century that most of the harvest of the industrial revolution was reaped, because it took several decades (from 1790 to 1850) to prepare the ground for the new economy (machine-tools, railroads, and steamships). The world-wide network made possible by coal, iron and steel, the transportation revolution, new technology, capital exports, international migration, and free trade entailed running down British agriculture to less than 5 percent of national income. This division of labor and specialization, although highly profitable, entailed great hazards for Britain and in the long run was destined to be a short-lived source of enrichment.

In short, Britain's industrial revolution was a drama in three acts.

Act I. 1760–1800   The energy shortage was solved through fundamental innovations by Henry Cort and James Watt.

---

5 Nicholas F. R. Crafts, "British Economic Growth, 1700–1831: A Review of the Evidence," *Economic History Review*, XXXVI (1983), 190.

Act II. 1800–1846    In the transition period investment in ma-
                     chine tools, railroads, and steamships laid
                     the foundations of a modern economy.
Act III. 1846–1900   Britain achieved economic fulfillment as the
                     workshop of the world and the center of the
                     Atlantic economy.

Space does not allow a full statement of the argument relating to
Acts II and III. This article confines itself to the structural impact
of the change in the energy base (1760 to 1800), the part played
by food imports (1815 to 1856), and a brief summary of the
resulting payoff in the second half of the nineteenth century.

FROM WOOD TO FOSSILIZED FUEL, 1760–1800    Despite the inad-
equacies of eighteenth-century records of prices and outputs, recent research has been able to throw new light on the structural
changes in the British economy between 1760 and 1800. An au-
thoritative contribution has been made by Feinstein in his work
on British capital formation from 1760 to 1860. I use his results
to explore the nature and extent of the strains on the economy in
a period of rapid population growth.[6]

One of Feinstein's most interesting findings refutes the standard notion about the subsidiary role of capital formation in the
early phase of the industrial revolution; total investment as a
proportion of gross domestic product rose from 8 percent in the
1760s to 13 percent in the 1780s and 14 percent in the 1790s. We
can quantify the competing pressures by disaggregating total capital formation into four components—agriculture, residential and
public building, industry and trade, and transportation. Between
the 1760s and the 1770s agriculture, in relative terms, increased
from 33 percent to 37 percent of the total, and transportation
(canals, ships, roads, and carriages) rose from 23 percent to 29
percent. The relative share of industry and trade, however, fell
sharply from 20 percent to 12 percent, and residential and public
building decreased from 25 percent to 22 percent.[7]

6  Charles H. Feinstein, "Capital Formation in Great Britain," in Peter Mathias and
Michael M. Postan (eds.), *Cambridge Economic History of Europe*, VII. *The Industrial Economies: Capital, Labour and Enterprise* (Cambridge, 1978), Pt. 1, 28–96.
7  *Ibid.*, 91. According to Crafts' revised estimates, the investment ratios are as follows:
1760 5.7%, 1780 7.0%, 1801 7.9%. Crafts, "British Economic Growth," 195. These new

A closer analysis of industrial investment between the 1760s and the 1770s is revealing. In absolute terms, investment in industrial and commercial building went down from £0.97 million to £0.73 million, industrial machinery and equipment from £0.27 million to £0.11 million, and mining and quarrying from £0.08 million to £0.04 million (see Table 1). The Phelps Brown-Hopkins index of the real wages of building craftsmen in southern England fell by about 20 percent between the early 1740s and the end of the 1780s. Since this series is for southern England, it ignores the rise in real wages in the textile areas of northern England. To overcome this deficiency, Wrigley and Schofield used a northern wage series as well as the Phelps Brown-Hopkins series to produce a composite national index, which shows a rise during the 1770s to a level about equal to that of the early 1740s. However, as the authors point out, if the 1770s and 1780s are averaged, even in this series real wages were probably little more than stationary, with the annual population growth rate just under 1 percent.[8]

The evidence suggests that something very odd was happening to the economy. In the 1770s as compared with the 1760s, the level of real investment in manufacturing (factories, machines, and equipment) and coal mining actually fell by one third, whereas in transportation it increased by over one third and in

---

estimates do not in themselves call into question Feinstein's figures on the sectoral composition of gross domestic capital formation. Since the analysis in this section is concerned with sectoral shifts, I have used Feinstein's orders of magnitude.

Feinstein's method of estimation is an exercise in "back projection" from 1860. "In almost every case we have had to rely on fragmentary evidence held together by a multitude of more or less arbitrary assumptions. In the main, however, these have been specific and self-contained assumptions. . . . With a few exceptions, we have not assumed a particular relationship between the level of growth of capital and the level of growth of population or of real national product." The one important exception is the assumption that "the volume of capital expenditure on industrial and commercial building and on machinery was proportional to the movement in the index of industrial production." Feinstein, "Capital Formation," 82, 647, fn. 212. The index used was Walther Hoffmann's (excluding building) from his book, *British Industry, 1700–1950* (Oxford, 1955). On balance, Feinstein is justified in his view that "there does not at present appear to be a better method of estimation." Feinstein, "Capital Formation," 56.

8 E. Henry Phelps Brown and Sheila V. Hopkins, "Seven Centuries of Building Wages," *Economica*, XXII (1955), 195–206; Wrigley and Roger S. Schofield, *The Population History of England, 1541–1871: A Reconstruction* (Cambridge, Mass., 1981), 432, 442. The Phelps Brown-Hopkins index was spliced with Gilboy's index of the real wages of building labor in Lancashire: Elizabeth W. Gilboy, "The Cost of Living and Real Wages in Eighteenth-Century England," *Review of Economic Statistics*, XVIII (1936), 140.

Table 1  Gross Domestic Fixed Capital Formation, Great Britain, 1761–1860, at Constant Prices (£m p.a., decade averages, at 1851–1860 prices)

| | 1761–70 | 1771–80 | 1781–90 | 1791–1800 | 1801–10 | 1811–20 | 1821–30 | 1831–40 | 1841–50 | 1851–60 |
|---|---|---|---|---|---|---|---|---|---|---|
| Residential and Social | | | | | | | | | | |
| 1. Dwellings | 1.49 | 1.38 | 2.17 | 3.35 | 4.58 | 5.82 | 8.91 | 10.28 | 7.60 | 10.25 |
| 2. Public buildings and works | 0.15 | 0.14 | 0.22 | 0.33 | 0.46 | 0.58 | 1.07 | 1.54 | 1.52 | 2.05 |
| Agriculture | | | | | | | | | | |
| 3. Farm buildings, improvements, and equipment | 2.18 | 2.62 | 3.31 | 4.26 | 4.06 | 4.45 | 4.08 | 4.71 | 6.16 | 6.90 |
| Industry and Commerce | | | | | | | | | | |
| 4. Industrial and commercial buildings | 0.97 | 0.73 | 2.13 | 2.20 | 3.04 | 4.16 | 6.81 | 8.52 | 8.15 | 10.99 |
| 5. Industrial machinery and equipment | 0.27 | 0.11 | 1.10 | 0.88 | 0.84 | 1.28 | 2.65 | 3.51 | 4.18 | 5.65 |
| 6. Mining and quarrying | 0.08 | 0.04 | 0.08 | 0.16 | 0.12 | 0.25 | 0.28 | 0.63 | 0.88 | 1.71 |
| 7. Gas and water | — | — | — | — | — | 0.19 | 0.23 | 0.45 | 1.05 | 2.32 |
| Total (industry and commerce) | 1.32 | 0.88 | 3.31 | 3.24 | 4.00 | 5.88 | 9.97 | 13.11 | 14.26 | 20.67 |
| Transport | | | | | | | | | | |
| 8. Railways | — | — | — | — | — | 0.10 | 0.10 | 3.67 | 14.11 | 8.78 |
| 9. Roads and bridges | 0.53 | 0.52 | 0.53 | 0.49 | 0.47 | 0.78 | 1.15 | 1.19 | 1.02 | 1.01 |
| 10. Carriages and coaches | 0.20 | 0.20 | 0.30 | 0.40 | 0.50 | 0.60 | 0.80 | 1.00 | 1.30 | 1.70 |
| 11. Canals and waterways | 0.22 | 0.30 | 0.25 | 1.04 | 0.70 | 0.57 | 0.52 | 0.47 | 0.19 | 0.17 |
| 12. Docks and harbors | 0.02 | 0.04 | 0.05 | 0.07 | 0.68 | 0.42 | 0.30 | 0.45 | 0.85 | 1.46 |
| 13. Ships | 0.53 | 0.77 | 0.98 | 1.13 | 1.12 | 1.31 | 1.39 | 2.17 | 2.42 | 5.00 |
| Total (transport) | 1.50 | 2.03 | 2.11 | 3.13 | 3.47 | 3.78 | 4.26 | 8.95 | 19.89 | 18.12 |
| Total | 6.64 | 7.05 | 11.12 | 14.31 | 16.57 | 20.51 | 28.29 | 38.59 | 49.43 | 57.99 |

SOURCE: Feinstein, "Capital Formation in Great Britain," 40. Reprinted from Cambridge Economic History of Europe, VII, with permission of Cambridge University Press.

*Fig. 1*  Gross Domestic Fixed Capital Formation, Great Britain,
1761–1860, at 1851–1860 Prices, by Sector

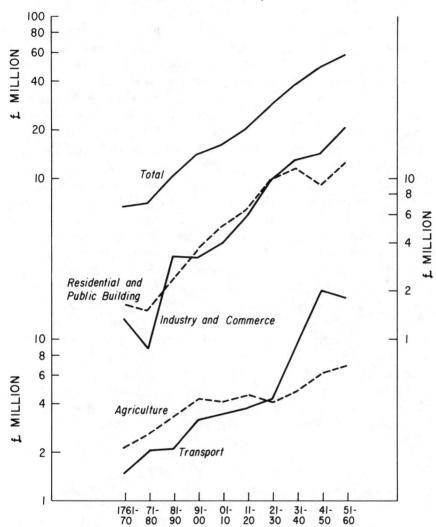

SOURCE: Table I.

agriculture by one fifth (Table I and Figure I). At the same time,
net investment abroad doubled in real terms, from £0.5 million
to £1.0 million per annum. How can one explain this extraordinary slump in industrial investment? Was it part of the economic
disruption caused by the American War of Independence? It is

difficult to think of any reason why the impact of that war should have been felt exclusively by manufacturing and mining.

A possible explanation is to be found in the increasing difficulties of the charcoal iron industry. Manufacturing depended on iron as its basic input; an estimate for 1788 shows that over a half of the iron consumed in Britain was made with charcoal, and about 75 percent of this charcoal iron was imported from Sweden and Russia. Between the 1740s and the 1770s the average price of charcoal went up by 45 percent, and imports of bar iron doubled from 22,500 to 44,100 tons. In the 1760s fuel costs per ton of pig iron in charcoal furnaces were substantially higher than in coke furnaces. Between the period 1765 to 1769 and 1770 to 1774 aggregate British output of pig iron remained stationary at 40,000 tons; production in the charcoal sector declined by 4,000 tons and this fall was exactly offset by a rise in the coke sector. The obsolescent charcoal iron industry was battling for survival, but the new coal-iron technology was not yet ready to take over both the refining and the smelting processes. It was a state of disequilibrium characterized by a dynamic shortage. In this situation the demand curve for charcoal moves to the right with increasing shifts, while the supply curve moves with only small shifts. Each time the market price rises toward a new equilibrium point, the demand curve has shifted again before the new equilibrium point is reached; disequilibrium persists and the market price keeps going up. The magnitude of the dynamic shortage depends on the extent of the demand shifts, the reaction speed in the market (the ratio of the rate of price rise to the excess demand), and the elasticities of demand and supply.[9]

9  Charles K. Hyde, *Technological Change and the British Iron Industry, 1700–1870* (Princeton, 1977), 79, 80, 93–94. Philip Riden, "The Output of the British Iron Industry before 1870," *Economic History Review*, XXX (1977), 448. The supply shifts of charcoal were small because charcoal could not benefit from the transportation revolution (the canals) as did coal. Most of the charcoal came from coppices planted near the iron furnaces and needed about 20–24 years to mature. Most of these coppices were isolated and could not be reached by wagons. Despite canals, charcoal carriers, using horses, remained in active employment until Cort's puddling process put them out of work. R. A. Lewis, "Transport for Eighteenth-Century Ironworks," *Economica*, XVIII (1951), 278–284. For a full account of the model of dynamic shortage, see Kenneth J. Arrow, "Price-Quantity Adjustments in Multiple Markets with Rising Demands" (Santa Monica, 1958); *idem* and William M. Capron, "Dynamic Shortages and Price Rises: the Engineer-Scientist Case," *Quarterly Journal of Economics*, LXXIII (1959), 292–308.

On another side of the picture, technical innovations in mining, together with the transportation revolution—particularly the building of canals—had a favorable effect on the supply of coal. The average cost per ton-mile of moving coal by canal was reduced to one quarter of the corresponding cost by land carriage. Between 1751 to 1755 and 1781 to 1785, the annual output of coal in Northumberland and Durham (most of which went by sea to London) rose by only 43 percent, whereas in the rest of the British coal fields, where canals were important, production doubled to 70 percent of the national total as against 30 percent for Northumberland and Durham.[10]

These substantial shifts in the supply curve of coal in the inland areas were accompanied by only small shifts in domestic demand, because the technical problem of using coal instead of charcoal in making bar iron had not been satisfactorily solved. Until this crucial bottleneck was overcome, the economy continued to be plagued by a paralyzing structural imbalance. In contrast to the rising price of charcoal, the price of coal, in the absence of monopolistic control, would tend to fall. That this was in fact what happened is shown in Figure 2, which plots the prices of charcoal and coal in relation to the index of the average price of producer goods between 1740 and 1799. A marked rise in the relative price of charcoal was accompanied by a downward trend in the relative price of coal, which was especially evident in the 1760s and 1780s when the coal market was not regulated.[11]

In 1784 Cort invented the puddling and rolling process, which overcame satisfactorily all the problems of substituting coal or coke for charcoal in refining pig iron into bar iron. This innovation removed the underlying cause of structural disequilibrium, but the full implications necessarily took time to unfold. The new process had hardly any influence on production in the 1780s. The main reason why real investment in industry and

10 William T. Jackman, *The Development of Transportation in Modern England* (London, 1966; 3rd ed.), 449; Sidney Pollard, "A New Estimate of British Coal Production, 1750–1850," *Economic History Review*, XXXIII (1980), 229.

11 The market price of coal reached such a low level by the end of the 1760s that the owners formed a cartel, the Limitation of the Vend, in 1772. By this means they were able to achieve an artificial rise in price, but, despite this interference, the fall in the *relative* price of coal still persisted until the end of the 1780s. See Paul M. Sweezy, *Monopoly and Competition in the English Coal Trade, 1550–1850* (Cambridge, Mass., 1938), 164.

*Fig. 2*   Charcoal and Coal Prices as Percentage of Producer Goods Price
Index, 1740–1800, Great Britain (Decade Averages)

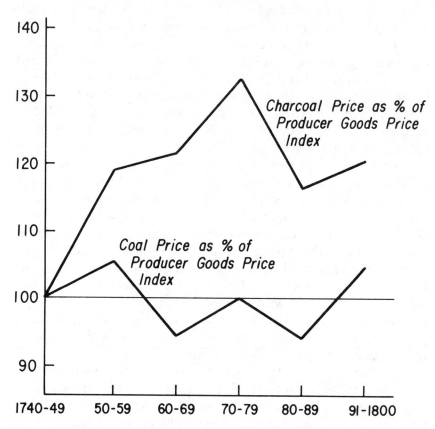

SOURCES: Charcoal price, Hyde, *Technological Change in the British Iron Industry,* 79. Coal
price, average of Westminster School and Navy Victualling series, William H. Beveridge,
*Prices and Wages in England from the Twelfth to the Nineteenth Century* (London, 1966; orig.
pub. 1939), I, 194–196, 577–578. Producer goods price index, 'Elizabeth B. Schumpeter,
"English Prices and Public Finance, 1660–1822," *Review of Economics and Statistics,* XX
(February 1938).

mining rose substantially in that decade was that the pressure of
dynamic shortage impelled many ironmasters to adopt the stamping and potting process developed by John and Charles Wood.
This process successfully substituted coal for charcoal in refining
pig iron into bar iron, but not in a reverberatory furnace; it was
a welcome second-best to the solution which Cort ultimately
achieved. It is estimated that, in the 1780s, about half the bar iron

produced in Britain was made with the potting process and that nearly all the forges adopting it were built during that decade. With the breakthrough of the new coal-iron technology, investment incentives in the manufacturing and mining sector during the 1790s were transformed. Coal output in the fifteen years between 1781 to 1785 and 1796 to 1800 increased by no less than 45 percent (from 7,750,000 to 10,960,000 tons) and then grew to 64,514,000 tons by 1854. Pig iron production rose from 62,000 tons in the early 1780s to 154,000 tons in 1796 to 1800 and reached 3,070,000 tons by 1854.[12]

In the revitalized iron industry, the adoption of steam power enhanced the momentum, as new puddling furnaces and a new generation of puddlers had to be brought into existence to keep pace with the unprecedented demands of the forges. That the price of south Wales bar iron fell from £14 a ton in 1804 to £7.5 a ton in 1824 in the face of enormous increases in demand demonstrates the dramatic impact of the innovation of 1784 on productivity. By 1804 British iron masters had taken over the bulk of the home market and by 1815 net exports were nearly a third of the output of 395,000 tons of pig iron. After the Napoleonic Wars, the British market for Swedish charcoal iron fell to 15 to 20 percent of Swedish exports (mainly bar iron with special qualities for steel-making), as compared to 40 percent at the end of the eighteenth century. Powerful linkage effects were felt throughout the economy, particularly in the introduction of new capital goods, machine-tools, and factory production methods. The age of fossilized fuel had begun with a vengeance; the industrial revolution had been achieved.[13]

ENGLAND'S FOOD IMPORTS, 1815–1856    The previous analysis has shown that there had to be a long transition before the industrial revolution could bring into existence an international economy transformed by railroads and steamships. A glance at

12   Hyde, "Technological Change in the British Wrought Iron Industry, 1750–1815: A Reinterpretation," *Economic History Review,* XVII (1974), 198. On the merits and defects of the stamping and potting process see C. R. Morton and N. Mutton, "The Transition to Cort's Puddling Process," *Journal of the Iron and Steel Institute* (1967), 723–724; Pollard, "British Coal Production," 229; Riden, "British Iron Industry," 448, 455.
13   Ernst F. Söderland, "The Impact of the British Industrial Revolution on the Swedish Iron Industry," in L. S. Pressnell (ed.), *Studies in the Industrial Revolution* (London, 1960), 58.

Figure 1 shows a dramatic expansion in annual investment in transportation from £4 million in the 1820s to £19 million in the 1840s and 1850s; most of this new capital went into the building of railroads and steamships. The steep gradient of this boom was the economic echo effect of the equally steep rise in investment in coal and iron between the 1780s and the 1830s. The outcome of this development in the second half of the nineteenth century— the Atlantic economy—explains why Britain's rapid population growth was accompanied by falling food prices and rising real wages. In earlier periods the problem was met in other ways and the outcome was not always so favorable. In their discussion of the issue, Wrigley and Schofield argue that, until about the end of the eighteenth century, rising population growth rates involved an even faster growth in food prices, but that at the turn of the century this longstanding relationship disappeared, even though population growth rates were rising to a peak. They remark that this change constituted a remarkably vivid tribute to the increase in the productive capacity of English agriculture in the period after about 1780.[14]

The outstanding importance of the English agricultural revolution, from 1750 to 1880, is accepted by most economic historians. The authors of a well-known textbook on the agricultural revolution write:

> The agricultural revolution . . . had performed its role in the process of industrialization. Output had risen almost as fast as population, and as late as 1868 it was estimated that no less than 80 percent of the food consumed in the United Kingdom by a highly urbanized and industrialized population had been grown at home.[15]

Yet, on the occasion of the Silver Jubilee of the British Agricultural History Society in 1977, Parker wrote an admirable article in which he pointed out that there are still some unanswered questions about the agricultural revolution:

14 Wrigley and Schofield, *Population History*, 404. Fig. 10.2 plots annual rates of growth of population and an index of the price of consumables (25-year moving averages).
15 Jonathan D. Chambers and Gordon E. Mingay, *The Agricultural Revolution, 1750–1880* (London, 1966), 207–208. No source is given for the 1868 estimate. For a vigorous attack on the received wisdom, see Eric Kerridge, "The Agricultural Revolution Reconsidered," *Agricultural History*, XLIII (1969), 463–475, and the reply by Mingay, 477–481.

By what means was Britain's growing population fed in these critical decades before the massive imports of overseas meat and grain? Could not some balance sheet be constructed to show the relative importance of dietary changes—whether restrictions or improvements—increased grain yields and meat supplies at home, Irish and other imports, and finally the new crops and abandonment of fallow?[16]

Clearly, these questions call for quantitative answers. In this section I examine one major aspect of the general question—the scale of Irish and other imports of food, concentrating principally on the period from the end of the Napoleonic Wars to the beginning of the steamship era.

Until 1826, British foreign trade statistics include imports from and exports to Ireland, and it is possible to see exactly how much food Britain imported from Ireland and how much from foreign countries. One of the first effects of the population explosion in England had been a sharp rise in the prices of livestock products; the resulting public clamor in the 1750s and 1760s forced the English parliament to repeal the Cattle Acts, which had long prohibited the import of Irish livestock and animal products in the interest of English breeders. The effect was spectacular. Between 1760 and 1790 the quantity of Irish shipments of beef to England went up threefold, butter sixfold, and pork sevenfold, and by 1796 Ireland was supplying 44 percent of Britain's imports of grain, butter, and meat. When England was facing the threat of starvation under Napoleon's blockade, she had even more incentive and opportunity than usual to take all she could from her Irish colony. No less than 35 percent of the total amount of grains, meal, and flour imported into Britain in the fifteen years between 1800 and 1814 came from Ireland. Between 1784 to 1786 and 1814 to 1816 British imports of grain, meat, and butter from Ireland went up four and a half times from £934,000 to £4,155,000 per annum in current values. Irish land was being called in to alleviate the mounting pressures on English land.[17]

16  William N. Parker, "From the Colonies: a Tempered Tribute," *Agricultural History Review*, XXV (1977), Pt. 2, 7.
17  When the British government stopped keeping records of Anglo-Irish trade, they made an exception of the trade in grains. George R. Porter, in *The Progress of the Nation* (London, 1851), 344; David Macpherson, *Annals of Commerce, Manufactures, Fisheries and*

Thanks to the valuable work of Davis, much-improved data relating to Irish trade are now available, and the comparison of the relative magnitude of Irish and other imports is no longer impeded by the change in the designation of Irish trade in 1826. The original records of imports and exports expressed in official values have been recalculated in terms of current prices, by commodity and area, for three years in each decade—from 1784–1786 to 1854–1856.[18]

Until 1824–1826, imports from Ireland to Britain by commodity were shown separately; after that date they were regarded as part of internal United Kingdom trade and no record was kept (except for grains). Table 2 sets out the values (at current prices) of imports of grains, meat, and butter into Britain from Ireland and from all other countries from 1814–1816 to 1844–1846. Re-exports were too small to make much difference. The basis of the estimates for 1834–1836 and 1844–1846 is explained in a note to the Table. The Irish contribution to total imports was 70 percent in 1814–1816 and 85 percent in 1834–1836. At the latter date total imports were about 11 percent of the estimated income in agriculture, forestry, and fishing.

These figures err on the low side, for they take no account of the substantial purchases of livestock. Porter gives an estimate of £3,397,760 as the value of live animals brought from Ireland to Liverpool in 1837. If we add this amount, the Irish contribution in the late 1830s must have been at least 13 percent of the entire output of English agriculture and over 85 percent of England's imports of grains, meat, butter, and livestock. The figures for 1844–1846 are affected by the Irish potato famine and the repeal of the Corn Laws; they register an enormous increase in imports from overseas—five times the amount in 1834–1836—due to the onset of free trade, but shipments from Ireland as a proportion of total imports fell to 52 percent. Total imports of grains, meat, and butter in 1844–1846 were about 15 percent of the estimated income in agriculture, forestry, and fishing. By 1854–1856 im-

*Navigations* (London, 1805), III, 308, 413; Louis M. Cullen, *Anglo-Irish Trade, 1600–1800* (New York, 1968), 70; W. Freeman Galpin, *The Grain Supply of England during the Napoleonic Period* (New York, 1925), Appendix 8; Ralph Davis, *The Industrial Revolution and Britain's Overseas Trade* (Leicester, 1979), 110, 116.
18   *Ibid.*, 77–126.

Table 2  Great Britain: Imports of Grains, Meat, and Butter from Overseas and from Ireland, 1814–1 to 1844–46 (Annual averages at current prices)

| | IMPORTS OF GRAINS, MEAT, AND BUTTER | | TOTAL IMPORTS (COLS. 1 AND 2) £000 | IMPORTS OF IRISH GRAINS AND MEAL[b] QUARTERS 000 | IMPORTS FROM IRELAND, COL. 2 AS % OF COL. 3 % | INCOME IN BRITISH AGRICULTURE, FORESTRY, AND FISHING[c] £000 | IMPORTS FROM IRELAND, COL. 2, AS % OF COL. 6 % | TOTAL IMPORTS, COL. 3 AS % OF COL. 6[d] % |
|---|---|---|---|---|---|---|---|---|
| | FROM OVERSEAS £000 | FROM IRELAND £000 | | | | | | |
| YEARS | (1) | (2) | (3) | (4) | (5) | (6) | (7) | (8) |
| 1814–16 | 1,714 | 4,155 | 5,869 | 847 | 70.1 | 91,700 | 4.5 | 6.4 |
| 1824–26 | 1,846 | 5,599 | 7,445 | 1,843 | 75.2 | 77,700 | 7.2 | 9.6 |
| 1834–36 | 1,512 | 8,427[a] | 9,939 | 2,774 | 84.8 | 89,700 | 9.4 | 11.1 |
| 1844–46 | 7,377 | 7,966[a] | 15,343 | 2,622 | 52.0 | 103,200 | 7.7 | 14.9 |

SOURCE: Davis, *Industrial Revolution and British Overseas Trade*, 116–123.

a  Estimated on the assumption that imports of meat and butter from Ireland were proportionate to the recorded imports of grains and meal (column 4).
b  Porter, *Progress of the Nation*, 345.
c  Mid-decade estimates based on Phyllis Deane and W. A. Cole, *British Economic Growth, 1688–1959* (London, 1962), 166.
d  Allowing for re-exports of grains, the percentages in column 8 would be: 1814–16 6.2%, 1824–26 9.5%, 1834–36 10.5%, 1844–46 14.6%.

ports of grains, meat, and butter from overseas had trebled compared with 1844–1846 (£22.3 million as against £7.4 million).[19]

An analysis of wheat imports in relation to English output is given in Table 3. The striking change after the repeal of the Corn Laws in 1846 is evident. A quarter of English wheat consumption was supplied by imports in 1847–1856 as against about a tenth in 1837–1846 (excluding Irish imports which would raise it to 12 percent), and this was long before the New World became the major supplier. In 1854–1856 about two thirds of the grain cargoes entering Britain came from Europe and the Near East and only one third from the United States. By 1867–1876 half of the wheat consumed in Britain came from abroad.

The statistics used so far have given an unduly ascetic impression of the British diet—as if the British consumed only bread, butter, and meat. To be realistic we must add tea, coffee, sugar, rice, cheese, fruit, spices, wine, spirits, and other food and drink. All of the above items are grouped together under "Food and

Table 3   England and Wales: Wheat Imports and Home Output, 1829–1868 (Annual averages, nearest 1,000 quarters)

| YEARS | WHEAT OUTPUT | WHEAT IMPORTS[c] | TOTAL CONSUMPTION | IMPORTS[d] AS % OF TOTAL CONSUMPTION |
|---|---|---|---|---|
| 1829–36 | 13,751 | 634 | 14,385 | 4.4 |
| 1836–46[ab] | 15,630 | 1,660 | 17,290 | 9.6 |
| 1847–56[a] | 13,443 | 4,520 | 18,063 | 25.7 |
| 1857–64[a] | 13,279 | 7,285 | 20,264 | 35.4 |
| 1867–76[a] | 10,811 | 10,775 | 21,586 | 50.0 |

SOURCE: Susan Fairlie, "The Corn Laws and British Wheat Production, 1829–76," Economic History Review, XXII (1969), 102.

a   These years were chosen in order to minimize possible errors from changes in the composition of the inspected market figures, on which the author based her output estimates.

b   The year 1842 was omitted for statistical reasons.

c   The author noted that "the imports were admitted officially to the United Kingdom as a whole, but in fact came mostly to England" (102).

d   Not including imports from Ireland. Adding the recorded imports from Ireland (and ignoring any foreign wheat that went into Ireland before 1845, which was negligible) makes total wheat imports as a proportion of consumption in England 8% in 1829–1836 and 12% in 1837–1846.

19   Porter, Progress of the Nation, 344.

Drink" in Table 4. During the Corn Law regime, from 1815 to 1846, Britain's gross imports of food and drink were about one third of the value of domestic agricultural output; allowing for exports and re-exports the proportion was about one quarter. In 1814–1816, the end of the Napoleonic Wars, re-exports of coffee and sugar to Europe were abnormally large. When the restraints of the Corn Laws were removed in 1846, imports of food and drink, excluding imports from Ireland, doubled in ten years, from £26,691,000 in 1844–1846 to £52,769,000 in 1854–1856, which was 47 percent of the approximate value of output in British agriculture, or 37 percent if we allow for exports and re-exports.

The analysis suggests the following conclusions about the period from 1815 to 1846. Notwithstanding the achievements of the agricultural revolution, the supply of grains, butter, meat, and livestock available to the English population would have been smaller by at least one sixth in the 1830s and early 1840s had it not been for imports, mainly from Ireland. This indispensable assistance was being drawn from a colony where little was being done by English landlords (many of them absentee) to bring about agrarian reform. There was no agricultural revolution in Ireland. Sluggish capital formation and technological backwardness, to-

Table 4    Great Britain: Imports of Food and Drink (including Imports from Ireland) in Relation to the Value of Agricultural Output 1814–1816 — 1854–1856 (Annual averages in current prices)

| | IMPORTS OF FOOD AND DRINK[a] | INCOME IN AGRICULTURE, FORESTRY, AND FISHING | COL. 1 AS % OF COL. 2 | COL. 1 MINUS RE-EXPORTS AS % OF COL. 2 | COL. 1 MINUS EXPORTS AND RE-EXPORTS AS % OF COL. 2 |
|---|---|---|---|---|---|
| | £1000 | £1000 | % | % | % |
| YEARS | (1) | (2) | (3) | (4) | (5) |
| 1814–16 | 31,127 | 91,700 | 34.0 | 23.2 | 17.5 |
| 1824–26 | 25,758 | 77,500 | 33.2 | 27.3 | 25.7 |
| 1834–36 | 28,465[b] | 89,700 | 31.7 | 27.2 | 25.5 |
| 1844–46 | 34,657[b] | 103,200 | 33.7 | 29.9 | 28.1 |
| 1854–56 | 52,769[c] | 112,700 | 46.7 | 41.7 | 36.6 |

SOURCES: as in Table 2.

a    Comprising grains, meat, butter, sugar, rice, cheese, fruit, spices, coffee, tea, wine, spirits, other food and drink.
b    Including imports from Ireland calculated as in Table 2.
c    Not including imports from Ireland.

gether with social unrest and the constraints imposed by heavy dependence on the potato, kept the Irish economy far behind the rest of Western Europe. Whereas Irish agriculture made a substantial contribution to England's food supply, average living standards in Ireland declined after 1815. Grain shipments from Irish ports continued throughout the famine years, from 1846 to 1849, albeit at a much reduced level; between 1.1 and 1.5 million Irish people died of famine-related causes and another 1 million emigrated.[20]

The achievements of the English agricultural revolution in the first half of the nineteenth century tend to be exaggerated. In that period England, as an interim measure, drew heavily on the land resources of her Celtic colony; but, substantial though this input was, it was not enough to alleviate severe strains, particularly in southern England. Despite the protection given by the Corn Laws, the level of real investment in buildings, improvements, and equipment in agriculture was stationary between 1800 and 1830 when the rate of population growth was at its height (see Table 1 and Figure 1).

The plight of the agricultural population of southern England, where the vast majority depended on wheat, was very serious. By 1850/51 average weekly wages in agriculture in southern England were 8s.5d., which was 26 percent lower than the average rate in northern England. The incidence of pauperism in the south was 12.1 percent of the population as against 6.2 percent in the north. Contemporary witnesses in the 1830s gave plentiful evidence of a shift by consumers away from wheat to the potato, particularly in the south of England. In this way many workers were able to survive on the lowest possible wage.[21]

At the beginning of the century, 94 percent of the people of southern and eastern England consumed wheat, but in Scotland 72 percent consumed oats; in Wales 80 percent ate barley or oats, and in the north of England 68 percent ate oats or barley. To

---

20 Joel Mokyr, *Why Ireland Starved* (London, 1983).
21 James Caird, *English Agriculture in 1850–51* (London, 1852; 2nd ed.); Redcliffe N. Salaman, *The History and Social Influence of the Potato* (Cambridge, 1949), 523–531. Referring to the low price of potatoes, Caird wrote in 1852: "There could be no greater evil befall the English agricultural labourer, than that any circumstance could compel him to depress his standard of comfort so far as to be content for his principal subsistence with the lowest species of food in this country, the potato." *Idem, English Agriculture,* 518–519.

interpret wheat consumption trends in the first half of the nineteenth century, we must realize that an increasing number of
people were switching from coarse grains to wheat. Between 1800
and 1850 it is estimated that the proportion of the population of
Great Britain who consumed wheat increased from 58 percent to
81 percent. In interpreting this fact one must recognize that "by
the same measure, and with possible implications for the 'cost of
living' debate, a disproportionate share of the increase in wheat
production during the first half of the nineteenth century was
probably absorbed by 'converts,' so that, while overall consumption per head may have been rising, *per capita* consumption among
existing wheat-eaters, who formed the majority of the population,
may have been falling." The converts were in Scotland, the north
of England, and Wales, and the traditional wheat-eaters were in
southern and eastern England where the white loaf had become
a necessity which poor people were reluctant to give up. There
is ample evidence that various adulterants, such as alum, were
added in order to whiten inferior grades of flour for the bread
sold to the mass of the people; the flour was often made out of
the worst kinds of damaged foreign wheat. More research is
needed on this important subject of dietary changes in different
regions of the British Isles in this crucial period.[22]

Much against the expectations of English landowners and
farmers, the quarter of a century after the introduction of free
trade in 1846 turned out to be a golden age for British farming,
based mainly on a shift to livestock production. There was a long
interval before the land resources of continents of new settlement
could be fully mobilized. The American Civil War delayed the
process; the completion of the first American transcontinental
railroad did not occur until 1869. Moreover, during this period,
until about 1870, there was increasing scarcity of foods on the
continent of Europe caused by the population explosion. The
supplies of foodstuffs from these new areas only began to hit
Europe like an avalanche in the 1880s.[23]

22   E. J. T. Collins, "Dietary Change and Cereal Consumption in Britain in the Nineteenth Century," *Agricultural History Review*, XXIII (1975), Pt. 2, 105, 114, 115. See also
Thomas, "Feeding England during the Industrial Revolution: A View from the Celtic
Fringe," *Agricultural History*, LVI (1982), 328–342. See Friedrich Christian Accum, *A
Treatise on Adulteration of Food and Culinary Poisons* (Philadelphia, 1820).
23   "Sometime after 1836 north-western Europe became collectively deficient in the bread
grains. Britain's traditional suppliers not only ceased to be able to meet her needs, but

FULFILLMENT     The delayed impact of the industrial revolution on the international economy was vividly described by Wells in 1889:

> The Bessemer rail, the modern steamship, and the Suez Canal have brought the wheat fields of Dakota and India, and the grazing lands of Texas, Colorado and Australia, and the Argentine Republic, nearer to the factory operatives in Manchester, England, than the farms of Illinois were before the war to the spindles and looms of New England.[24]

The tremendous effects of freight rates on world supplies of wheat are shown in Table 5. Between 1870 to 1874 and 1895 to 1899 freight rates from Chicago to New York fell from 113 to 47 pence per quarter and from New York across the Atlantic to Liverpool from 66 to 23 pence per quarter; the price of American wheat in Liverpool fell by 43 percent. United States wheat exports expanded threefold from 59 to 184 million bushels, and exports from Russia doubled from 55 to 107 million bushels. At last Britain was reaping the benefits of her industrial revolution. By 1870 she reached her peak, being responsible for no less than 32 percent of the world's manufacturing production. Between 1860 and 1910 United Kingdom food imports in real terms rose from £57 million to £260 million; the proportion of her wheat supply coming from overseas rose from 36 percent to 80 percent; meat imports grew from 1 million hundredweights in 1850 to 19 million hundredweights in 1900.[25]

The proportion of Britain's occupied population engaged in agriculture had fallen to 8 percent by 1911, and agricultural rents as a proportion of domestic income had declined from 7 percent in 1855 to 2 percent in 1910. In the half-century ending in 1911,

---

were to some extent competing for available supplies from elsewhere (that is, principally the Russian Black Sea and Volga Steppes and the United States of America)." Fairlie, "The Nineteenth-Century Corn Law Reconsidered," *Economic History Review,* XVIII (1965), 568.

24  David A. Wells, *Recent Economic Changes* (New York, 1889), 91.

25  For a model of the process of interaction between Great Britain and the overseas countries of new settlement, see Thomas, *Migration and Economic Growth: a Study of Great Britain and the Atlantic Economy* (New York, 1973; 2nd ed.), 249–289. League of Nations, *Industrialization and Foreign Trade* (Geneva, 1945), 13; John P. Huttman, "British Meat Imports in the Free Trade Era," *Agricultural History,* LII (1978), 247.

*Table 5*  Freight Rates, Wheat Exports, and Prices, 1870–1899 (Annual averages)

| | FREIGHT RATES | | PRICE OF U.S. WHEAT FROM ATLANTIC PORTS C.I.F. LIVERPOOL | WHEAT EXPORTS (MILLION BUSHELS) FROM: | | | |
| | CHICAGO TO NEW YORK BY RAIL | NEW YORK TO LIVERPOOL BY STEAMER | | USA | CANADA | RUSSIA | INDIA |
| YEARS | PENCE PER QTR. | PENCE PER QTR. | PENCE PER QTR. | | | | |
|---|---|---|---|---|---|---|---|
| 1870–4 | 113 | 66 | 625[a] | 59 | 1 | 55 | 1 |
| 1875–9 | 72 | 60 | 568[a] | 107 | 3 | 71 | 6 |
| 1880–4 | 63 | 35 | 531 | 136 | 4 | 65 | 29 |
| 1885–9 | 61 | 25 | 402 | 110 | 3 | 95 | 36 |
| 1890–4 | 53 | 20 | 379 | 170 | 9 | 104 | 30 |
| 1895–9 | 47 | 23 | 356 | 184 | 16 | 107 | 15 |

SOURCE: Michael Tracy, *Agriculture in Western Europe* (New York, 1964), 22–23.

a  Including wheat from Pacific ports from 1871 through 1875.

the population of the United Kingdom increased by 55 percent and average real wages went up by 96 percent (see Table 6). In the words of an authority on the history of the standard of living, "from some date around the Great Exhibition [1851] onwards the wealth derived from Britain's predominant industrial and commercial position began to be shared to a growing extent by all sections of the community."[26]

Marshall stressed the transportation revolution rather than the rise of manufacturing as the factor facilitating the transformation of England.

> Probably more than three fourths of the whole benefit [England] has derived from the progress of manufactures during the nineteenth century has been through its indirect influences in lowering the cost of transport of men and goods, of water and light, of electricity and news: for the dominant factor of our own age is the development not of the manufacturing, but of the transport industries.[27]

The progress of transportation transformed the food supply situation. What became known as Ricardo's paradox—that technical innovations would have the effect of lowering rents—proved to be historically accurate, in that the world created by the switch from organic to fossilized fuel added immeasurably to the supply of land available to satisfy the wants of Great Britain. In the first half of the nineteenth century, when England's own agricultural productivity barely kept pace with its population increase, it was fortunate to be able to draw on her Celtic periphery; complete fulfillment came in the second half of the century, when her industrial revolution had equipped her to draw on the land resources of the whole world. The expected effect on the course of rents materialized (see Table 6). The process entailed a unique degree of industrial specialization, which, however, brought severe problems for Britain as time went by and the international environment changed fundamentally to her detriment.[28]

26 John Burnett, *Plenty and Want: A Social History of Diet in England from 1815 to the Present Day* (London, 1968), 123.
27 Alfred Marshall, *Principles of Economics* (London, 1920; 8th ed.), 674–675.
28 In the early 1880s, Toynbee observed that "as means of communication improve, we

Table 6  United Kingdom: Food Imports, Real Wages, and Rent, 1860–1910

| YEARS | POPULATION[a] | WHEAT SUPPLY[b] | | % OF WHEAT SUPPLY IMPORTED | REAL WAGES[c] (DECADE AVERAGES) | AGRICULTURAL RENT[d] | AGRICULTURAL RENT AS % OF DOMESTIC INCOME[e] |
| | | IMPORTS | OUTPUT | | | | |
| | MILLION | MN. QTRS. | MN. QTRS. | % | 1850–9 = 100 | £ MILLION | % |
| --- | --- | --- | --- | --- | --- | --- | --- |
| 1860 | 29.0 | 7.4 | 13.1 | 36 | 100 | 45.8 | 6.8 |
| 1870 | 31.6 | 8.6 | 13.4 | 39 | 111 | 48.4 | 5.3 |
| 1880 | 34.9 | 16.0 | 5.9 | 73 | 130 | 50.5 | 4.8 |
| 1890 | 37.8 | 19.2 | 9.4 | 67 | 145 | 41.3 | 3.4 |
| 1900 | 41.5 | 23.0 | 6.8 | 77 | 171 | 37.3 | 2.2 |
| 1910 | 45.3 | 27.8 | 7.1 | 80 | 196 | 36.8 | 2.0 |

SOURCES:

a  For population census years 1861, etc.: Deane and Cole, *British Economic Growth*, 8.

b  *Report of the Agricultural Policy Sub-Committee of the Reconstruction Committee* (London, 1918), Cd. 9079, 9.

c  Decade averages, 1850–1869, 1860–1869, etc.: Pollard, "Labour in Britain," in Mathias and Postan (eds.), *Cambridge Economic History of Europe*, VII, 171.

d  Estimates for England and Wales: Avner Offer, "Ricardo's Paradox and the Movement of Rents in England, c. 1870–1910," *Economic History Review*, XXXIII (1980), 250.

e  Domestic income: Feinstein, *National Income, Expenditure, and Output of the United Kingdom, 1855–1965* (New York, 1972), 74–75.

For the globe as a whole, in the long run, the Malthusian dilemma is part of the human predicament, but in the course of history different corners of the earth have from time to time enjoyed bountiful periods of respite. Britain's industrial revolution was one of these success stories that could not last. Jevons saw the writing on the wall even as Britain was reaching her prime. "For the present," he declared, "our cheap supplies of coal and our skill in its employment, and the freedom of our commerce with other wider lands, render us independent of the limited agricultural area of these islands, and apparently take us out of the scope of Malthus' doctrine." (For "coal" in this sentence, we should now read "fossilized fuels.")[29]

It is interesting to note that, in the first and second editions of *The Coal Question,* Jevons did not insert the word "apparently" in the above sentence. He began to plan a revised third edition but did not live to see it completed. According to Alfred W. Flux, editor of the third edition (1906), "a copy of the volume, on the margins of which Jevons had begun the work of revision, was found by Mrs. Jevons." Revision had only got as far as some verbal changes in four chapters. One of these was the addition of the word "apparently" in the above sentence. It was an important change of meaning. By saying that "our cheap supplies of coal . . . apparently take us out of the scope of Malthus' doctrine," Jevons seemed to point to the transient nature of the benefits bestowed on Britain by her industrial revolution.[30]

Half a century later, when World War I was over, Keynes reaffirmed Jevons' prophetic vision.

> Up to about 1900 a unit of labour applied to industry yielded year by year a purchasing power over an increasing quantity of food. It is possible that about the year 1900 this process began to be reversed, and a diminishing yield of Nature to man's effort was beginning to reassert itself.

add more and more to the supply of land available for satisfying the wants of a particular place." Arnold Toynbee, *The Industrial Revolution* (Boston, 1956; orig. pub. 1884), 109. Offer, "Ricardo's Paradox and the Movement of Rents," 236–252. See also Peter Lindert, "Land Scarcity and American Economic Growth," *Journal of Economic History,* XXXIV (1974), 876–877.
29  W. Stanley Jevons, *The Coal Question* (New York, 1965; orig. pub. 1865), 199–200.
30  *Ibid.,* xxvii.

Before the eighteenth century mankind entertained no false hopes. To lay the illusions which grew popular at that age's latter end, Malthus disclosed a Devil. For half a century all serious economical writings held that Devil in clear prospect. For the next half-century he was chained and out of sight. Now perhaps we have loosed him again.[31]

It is over sixty years since those famous words were written. After the close of the Atlantic economy and the enormous drain of two World Wars, Britain is once more confronted with the constraint of her "limited agricultural area," although the pressure is temporarily alleviated by North Sea oil. One cannot help thinking that this interpretation may be more realistic than the one suggested by Wrigley and Schofield—that in 1798 "by an ironic coincidence Malthus had given pungent expression to an issue that haunted most preindustrial societies at almost the last moment when it could still plausibly be represented as relevant to the country in which he was born."[32]

31  John Maynard Keynes, *The Economic Consequences of the Peace* (London, 1920), 10.
32  Wrigley and Schofield, *Population History,* 404.

*Ann Kussmaul*

# Time and Space, Hoofs and Grain: The Seasonality of Marriage in England

Marriage, argue Wrigley and Schofield, was the most socially and economically determined of registered demographic events. Rates of nuptiality, for example, depended in part on the relative numbers of men and women in localities, which in turn was a function of local employment opportunities and social definitions of economic roles. The decision to marry was often related to the decision to establish a household as a unit of production as well as reproduction. And on the level more of demographic curiosity, the timing of weddings within the year was sensitive to the annual rhythm of work: spatial variations in its seasonality "exhibit a basic structure which reflects the exigencies of the changing seasonal demand for labour in agriculture," with autumn and spring/summer peaks in marriages mirroring "the slack seasons after the gathering of the 'harvest' of crops and young animals, respectively."[1]

I here propose to exploit this last, most demographically trivial relationship between marriage and the economy. A tool for economic history can be fashioned from the raw materials of historical demography: parish registers. Their spatial breadth and temporal depth are unparalleled as a source for preindustrial history; the seasonality of marriage can be made to reveal both the dominant patterns of work and, more important, the timing of changes in primary economic activities. Forging the tool is not free from difficulties. Influences other than the seasonality of work affected the timing of marriages; these influences represent inter-

Ann Kussmaul is Associate Professor of Economics at Glendon College, York University, Toronto. She is the author of *Servants in Husbandry in Early Modern England* (Cambridge, 1981).

The author wishes to thank the Social Sciences and Humanities Research Council of Canada for its financial support of the research and the Economic and Social Research Council—Cambridge Group for the opportunity to use their aggregative marriage file.

1 E. Anthony Wrigley and Roger S. Schofield, *The Population History of England, 1541–1871: A Reconstruction* (Cambridge, Mass., 1981), 303.

ference with the potential applications and are a major consideration of this article.[2]

PATTERNS OF SEASONALITY     The great regularity in the timing of weddings, their peaks and troughs within the year, is clearly visible in the evidence presented in *Population History*. As a relatively minor aspect of the preindustrial demographic regime, it was accorded only a brief mention. Yet, as this article shows, the seasonality of marriage varied systematically over the long course of registration, and its main driver was changes in the seasonality of work.

National seasonal marriage patterns are summarized in Figure 8.3 and Table 8.5 of *Population History*. The parallel figures and tables for baptisms and burials reveal that marriages changed more in their seasonality than did these two other registered events, and displayed other unusual features. First, the indexes for March and December increased strongly, with the decline in the observance of Lent and Advent as seasons during which the celebration of marriage was prohibited. Second, the change in overall marriage seasonality did not approximate a simple linear decline. Baptisms simply became less seasonal over time, but marriage patterns changed in their seasonality, especially with respect to marriage in the spring and early summer. The most pronounced spring/summer peak in Figure 8.3 does not occur until 1650 to 1699, and that peak is bracketed by secondary peaks in 1600 to 1649 and 1700 to 1749. Finally, the temporal findings suggest the possibility that there was no single national pattern: the distribution of the national sample of marriages is not single-peaked, but bimodal, or even trimodal, with peaks in the autumn, spring/summer, and February.[3]

2   That the pattern of agricultural seasonality changed with time first came to my attention in investigating the decline of farm service. See Kussmaul, *Servants in Husbandry in Early Modern England* (Cambridge, 1981), 105–111.
3   Wrigley and Schofield, *Population History*, 288–300. Monthly index values of 100 would result had marriages been evenly distributed over the days of the year. $\text{Index}_i = ((T_i/T)/(N_i/365.25))100$, where $T_i$ is the number of marriages in month i, T is the number of marriages in the year, and $N_i$ the number of days in month i. The use of indexes allows immediate comparison between places with different annual numbers of marriages and months with different numbers of days. Marriages were not, strictly speaking, prohibited under church law during Lent and Advent. See *ibid.*, 298.

The spatial distribution of marriage seasonality is also discussed in *Population History*. The map of Figure 8.4 shows each of the 404 sample parishes with a symbol indicating the season in which the most important marriage month fell, measured over the long period from 1601 to 1720. Spring/early summer marriage peaks were found in parts of the southeast, the west, and sporadically near the east coast; autumn peaks were predominant in the east and most of the midlands; February peaks, probably representative of strong adherence to the prohibition of marriage in Advent and Lent, were limited to the band of western counties running north from Staffordshire to Lancashire.[4]

SECTIONING THE SAMPLE    In northwest Europe as a whole, differences in marriage seasonality reflect "the changing seasonal demand for labour." It is likely that, within the narrower geographical compass of England, the seasonal demand for the labor of young adults had itself changed over time. The map representing the regional pattern of peak marriage seasons, from 1601 to 1720, in *Population History* (Fig. 8.4) obscures these changes, just as too long a time exposure increases the likelihood of a blurred photograph. That the subject moved can be seen in Figures 1 and 2. Each map covers a forty-year period, 1561 to 1600 and 1681 to 1720 respectively; the movement between the shorter periods can be captured. Figure 1 is dominated by the A's of autumn peaks, except for parts of the southeast, the Wash, and the February band of western counties. In Figure 2, in contrast, A's are almost absent from the west; spring/early summer peaks predominate, and only a hint of this pattern can be seen in the earlier period. Similarly, the tendency for parts of the northwest to display February peaks, barely detectable from 1561 to 1600, was much more pronounced a century later.[5]

4   *Ibid.*, 302. Figure 8.4 is the only spatial representation in the book, aside from the 13 maps of crisis mortality in Appendix A.10. In France, for instance, February marriages were common. *Ibid.*, 393n.
5   See Appendix for differences in method; briefly, the present sample excludes market towns, includes September in eligibility for the Autumn index, and drops from observation in any period parishes with fewer than 60 marriages. A crude system of regional division is employed in Figure 1. The country was arbitrarily sectioned into regions by drawing boundaries at National Grid coordinates ending in 000, that is, at 100-kilometer intervals. Where this division would have produced small coastal strips, they have been included in the adjacent inland region.

*Fig. 1*   Peak Marriage Seasons, 1561–1600

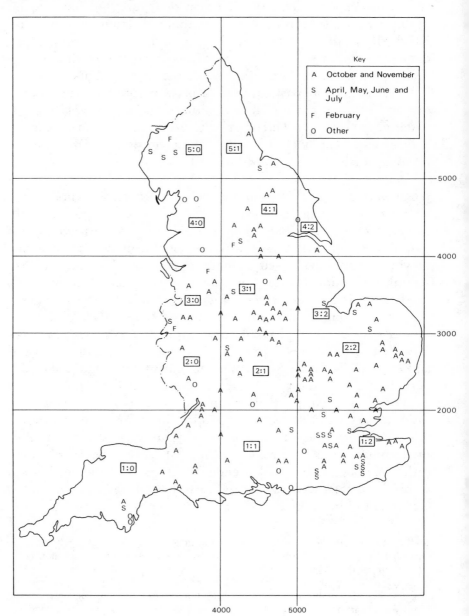

*Fig. 2*  Peak Marriage Seasons, 1681–1720

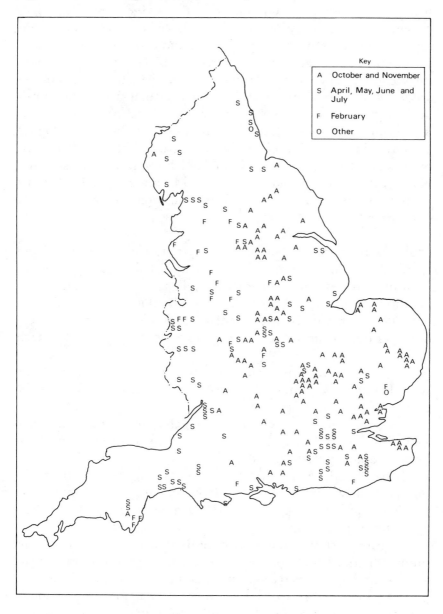

If these peaks represent "the exigencies of . . . seasonal demand for labour in agriculture," the exigencies themselves changed. The grain harvest appears to have been the predominant seasonal influence in the late sixteenth and early seventeenth centuries, but great change had occurred by the later seventeenth and early eighteenth centuries. In Figure 1, no parish except those in areas poorly represented in the sample is distant from an autumn-peaked parish; the greatest diversity of seasonal patterns in well-represented areas occurs nearest to London. By the time of Figure 2, 1681 to 1720, a bifurcation has appeared, with broad sections of western England newly dominated by spring/early summer peaks, the presumed tokens of pastoral farming. Strictly in terms of marriage seasonality, regional specialization on a national scale has emerged.

Multiple maps are cumbersome, and variation along temporal and spatial lines can be more easily manipulated when the twelve monthly indexes for each parish are collapsed into a smaller number of variables. Accordingly, three continuous seasonal indicators have been constructed and calculated for ten overlapping forty-year periods, from 1541 to 1580 until 1721 to 1760, for each parish:

$S_x$, the spring/early summer maximum, the value of the maximal individual monthly index, April to July (a proxy for the degree of broadly pastoral activities);

$A_x$, the autumn maximum, the value of the maximal individual monthly index, September to November (a proxy for broadly arable practice); and

IND, based on the first two indexes, the distance from the no-seasonality coordinates of (100,100) to the combination $(A_x, S_x)$, and inverse proxy for the degree of less seasonal non-agricultural practices.

Figure 3 shows the distribution of parochial observations pulling apart with the passage of time. It is based on plots of the autumn and spring/early summer maxima $(A_x, S_x)$, for periods 1, 3, 5, 7, and 9, 1541 to 1580 until 1701 to 1740. Each "Cloud" was drawn by connecting the outliers, the outermost observations for a single period, to encompass all the observations for that period. The successive clouds were then superimposed on one another. The resulting composite, shaded to indicate the areas of the graph gained by each successive period, shows the growth

*Fig. 3*   Clouds: Outlines of Distributions of (A$_x$, S$_x$)
1541–1580 to 1701–1740

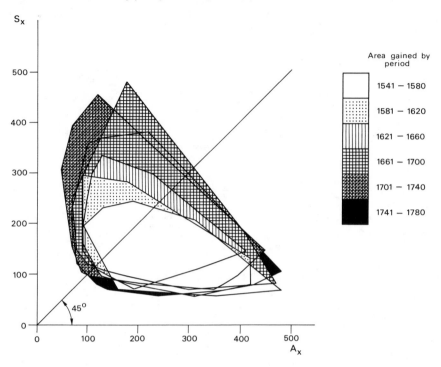

over time of a spring/early summer leg and, less clearly, an implosion toward the nonseasonal point of (100,100). Included in the diagram is a diagonal reference line: along it the spring/early summer and autumn indexes are equal. The figure echoes the change implied in the maps of Figures 1 and 2: above the reference line, the spring/early summer index is greater. The national distribution thus pulls apart in two directions: up, toward early summer; and in, toward aseasonality. The graph is defective in that it is based on the outliers of the distributions, but there is no more graphic way of showing the emergence of a strong differentiation in seasonal marriage behavior.

Figure 3 resembles a growing cloud; Figure 4 might represent two flocks of birds in flight. The scatter diagrams of the autumn and spring/early summer indexes for two regions are plotted on its panels; the observations for 1601 to 1640 are marked as "." and as "x" for 1701 to 1740. In the first panel, the west (regions 1:0, 2:0, and 3:0 on Figure 1), the whole distribution drifts away

*Fig. 4* Scatter Diagrams of ($A_x$, $S_x$), 1601–1640 and 1701–1740, Two Regions

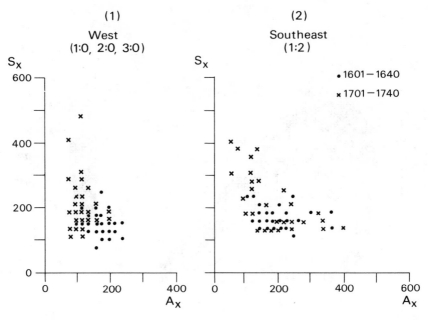

from autumn marriages toward either spring/early summer marriages or aseasonality. In the second panel, the southeast (region 1:2, which includes the de-industrializing Weald), the clumped observations of 1601 to 1640 scatter over the next century in one of three directions, out toward greater autumn seasonality, up toward greater spring/early summer seasonality, or in toward even greater aseasonality. The arbitrary regions employed in this article may not always delineate homogeneous areas, but regions homogeneous in one period may not be so in another.[6]

Two more formal statistical methods show the differentiation over time and space, and the mutual influence of time and space,

6 Other regions show somewhat similar patterns. Region 4:0 moves up and to the left, in a pastoral direction, as did its southern neighbors; so does the northeastern region (5:1). The north midlands (3:1) drifts down, away from early summer, as does East Anglia. The Wash (3:2) scatters in the arable and pastoral directions, as the southeastern region did. Three other regions show a different pattern: the distributions for the south midlands (2:1), Yorkshire (4:1), and the northwest (5:0) all draw in toward aseasonality between the two periods.

on the national series. Table 1 contains the means of the parochial indexes for autumn and spring/early summer in each forty-year period from 1541 to 1580 until 1721 to 1760, and the associated coefficients of variation. The mean spring/early summer index grows until the later seventeenth century, as most of the previous evidence suggests that it must; the mean autumn index declines until the mid-seventeenth century before regaining some of its earlier strength. The two means, therefore, usually display opposite trends. The coefficients of variation, in contrast, move in parallel. Parishes became more differentiated in their seasonality; their distribution widened around the mean values, but this tendency only established itself after the mid-seventeenth century. Figure 5 helps illustrate this latter point: in it are plotted the mean indexes for two of the regions of Figure 1, and the spatially different behavior can be seen. In East Anglia, region 2:2, the autumn index declines towards the mid-seventeenth century and then recovers, whereas the spring/early summer index rises somewhat, only to fall; in the west midlands, region 2:0, the autumn index also falls to the mid-seventeenth century, but then continues to drop, whereas the spring/early summer index rises until the early eighteenth century before declining (but not to its original level).

Table 1    Mean and Coefficient of Variation, Autumn and Spring/Early Summer Indexes of Marriage Seasonality, 1541–1580 to 1721–1760

| | | AUTUMN MAXIMUM | | SPRING/EARLY SUMMER MAXIMUM | | |
|---|---|---|---|---|---|---|
| PERIOD | DATE | MEAN | C.V. | MEAN | C.V. | N |
| 1. | 1541–1580 | 230.4 | 31.5 | 153.7 | 26.5 | 111 |
| 2. | 1561–1600 | 229.2 | 33.0 | 148.0 | 24.0 | 173 |
| 3. | 1581–1620 | 214.8 | 31.6 | 149.9 | 26.3 | 208 |
| 4. | 1601–1640 | 210.4 | 31.0 | 155.3 | 23.4 | 234 |
| 5. | 1621–1660 | 180.9 | 30.2 | 163.9 | 25.5 | 206 |
| 6. | 1641–1680 | 173.9 | 33.6 | 172.1 | 32.8 | 203 |
| 7. | 1661–1700 | 186.6 | 39.1 | 177.4 | 30.9 | 220 |
| 8. | 1681–1720 | 191.6 | 44.8 | 172.2 | 33.6 | 236 |
| 9. | 1701–1740 | 187.9 | 40.4 | 168.6 | 38.4 | 238 |
| 10. | 1721–1760 | 190.1 | 39.4 | 154.0 | 39.9 | 251 |

*Fig. 5*  Mean Seasonal Indexes of Marriages, West Midlands (region
2:0) and East Anglia (regional 2:2), 1541–1580 to 1721–1760

(a)  Autumn  Maximum

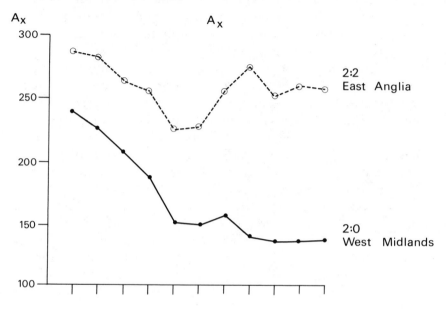

(b)  Early  Summer  Maximum

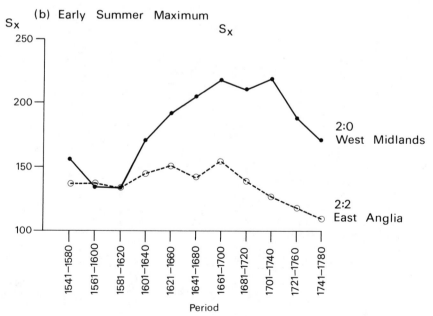

Analysis of variance, finally, demonstrates compactly the changes under investigation. Table 2 presents the results of two runs showing marriage seasonality varying as a function of time and space. In both runs, the independent class variables are PE-RIOD (the odd-numbered forty-year periods of Table 1) and RE-GION (the regions of Figure 1). In the first run, the dependent variable (ANG) is the ratio of spring/early summer marriages to autumn marriages, transformed into the angle formed by a line drawn from the origin to the observation: $ANG = ATAN(S_x/A_x)$. The variable captures swings between predominantly autumnal, arable, and predominantly vernal, pastoral, seasonality. The second dependent variable is IND, as defined above; it shows tendencies toward the loss of all agricultural seasonality.

The analysis exposes the statistical significance of the effects of time (Figure 3), place (Figures 1 and 2), and, at least in the case of the first dependent variable, ANG, of the interaction between

*Table 2*  Analysis of Variance, Two Models

(a)
Dependent Variable: $ANG = ATAN(S_x/A_x)$

| SOURCE | D.F. | F VALUE | PROBABILITY OF GREATER F |
|---|---|---|---|
| Period | 4 | 20.79 | 0.0001 |
| Region | 12 | 21.52 | 0.0001 |
| Period * Region | 48 | 2.04 | 0.0001 |

Model:  F value  7.65
       Prob. > F  0.0001
       $r^2$  0.349

(b)
Dependent Variable: $IND = \log((S_x - 100)^2 + (A_x - 100)^2)^{1/2}$

| SOURCE | D.F. | F VALUE | PROBABILITY OF GREATER F |
|---|---|---|---|
| Period | 4 | 6.18 | 0.0001 |
| Region | 12 | 17.19 | 0.0001 |
| Period * Region | 48 | 1.35 | 0.0572 |

Model:  F value  5.61
       Prob. > F  0.0001
       $r^2$  0.281

time and space after accounting for the separate effects of each independent variable. The results are gratifying, especially because the dependent variables represent only two aspects of seasonal change, the class variables capture only a few of the possible influences on patterns of work and seasonality, and place was defined so arbitrarily according to grid reference boundaries, necessarily obscuring systematic regional patterns.[7]

ALTERNATIVE EXPLANATIONS    The strong and ordered movements over time and space in the seasonality of marriage had as their primary cause shifts in regional patterns of work. The spatial change is consistent with increasing regional specialization and wider integration of commodity markets; the change over time of the aggregate national indexes tracked reversals in the relative prices of arable and pastoral products. But what if the observed changes in seasonality could be fully accounted for in ways unrelated to the seasonality of work? Alternative explanations must be considered.

Changes in religious practice are an obvious possibility. The most striking seasonal pattern of Figure 8.3 in *Population History,* the monthly indexes for the sample of 404 parishes, is not a peak, but the early trough of March (the month most affected by Lent); March gradually filled with marriages with the passage of time. Lent and Advent were fairly scrupulously observed as periods of abstinence from weddings in the sixteenth and early seventeenth centuries; the March and December indexes then rise sharply in the Interregnum, and subside somewhat with the Restoration before beginning their secular rise. By the nineteenth century December had become one of the most popular marrige months. The problem is that the changes in temporal and spatial patterns that have been described may represent nothing more than the removal of a religious mask that had hidden the true seasonality of work.

This argument has two parts. Avoidance of marriage in December (Advent) might have caused a rush to marry in November, and since November is one of the months used to measure the autumn peak, it is possible that the autumn index might be

---

7  The crossed effect of Region * Period for the dependent variable IND misses the customary cutoff for error of 0.05 by 0.0072.

high everywhere in the early periods for no reason other than religious observance. Something of the sort seems to have affected the southwestern region (1:0) more strongly than any other: the sum of November and December indexes is nearly constant over 300 years, with the balance between the two months simply shifting toward December. But the earlier autumn domination of the region's seasonality is still not simply religious: the October and November indexes are each higher than any spring/early summer index until the later seventeenth century.[8]

More complex is the interpretative problem posed by Lent and Rogationtide, the three weeks between Rogation Sunday (five weeks after Easter) and Trinity Sunday, because their dates move. The worst case would be if the oscillation of Lent into April (April 25 is the latest day upon which Easter can fall) and of Rogationtide back and forth through April, May, and June, removed marriages from the spring and early summer, even when it was a true post-peak season in a pastoral economy, so that the pastoral marriage seasonality could not emerge until Lent and Rogationtide filled with marriages.

The worst case, however, is unlikely. Marriages could have crowded into the non-prohibited weeks in the spring and early summer months: in any year, five to thirty days of April were not Lenten, and Rogationtide left free twenty-five to thirty days in April, ten to twenty-nine days in May, and ten to thirty days in June. If this were not the case, April marriages should have paralleled the movement of March marriages throughout the abrupt changes of the seventeenth century. The drop in the observance of Lent in the Interregnum and its modest recovery at the Restoration are clearly etched into the graph of March marriages (Figure 6), but April marriages show no discontinuity in their trend during the relevant periods: they simply continue their imperturbable rise.

Rogationtide creates a more difficult empirical problem: no month was affected by its three weeks as March was by Lent. A small test of the observance of Rogationtide in the period when

8  November plus December indexes for the southwestern region range narrowly from 191 to 236, from 1541–1560 to 1741–1760 (calculated in 20-year periods, over the region, not the parishes). November's share of these marriages dropped from 93% at the beginning of the period to 45% at its end. But in 1561–1580, for example, the June index of 130, the highest early summer index in the region, was well below the October index of 192.

*Fig. 6*  Mean Indexes of Marriages, March and April, 1561–1600 to
         1681–1720

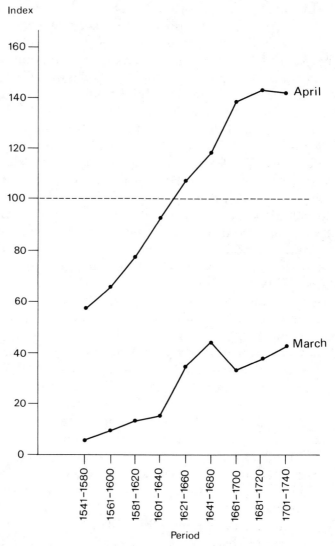

Lent was being well observed is, however, possible. The years
between 1539 and 1639 were divided into three samples. In the
first were those eleven years in which seven days or fewer of May
and fifteen or more of June were in Rogationtide (Easter having
fallen between April 20 and 25); the second included the sixty-
seven years in which fifteen or more May days and seven or fewer

June days were in Rogationtide (Easter March 22–April 12); the third, the remaining twenty-three years, were ignored in the following computation. If the observance of Rogationtide had the power to mask the work-induced seasonality, we would expect May marriages, as a proportion of May–June marriages, to be significantly higher in the first group of years (that is, when most of Rogationtide fell in June) than in the second group. The May proportion was indeed higher in the first group. When most of Rogationtide fell in June, 53.1 percent of May–June marriages occurred in May; when most of Rogationtide fell in May, only 45.4 percent of May–June marriages were celebrated in May. But the small difference in proportions is not statistically significant, according to the usual standards of acceptable errors: the probability of erring in declaring the first proportion larger than the second is 0.32, or 32 percent.[9]

There is stronger evidence that the timing of Lent and Rogationtide affected the distribution of marriages *within* the early summer. In the earlier forty-year periods under observation, April was seldom the month with the highest early summer index (see Figure 7). One hundred years later, in the early eighteenth century, July held the maximal early summer index in far fewer parishes; in general, July peaks had shifted back into June, June into May, and May into April. The evidence appears consistent with the notion of the bunching of marriages following both the peak work season and the prohibited marriage season before 1640, and the later decline of the religious impediment. Had all England grown warmer between 1580 and 1680, the earlier growth of grass would eventually have produced earlier lambing and calving, and would have pulled the pastoral work peak back toward Easter, but this change is hardly likely: the period is generally characterized as a little ice age.[10]

9 The data were drawn from Wrigley and Schofield, *Population History,* 519–521, Appendix 2, Table A2.4. The number of marriages in the early Easter group was 485,879, that in the late Easter group 78,826. The Z-value for the test between proportions was 0.471. See Hubert M. Blalock, *Social Statistics* (New York, 1960), 176–178.
10 Squares within the grid in Fig. 7 are shaded according to the regional maximum monthly index, calculated on the basis of mean values for the region's parishes. Regions with fewer than 4 parishes with at least 60 marriages in a 40-year period are indicated with "NA." On the little ice age, see the special number of this Journal on climate, esp. Reid A. Bryson and Christine Padoch, "On the Climates of History," *Journal of Interdisciplinary History,* X(1980), 583–598.

*Fig. 7* Maximal Spring/Early Summer Marriage Months, by "Region," 1541–1580 to 1721–1760

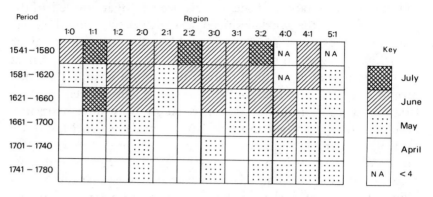

Three further explanations of at least part of the observed changes in marriage seasonality are possible. The first is a change in the social aspects of nuptiality. Within this category are changes in the proportion of clandestine to recorded marriages, and of remarriages to first marriages. Clandestine marriages, which escaped registration, surged in the later seventeenth century. It would have to be shown, however, that there was a systematic tendency for the non-registered to marry at a different time from the registered, and the strongest reason for their so doing lends support to the hypothesis of economic change, for which a path is being cleared. A major motive for concealing a marriage from the church was the selection of a date that fell during a prohibited season. The effect of a rise in clandestine marriages would then have been to lessen the recorded numbers marrying in April, May, and June, but these are the months that gain recorded marriages in the later seventeenth century. Instead of this aspect of England's demographic past having distorted the trend in the recorded seasonality of marriage, is it not possible that real changes in the pattern of work caused changes in the seasonality of marriage, which in turn could accont for another well-known demographic feature of the later seventeenth century, the drop in prenuptial conceptions? The seasonal pattern of first postnuptial conceptions closely followed the pattern of marriage seasonality, but all other classes of conceptions (relative to marriage and parity) including both prenuptial and (ultimately) illegitimate conceptions peaked in early summer. Where marriage peaks moved from the autumn to spring and early summer, the timing of marriage there would have become coincident with the natural timing of conception. Thus, conceptions that would have been prenuptial, had the wedding occurred in October, would become postnuptial with a May wedding, and the recorded number of prenuptial conceptions would fall.[11]

Second, remarriage most likely declined as a proportion of all marriages after the mid-seventeenth century, and the seasonality of the marriages of widows and widowers may well have been affected by different circumstances from that of bachelors and spinsters. For example, had there been a fixed interval between widowhood and remarriage, the seasonality of remarriage might have been determined as much by the seasonality of death of spouses as by the seasonality of work. In general, we might expect remarriage to have been less seasonal than first marriages, and this pattern appears in one unusual marriage register, which includes marital status. The impact of a decline in remarriage, therefore, would have been to sharpen the observed seasonality of marriage. But the impact should stop there: it is difficult to imagine the circumstances in which a decline in remarriage could have shifted the seasonal peaks from autumn to the spring and early summer, and could have done so selectively, with respect to space.[12]

Finally, in earlier work on servants in husbandry, I argued that the most important influence on October marriages in the rural east was the changing proportion of farm servants to day-laborers. Servants in husbandry were released from their annual

11 Wrigley and Schofield, *Population History*, 263; Martin Ingram, "Spousals Litigation in the English Ecclesiastical Courts, c.1340–c.1640," in R. Brian Outhwaite (ed.), *Marriage and Society: Studies in the Social History of Marriage* (London, 1981), 56; Wrigley, "Marriage, Fertility, and Population Growth in Eighteenth-Century England," in *ibid.*, 165.

12 Wrigley and Schofield, *Population History*, 258. The parish with the unusual marriage register is Beccles, Suffolk; it would not be my first choice as a test, from the point of view of this study. First, it was a market town; second, its main non-mercantile activity appears to have been fishing, and tides, currents, and the reproductive cycles of fish are beyond the present scope of this study; finally, as the footnote on p. 258 of Wrigley and Schofield reveals, remarriages did not decline in Beccles. The sum of the monthly deviations of the indexes from the nonseasonal 100 (divided by 12) for first marriages (both spouses single) in Beccles, 1568–1640, was 35.9; that for remarriages (at least one spouse widowed) only 24.4. In 1661–1700, both aggregate measures of seasonality had declined, slightly: the mean sum for first marriages was 34.5; that for remarriages 20.3. The register is in the Suffolk Record Office, Ipswich.

contracts (and their implied celibacy) each Michaelmas, and were more likely to marry then, in October, than were day-laborers, whose shorter contracts were in any case no impediment to marriage. The rise in the October index in the later seventeenth century was taken as indicating an increase in the proportion of young adults entering marriage from farm service, and this in turn was related to changes in the general supply of labor and to changes in relative prices.[13]

Could such a change account for the variation detailed in the first parts of this article? It could and it could not: increases in the proportion of farm servants would have intensified the existing pattern of seasonality, but could not have shifted the location of the peaks in marriage within the year, from one season to the other. The annual hiring dates of servants were not arbitrary: they occurred in the slack season following the peak in the local work year. For example, Martinmas, in November, was the hiring time in arable parts of the north, with its later harvests. In some regions, eighteenth-century sources reveal annual hiring at six-month intervals; concentration of hiring could easily have moved from the autumn (or early summer) to the opposite season had the needs of the work-year changed.[14]

All the findings that depend on the absolute strength of the seasonal indexes (the coefficient of variation, most notably) may well have been caused, at least in part, by two influences operating independently of changes in the underlying pattern of work— namely changes in the proportions marrying as farm servants and as former spouses—but neither could have affected the timing of seasonal peaks. Remarriage and day-laboring act, at most, as dampers on marriage seasonality.

Non-economic factors, including the mode of hiring labor, could only have modified, and not significantly altered, the seasonality of marriage as measured in the autumn and spring/early summer indexes. The precise dating of the peaks within a season (for example in May or in June) may have been influenced by religious observance, and the intensity of peaks by the extent of

13  Kussmaul, *Servants in Husbandry*, 105–111.
14  In the Lincolnshire fens, hiring fairs were held at May Day and again at Martinmas; in parts of eighteenth-century Wiltshire, Worcestershire, Dorset, Somerset, and Gloucestershire, contiguous parishes often hired most of their servants at different seasons. See *idem*, "Statute Sessions and Hiring at Fairs," unpub. ms. (1982).

remarriage and farm service, but none of the probable disturbances could have moved the peaks from one season to another. The field has thus been at least partially cleared for an explanation couched in terms of changing economic exigencies.

PRELIMINARY ECONOMIC IMPLICATIONS    The timing of marriage was not rigid in the English past. If the changes in English marriage seasonality between spring/early summer and autumn had as their primary cause changes in underlying patterns of work, the implications of these findings are far-reaching. They constitute evidence for the emergence of economic integration and growing regional specialization at a reasonably indentifiable time (and, *inter alia,* evidence for the flexibility of what the nineteenth century saw set into interpretative concrete as custom).[15]

In a simple argument for economic integration as prime mover, assume, at a high level of abstraction, that there are only two possible patterns of work to be observed: grain production, harvest-dominated, yielding a high autumn index of marriage seasonality; and pastoral production, dominated by the rearing of lambs and calves, yielding high spring/early summer indexes. To do so is to unlearn English agrarian history, in all its complexity, and to ignore, among other practices, fattening, dairying, alternative husbandry, fishing, and rural industry.[16]

The argument hinges on the two general and different cases in which high autumn seasonality could have been attained. First, high employment in grain production could have resulted from a lack of market integration between places, either for institutional reasons or because of high transportation costs. In this case, parishes would have produced grain, no matter what other additional employments might have been practiced, because grain, the main foodstuff, was not being obtained from more distant suppliers. It

15    I suspect that June would not have gained its romantic aura in North America had school terms ended in April, or September.
16    Fattening without rearing would have no early summer work peak; the seasonality of dairying would be more governed by the summer harvest of hay and the cessation of milking and cheese- and butter-making in the late autumn, except where adequate high-quality fodder was provided for winter feeding and milking. Alternate husbandry might be marked by the bimodal pattern of high autumn and high early summer peaks. The seasonality of fishing depends on the greatly variable seasonality of the reproduction and movement of the fish. Rural industry might be expected to be, in general, aseasonal.

was a case of the "bound and localized" economy, discussed by de Vries, with grain as the subsistence crop.[17]

In the second case, high harvest seasonality could have been the result of high employment in commercial grain production for integrated markets and extra-local consumption. With regard to economic integration and regional specialization, low autumn indexes are, by contrast, amenable to a single interpretation. Especially in the case where low autumn seasonality prevailed throughout a region, it can only mean that the region was dependent on interregional trade for its supply of breadstuffs, and in turn specialized in the production and sale of the products of non-arable activities. As de Vries put it, "one cannot live on butter, cheese, and cabbage alone; and one cannot live on hemp, madder, flax, and coleseed at all." Low autumn seasonality is thus *prima facie* evidence of market orientation; high autumn seasonality is not.[18]

The observed shift away from autumn seasonality in some regions, and its retention in others, can therefore be explained in several different ways, or, more reasonably, in some combination of ways. First, households in areas less suited to grain production could have become better integrated with market production, dropping the subsistence production of grain in favor of other products; second, regions could have become better integrated with supraregional or international markets, dropping their dependence on local grain supplies; or, third, thoroughly integrated regions could have readjusted their market-oriented specializations in response to changes in relative prices.

What case could be made for these explanations for the later seventeenth century? In the model of household specialization proposed by Hymer and Resnick and later applied to early-modern development by de Vries, peasant householders were induced by rising agricultural prices to drop production of non-agricultural subsistence goods for their own use, and to use their land and labor for the commercial production of grain. In this form, the model is poorly suited to the English case, since the later

17  Jan de Vries, *The Dutch Rural Economy in the Golden Age, 1500–1700* (New Haven, 1974), 1.
18  *Ibid.,* 64.

seventeenth century was a time of falling relative prices of cereals. What demands explanation is the dropping of grain production.[19]

One aspect of the model can be salvaged, however. The offer of new goods, products of industry or of international trade, might have induced farmers to increase their production of marketable agricultural goods in order to purchase the new goods. In doing so, they would have concentrated on the production of the goods to which their land and other resources were best suited. Falling cereal prices would have biased this choice away from grain. This argument is de Vries's "capitalism creating its own demand," a demand, in this case, for money income. The later seventeenth century was as likely a time as any for such a process to have occurred, and, by inference, it was there that de Vries located it.[20]

The simplest opening of trade model, in which two regions with different resource endowments enter into trade, fits the available evidence of marriage seasonality neatly. Before the opening of trade, both regions would have produced both arable and pastoral goods; as trade became established, the region with higher-cost grain production would have moved factors out of this field into others, while the lower-cost region would have moved factors into grain production. This pattern fits, roughly, the evidence of Figures 4 and 5, in which the regions that became specialized grain producers saw their spring/early summer marriages drop in the later seventeenth century, while those that specialized in pastoral production saw their autumn indexes decline. Such a finding would have the further advantage of being consistent with many recent suggestions concerning the changes wrought in the later seventeenth and early eighteenth centuries by transportation improvements, and the growth of London as a center of consumption, both absolutely and relative to English population growth.[21]

19 Stephen Hymer and Stephen Resnick, "A Model of an Agrarian Economy with Nonagricultural Activities," *American Economic Review,* LIX (1969), 493–506; de Vries, *Dutch Rural Economy,* 17–21.

20 *Idem, The Economy of Europe in an Age of Crisis* (Cambridge, 1976), 236–254; cf. Joel Mokyr, "Demand vs. Supply in the Industrial Revolution," *Journal of Economic History,* XXXVII(1977), 985. See also, de Vries, "Capitalism Creating its own Demand," in *Economy of Europe,* 176–209.

21 See John Chartres, *Internal Trade in England, 1500–1700* (London, 1977); Wrigley, "A

The simplest version of the third explanation, readjustments in commercial specializations, cannot be wholly true. Most pastoral products, except, most notably, wool, increased in price relative to grain in the later seventeenth century. The problem, however, is to explain the observed regional disparity of response to changing relative prices. All that would be needed to improve the logical power of the third explanation, however, is a certain orderliness of response to the changed relative prices, in which the highest cost producers of grain dropped out first. If grain producers in the west faced higher costs than those in the midlands and east, the As of grain production would have selectively disappeared from the west (Figure 2).[22]

The three explanations, taken singly, have very different implications for our understanding of England's economic development. The third leaves relatively little to be done in terms of national economic integration of commodity markets after, say, 1600, for its posits a thorough integration in the early-seventeenth century. Such a result is extreme. The first explanation, a general shift from subsistence to commercial orientation in the later seventeenth century, errs in the opposite direction: no one could deny the presence of active English markets in wool, grain, or indeed in most agricultural commodities before that time. If one explanation had to be preferred, then it is that of the opening of trade; taken alone, it is consistent with prior research. The modification that would be proposed would only be to place the greater national integration of grain markets back into the seventeenth century, the direction pointed to in the forthcoming volume of the *Agrarian History of England and Wales*. Without doubt, however, even in terms of the overly simple assumption of a two product world, all three processes were at work: the pace of economic development (taken here narrowly to mean greater commercial orientation of production and regional specialization) had not yet occurred evenly throughout England as the seventeenth century dawned. In this regard, the greater dif-

Simple Model of London's Importance in Changing English Society and Economy, 1650–1700," *Past & Present,* 37(1967), 44–70.

22 The difference might have been imposed, for example, by differential labor costs, differential rainfall, or differential transportation costs. See Kussmaul, "Agrarian Change in Seventeenth-Century England," *Journal of Economic History,* XLV (1985), 1–30.

ferentiation closer to London in the earlier map points to a diffusion of specialization with London as its focus.[23]

Parish registers are not among the classic sources for economic history. Were it not for the occasional notation of occupations in some registers, their use would be reserved for demographers and genealogists. But because the timing of marriages within the year was economically sensitive, marriage seasonality commends itself as an indirect indicator of economic activities. And because the events were routinely recorded, from the late 1530s, this source is unparalleled in its spatial breadth, temporal and social depth, and consistency for pre-census, preindustrial England.

The article has mentioned two of the uses to which marriage seasonality could be put: the observation of the timing of regional specialization, and the testing of explanations of the timing and nature of change. The spatial design traced by marriage seasonality conforms to generally accepted views of regional activities far better for the late seventeenth and early eighteenth centuries than it does for the sixteenth and early seventeenth; the observed spreading out from London, over time, of differentiation in seasonal weddings gives weight to the central place approaches to regional economic development. Furthermore, it may be possible to learn more about rural industry, its location, growth, and decline, through the use of indexes of non-seasonality. Finally, it would be feasible to develop a diagnostic technique from marriage seasonality to supplement the traditional sources of local history.

Studying the seasonality of marriage provides some illumination on traditionally dark areas of economic history (such as the timing of economic integration, or regional specialization) that require precisely dated sources, of reasonable consistency over time and space, from many places, over long periods of

23 Eversley, for example, finds the period after 1750 to have been the most important in forming national integration from distinct regional markets. David E. C. Eversley, "The Home Market and Growth in England, 1750–80," in Eric L. Jones and Gordon E. Mingay (eds.), *Land, Labour, and Population in the Industrial Revolution* (London, 1967), 217.Chartres, "The Marketing of Agricultural Produce," in Joan Thrisk (ed.), *The Agrarian History of England and Wales*, V, forthcoming. Cf. C. W. J. Granger and C. M. Elliott, "A Fresh Look at Wheat Prices and Markets in the Eighteenth Century," *Economic History Review*, XX(1967), 257–265.

time. Marriage seasonality has the obvious disadvantage of being indirect, as a source for economic, rather than demographic, history, but no more direct source has longer runs, wider coverage, or greater consistency.

## APPENDIX

I used the "uncleaned" version of the Cambridge Group's aggregative marriage file: no corrections have been made for underregistration. Their method of correcting for underregistration was to apply a national template of the seasonal distribution of marriages to the defective registers, but this method would have defeated my purpose in demonstrating the differences in regional patterns, especially in periods of high underregistration, most notably in the Interregnum. I prefer to accept the spurious seasonality that underregistration may create (if, for instance, more Octobers happened to be underregistered than were other months), rather than to have a national average imposed on a study based on the changing distribution about that average.

A close comparison between the marriage map of *Population History* and Figures 1 and 2 reveals the relative sparseness of the sample of the Cambridge Group's data used in this study. The difference springs from two main causes:

1. I eliminated the market towns identified by Everitt and Adams from the 404 parish sample, in order to focus on rural change. The sample was thus reduced to 275 parishes. The price of so doing was the loss of predominantly rural places with defunct market charters, along with the loss of the true towns that I intended to be dropped from observation.[24]

2. In order to observe change, some compromise had to be struck between the large spurious variation in parochial indexes in very short periods and the invisibility of change in overlong periods. Forty-year periods were selected. Since parishes sometimes registered very few marriages in a period, a wholly arbitrary cutoff point of sixty marriages was adopted to mitigate the problem of spurious indexes: unless sixty marriages were celebrated in the forty-year period under consideration, the parish was dropped from observation for that period. The number of parishes in observation in each period is shown in Table 1 above.

Autumn was also lengthened to include September. Harvests in the south could end as early as late July, as was reflected in the clustering of September as the maximum marriage month only in the extreme south.[25]

24 John Adams, *Index Villarum* (London, 1690); Alan Everitt, "The Marketing of Agricultural Produce," in Thirsk (ed.), *Agrarian History* (Cambridge, 1967), IV, 467–475.
25 Christopher W. Chalkin, *Seventeenth Century Kent: A Social and Economic History* (London, 1965), 84.

I chose the parish rather than, for example, the county or region of Figure 3 as the unit of observation to avoid a subtle bias toward observing reduced seasonality in a larger aggregate out of all proportion to the reduction in seasonality over space. Parishes with relatively low seasonality tended to be larger, at least in the sense of celebrating more marriages in any period.[26] This relationship should come as no surprise given, first, the reasonable assumption that non-agricultural work, however seasonal it might have been by modern standards, was necessarily less seasonal than most agricultural work; and, second, the recent wealth of information on the positive relationship between rural industrialization and rates of family formation. Any tendency toward industrialization in some parishes would therefore bias the regional observations toward suggesting a general decline in seasonality, if monthly and annual totals of marriages were summed over that larger region.[27]

26  IND, as defined above as the logged distance of the early summer and autumn maximums from (100,100), was negatively correlated, in every period, with the annual marriage totals for the period.
27  Cf. Jones, *Seasons and Prices: the Role of the Weather in English Agricultural History* (London, 1964), 21. See also Alec N. Duckham, *Agricultural Synthesis: The Farming Year* (London, 1963). David Levine, *Family Formation in an Age of Nascent Capitalism* (New York, 1977), 58–87; Hans Medick, "The Structures and Function of Population-Development under the Proto-industrial System," in Peter Kriedte et al. (trans. Beate Schempp), *Industrialization Before Industrialization: Rural Industry in the Genesis of Capitalism* (Cambridge, 1981).